GW00726041

ALSO BY TC LUOMA:

Atomic Dog: The Testosterone Principles

The Testosterone Principles 2: Manhood and Other Stuff

TC LUOMA

BALBOA.
PRESS

A DIVISION OF HAY HOUSE

Copyright © 2012 TC Luoma

Cover Art: Leah Devora

All rights reserved. No part of this book may be used or reproduced by any means,
graphic, electronic, or mechanical, including photocopying, recording, taping or by any
information storage retrieval system without the written permission of the publisher
except in the case of brief quotations embodied in critical articles and reviews.

Balboa Press books may be ordered through booksellers or by contacting:

Balboa Press
A Division of Hay House
1663 Liberty Drive
Bloomington, IN 47403
www.balboapress.com
1-(877) 407-4847

Because of the dynamic nature of the Internet, any web addresses or links contained
in this book may have changed since publication and may no longer be valid. The views
expressed in this work are solely those of the author and do not necessarily reflect the views
of the publisher, and the publisher hereby disclaims any responsibility for them.

The author of this book does not dispense medical advice or prescribe the use of any technique as a form of
treatment for physical, emotional, or medical problems without the advice of a physician, either directly or
indirectly. The intent of the author is only to offer information of a general nature to help you in your quest
for emotional and spiritual well-being. In the event you use any of the information in this book for yourself,
which is your constitutional right, the author and the publisher assume no responsibility for your actions.

Any people depicted in stock imagery provided by Thinkstock are models,
and such images are being used for illustrative purposes only.
Certain stock imagery © Thinkstock.

ISBN: 978-1-4525-4372-7 (sc)
ISBN: 978-1-4525-4373-4 (hc)
ISBN: 978-1-4525-4371-0 (e)

Library of Congress Control Number: 2011962524

Printed in the United States of America

Balboa Press rev. date: 01/27/2012

The Testosterone Principles 2

For Laurie

He ate his dinners, usually, at the Englischer Hof. At the beginning of each meal he would put a gold coin upon the table before him; and at the end of each meal he would put the coin back in his pocket. It was, no doubt, an indignant waiter who at last asked him the meaning of the invariable ceremony. Schopenhauer answered that it was his silent wager to drop the coin into the poor-box on the first day the English officers dining there should talk of anything else than horses, women, or dogs.

-- *The Story of Philosophy*, by Will Durant, page 398

Contents

Preface

So here's the story.

Back in 1998, I was contracted to be the Editor-in-Chief of a website with the unlikely but highly appealing (at least to me) name of *Testosterone*.

It was a website owned by a supplement company named Biotest, and the innocent but effective business plan was to provide all kinds of free information about exercise, weight lifting, and nutrition that would backend the supplements.

People would soak in the info, and if the supplements mentioned in the articles appealed to them, they'd buy them. It was a win-win, as they say.

I took the job because I had extensive experience in nutrition, supplements, and exercise, but I saw the site as something more. I felt, given the right tone and delicate touch, that the site could also espouse a new philosophy of sorts, and that philosophy was *manhood*.

Oh, I know what you're thinking. You're thinking the type of manhood that worships monster truck rallies and nacho fries and fast cars; that paints its bare chest green and sits in the subzero stands of Lambeau Field with a hunk of plastic cheese on its head while bellowing like a gutted Klingon; that communicates largely by grunting, belching, or telling fart jokes; that once loved a woman so very, very much that he *almost told her*; that drank the 12-pack of beer that killed the rat that ate the malt that lay in the house that Jack built!

You know, all that stereotypical crap.

But that's not what I had in mind. In fact, I had this quaint notion of manhood that's sort of a blend of the chivalrous Knights of the Round Table combined with, I don't know, the bawdiness of that French rascal Rabelais, or, for those of you unfamiliar with historical archetypes, a type of manhood that combines the do-goodedness of the Boy Scouts with some heaping doses of self-determination and pragmatism, sprinkled with a dollop of Testosterone, and seasoned with a few fistful-size pinches of Howard Stern.

From my experience and observations, men and boys were in some serious need of a new definition of manhood. Men by and large don't have a masculine identity that's much different from the one-dimensional and infantile masculinity epitomized by professional athletes or by the characters in Hollywood action movies or, worse, yet, television sitcoms.

But there's a yin to the masculine yang I just described, and neither side is very pretty.

There's a whole other breed of man who, despite rejecting silly *Maxim Magazine* notions of manhood, has gone completely in the other direction, only slowing down to do some occasional antiquing. They're the modern-day castrati, only they don't sing (unless they're watching *Glee*). Their balls were either cut off metaphorically by society, circumstance, or disapproving wives who put them in a Mason jar and stored them in the shed behind the pickled beets.

This species, by and large, is what American women have been saddled with, sometimes by their own doing, and sometimes because, like Eskimos eating at the Eskimo Buffet, they have little to choose from other than walrus blubber.

As a result, kids don't have fathers anymore; the traditional American family consists of two "moms," one with a traditional vagina and one with a penis and testicles that acts like a mom. Wives, by and large, don't have husbands anymore – they gave their wedding vows to yet another son who, despite being in his 30's or 40's or beyond, has to be told what to do and scolded when he's bad.

The other type of man I described earlier, the beer-swilling, monosyllabic slobs? Oh, they get married and have kids, too, but they don't stay married very long -- if their wives have any sense, that is. They're the ones responsible for generating most of the restraining orders in this country.

So I began writing a weekly column called *The Atomic Dog*. Most of the articles were about some aspect of my version of manhood, along with the occasional observation about new developments in science or psychology, along with a healthy dose of popular culture and sex.

While the sex was unsettling to some, *offensive* to some, I make no apology for my biology. I'm a man. I have a penis. I know how to use it. It's best you sensitive types come to grips with that fact.

But what made me think I was qualified to write about manhood? I'm qualified to write about the subject the same way a sportswriter is qualified to write about baseball – I've spent thousands of hours watching it, reading about it, studying it, and talking to thousands of "players."

What I saw/read/heard wasn't good. The good aspects of malehood, the good aspects of our great Father Hormone, Testosterone, have been sullied by civilization. Heroism, passion, drive, intensity, and chivalry are obsolete. And that, I think, is sad.

So I began writing about Testosterone, manhood, and other stuff. And you know what? The column seemed to help people. Either they took pleasure in the alleged humor, or they actually took some of the lessons – some understated and some not – to heart and changed their lives.

Who'da thunk?

In any event, it was hugely satisfying to me and I wanted to continue writing the column. It grew in popularity and resulted in a book called *Atomic Dog: The Testosterone Principles* that featured the most popular early columns. The book became sort of a Bible of manhood for a small army of appreciative men.

It also became somewhat of a "user's guide" to a number of tremendous, must-be-sent-from-heaven women who wanted to know what goes through the hearts and minds of the men they love.

This book, *The Testosterone Principles 2: Manhood and Other Stuff*, is its sequel. I hope it's received as well as the first one.

Remember, don't let your balls go the way of the appendix.

--TC

Why You Suck

There it was again, hours of practice accrued equates to success. Nothing magical. The more psychologists in Gladwell's book looked at the careers of the gifted, the smaller the role innate talent seems to play and the bigger the role preparation seems to play.

It seems the universe has done some of you an injustice. Like a malicious, pimply-faced McDonald's employee, the universe has surreptitiously hawked a loogie into your Diet Coke and you never even knew it.

As unlikely as it may first sound, whether you were conceived during your parents' coupling on the first warm day of spring or summer -- perhaps in a field of daisies after they shared a cheeky Pinot Noir -- or whether your conception instead occurred in a warm ski lodge during winter -- your parents underneath a couple of bear skins and smelly all-day skiing socks still covering their cold, cold feet -- could have played a huge part in whatever success or lack of success you're experiencing now.

That's right, the *month* your shiny, blood-slick bawling baby self emerged into the world either gave you a huge advantage in life, or affixed a huge metaphorical two-ton career anchor to your ass.

But don't worry, I'm not going to go all astrology on you. Your possible problems are a lot more terrestrial, at least as explained in the new book, *Outliers*, by Malcolm Gladwell.

The story, or at least my abbreviated version of it, starts in southern Alberta, Canada, in the mid 1980's. Psychologist Roger Barnsley was attending a junior hockey game with his wife when they noticed something a little spooky about the program --for some reason, there were a disproportionately large number of January, February, and March birth dates.

Barnsley went home that night and looked up the birth dates of as many junior and professional Canadian hockey players as he could find and he saw the same pattern. More players were born in January than any other month. The second most frequent birth month? February. The third? March.

In fact, there were almost five and a half times as many players born in January as were in November.

When Barnsley looked at any elite group of hockey players, 40 percent of the absolute best were born between January and March, 30 percent between April and June, 20 percent between July and September, and 10 percent between October and December.

Here's a hint: in Canada, the eligibility cut-off date for any junior division of hockey is January 1st. That means that if you turned 10 on January 2nd, you'll be playing with some boys that don't turn 10 until the end of that year, which constitutes an enormous difference in physical maturity. They are Nelson Muntz compared to Milhouse.

Nine or ten is also the age at which coaches start picking hockey all-star teams. Invariably, the comparatively older, bigger players are picked. Those players get better coaching, they get to play against better players, and perhaps most importantly, they get to play in 50 or 75 games instead of 20.

The same sequence invariably occurs as they move from age division to age division, league to league.

What starts out as a small but distinct advantage snowballs year after year, until those that were born earlier in the year are almost invariably much, much better.

Football and basketball don't select, stream, and differentiate to the same degree as hockey, but baseball does.

The cutoff for nonschool baseball leagues is July 31st and more players are born in August than any other month. In 2005, there were 505 major leaguers born in August, compared with 313 in July.

You can find the same temporal injustice occurring in European soccer. In England, the cutoff date is September 1st, and at one point in the 1990's, 288 professional players were born between September and November and only 136 were born between June and August.

Likewise, in international soccer, the cutoff date used to be August 1st and in one recent Junior World Championship, 135 players were born in the three months after August 1st and only 22 were born in May, June, and July.

Unfortunately, these temporal death zones aren't the exclusive purview of sport; a big one also dogs our educational system.

Again, kids who are born in the early part of the year are lumped in with those that were born in the summer, fall, or winter of that year. The older kids are put in an advanced stream where they learn better skills and the next year, because they're in a more advanced group, they do even better. What starts out as a small advantage persists, year after year.

Teachers invariably confuse comparative maturity with ability, and kids are locked into patterns of achievement and underachievement, encouragement and discouragement, that stretch on and on.

As evidence, Gladwell points to a study of 4-year colleges in the United States where students in the youngest group are under-represented by 11.6 percent!

This lopsided success rate demonstrated by the older students is called "accumulative advantage" by sociologists, and it's a kind of cold, sterile term for those millions of potential superstars that were pushed into athletic or academic oblivion just because of a silly, arbitrary bureaucratic whim based on the calendar.

The main reason all this "accumulative advantage" ends up damaging the prospects of millions of kids around the world has partly to do with the 10,000-hour rule.

In the 1990's, psychologist K. Anders Ericsson conducted an experiment with the Berlin Academy of Music. He divided the school's violinists into three groups: the elite, the good, and those that were unlikely to ever play professionally.

All of the kids had started playing when they were 5 years old, but what divided them, aside from ability, was simply how many hours each had spent practicing. The really good ones had totaled 10,000 hours of practice, while the good ones had only managed to squeak away on the catgut for 8,000 hours or so.

The underachievers? Just 4,000 hours of practice.

The most surprising thing was that they really couldn't find any "naturals." Nor could they find any grinders, people who just worked harder than everybody else but just didn't have the talent to become elite.

The thing that distinguished one from another was simply hard work, nothing else.

But the weird thing is that 10,000 hours — roughly the amount of practice a truly committed devotee could accrue over 10 years — keeps popping up in different fields. Whether you're a writer, a concert pianist, a basketball player, computer programmer, or chess master, true greatness seems to pivot on that magic number.

Gladwell notes only one exception -- chess player Bobby Fisher, who took only *nine* years to achieve Chess Master status.

The Beatles are an old-fogey rock band anachronism to most modern music lovers, but few would probably deny their influence on the world's music. Interestingly, the Beatles were afforded certain circumstances that allowed them to become great.

Early in their career, before anybody had heard of them, they got the opportunity to fly from their England homes to Hamburg, Germany, where a strip club owner had gotten the idea to have bands play non-stop music while sexy Sadie did a little helter skelter on stage.

And play non-stop the Beatles did, for seven days a week, eight hours a night. They made five trips to Hamburg between 1960 and 1962. By the time they had their initial taste of success, they'd performed live approximately 1200 times, which is extraordinary in that most bands never play live 1200 times over their entire careers.

Writer Philip Norman, who wrote the Beatles' biography *Shout,* explained it this way:

> *"They learned not only stamina. They had to learn an enormous amount of numbers — cover versions of everything you can think of, not just rock and roll, a bit of jazz too. But when they came back, they sounded like no one else. It was the making of them."*

There it was again, hours of practice accrued equates to success. Nothing magical. The more psychologists in Gladwell's book looked at the careers of the gifted, the smaller the role innate talent seems to play and the bigger the role preparation seems to play.

Those hockey, baseball, and soccer players who weren't good enough to make it? They might have been too young to compete with older, more physically mature players, so they weren't picked to all-star teams, didn't get the extra coaching, never got close to hitting 10,000 hours of practice by the time the professional teams came around looking for players.

One can't help but wonder how many Gretzkys, A-Rods, or Ronaldos got left behind because of the calendar. One wonders how many Einsteins, Steve Jobses, or Bill Gateses got lumped in with the "less mature" students because they had the bad luck to be Sagittarius instead of Aquarius.

Gladwell encapsulates the problem thusly:

> *"Because we so profoundly, personalize success, we miss opportunities to lift others onto the top rung. We make rules that frustrate achievement. We prematurely write off people as failures. We are too much in awe of those that succeed and far too dismissive of those who fail."*

The answer might be that often, your perceived failures might not be so much genetic as they are sociological, might not be so physiological as they are psychological, and armed with that knowledge, maybe you're not necessarily destined to be the loser society thought you were.

-- 2008

A Mobius Strip Life

For the first time in a long time, he felt despair. His goal, the one thing that kept him going, was moving further from his reach. It's like he's in a prison cell and he's managed to coldcock the screw with a rolled up copy of Popular Mechanics, but he can't quite reach the keys attached to the guard's belt. Just when he's about to snare them with a rolled up poster of Rita Hayworth, the guard twitches and kicks the keys further away.

There were five of them, all probably under 21, all wearing their best Las-Vegas-out-on-the-town-slut-wear.

They walked towards him in a row, almost like they were the opening sequence for some new television action series.

Sure, new from the WB network this fall, *Fox Force 5*.

And they were all pretty. Real-life Bratz dolls. And each was wearing stiletto-heeled shoes so colorful they must have been candy-coated by the M&M people. Their dresses or skirts were CD cellophane-wrapper tight and they collectively showed yards of tanned, coltish leg.

The people-watching was one of Jason's favorite things about Vegas. He'd sat down next to the motorized walkway outside the Bellagio hotel to sip his Slurpie, contemplate his life, and of course watch the people, or in this case, the babes.

He'd just spent seven hours at the poker table and he was up a few hundred dollars. Still, he didn't know if he'd made the right move; not the right move at the poker table, mind you, but the right move in *life*.

Back home in San Diego, Jason owned a little neighborhood café that served coffee drinks, sandwiches, and pastries. He was a success, but my God how he had to work! He woke up at 3:45 in the morning and he usually didn't get home until 9 or 10 at night.

Weekends were a little better, 12-hour days instead of 18-hour days, but he still felt like the walking dead. Luckily, he had the alarm clocks, 6 of them. The first one, right next to him, would hopefully start to rouse him from what was closer to a coma than sleep. He'd take a bear-paw swipe at it, either turning it off or knocking it across the room, but it was hardly enough to rouse him.

Then the others would start to buzz, trill, drone, or clang. Sometimes they'd go off for 15 minutes before he woke completely, or what passes for completely in someone so perpetually sleep deprived.

For Jason, life was all about schedule, highly orchestrated 15-minute chunks of time. Botch up one and it has a cascade effect on the remaining

15-minute blocks of time until they start piling up on each other like delicate ceramic dolls on a runaway conveyor belt.

If he did everything right, if nothing screwed up his delicate schedule, if no pudknocker stopped to ask him about his goddam day, he had two 15-minute blocks of time to study Texas Hold 'Em at the end of his obscenely long day.

He didn't drink during the day because that meant he'd eventually have to take time out to pee. Eating consisted of jamming bits of pastry or lunchmeat down his throat as he worked.

He didn't do laundry; he just bought boxes of shirts from Costco. He'd throw the one he was wearing away at the end of the day and he'd unbag a new one in the morning. He didn't make his bed because he didn't have one. Having a bed requires washing sheets and pillowcases, so he slept on a mat on the floor. Besides, he worried that sleeping on a bed would make him "soft."

It was all because of what he called his 80-month plan. He'd continue working at the same pace for the next 80 months until he had his bankroll. At that point he'd sell the café and move to Las Vegas to become a professional poker player.

You're probably thinking that there's no way he can do it; there's no way he can keep it up, but he'd already kept that pace for *five years*.

You can keep your DiMaggio's and Ripken's; those iron men had *nothing* on Jason.

But then the economy got funky. Household income dropped for the sixth year in a row, gas prices soared, companies laid off people everywhere, and the mortgage crisis kicked us in the balls.

Traffic to the café slowed down. People started staying home and drinking Maxwell House Instant Coffee instead of schlepping down to the coffee shop for a three or four dollar coffee drink.

It was bad enough that the cost of his raw supplies like flour and milk had almost doubled in the last year or two, but when the economy put a chokehold on his customer life line, Jason started to worry; he could see his 80-month plan turning into the 100 Year War.

For the first time in a long time, he felt despair. His goal, the one thing that kept him going, was moving further from his reach. It's like he's in a prison cell and he's managed to coldcock the screw with a rolled up copy of *Popular Mechanics*, but he can't quite reach the keys attached to the guard's belt. Just when he's about to snare them with a rolled up poster of Rita Hayworth, the guard twitches and kicks the keys further away.

So he experiences a few dark nights of the soul, arranged in 15-minute blocks, of course. He decides to make the best of the situation. Rather than see his 80-month plan turn into a repeating one-sided loop, a Mobius strip, he makes a bold decision.

Monday through Friday, he'll work at the café. Friday night after work, he'll hop the red eye to Vegas, get a cheap room, and play as many hours of poker as he can until he flies back on Sunday night. He'll let his employees run the store while he's away.

It's not exactly what he wanted to do, but it's not bad. He gets to keep the sure income stream in the café and he gets to see if he's cut out to play poker.

He's into the third week of his grand experiment but he's not sure he's on the right track. He's a little short of his poker goals, money-wise, and he's worried.

And that brings him to the front of the Bellagio, sipping a Slurpie and watching the living Bratz dolls. The girls get to within ten feet of him when one of them, unnoticed by the others, falls a step or two behind them. She tiptoes up behind a dark-haired one wearing a fuchsia tank dress and like a hockey goon, she pulls her friend's dress up over her head in one deft motion.

The others back off, hands over their mouths to stifle their shrieks of laughter while the victim of the prank starts screaming like Oprah had just given her a Toyota. She's clearly embarrassed but her embarrassment goes beyond the pale because, lordy, lordy, she's not wearing any *underwear*! Instead of thongs, Jason sees a dark bacon strip of pubic hair against the one part of her body that isn't tan.

To make things more embarrassing, the perpetrator of the prank has gathered up the material of the poor booty-exposed girl's frock over her head and she's gripped it tightly with her clenched fist like she's trying to prevent a weasel from getting out of a gunnysack.

And she won't let go.

The victim is thrashing around and flailing her arms like she's Frankenstein's monster and a villager just set her aflame with a torch.

The other girls don't even think of coming to her aid. They're in spasms; they can't breathe. In between their shrieks of laughter they yell at the girl in the gunnysack, "I can't *believe* you're not wearing any underwear!" "Why aren't you wearing any underwear!?!

After 10 or 15 seconds, the prankster lets go of the dress and the victim, red-faced but none the worse for wear, smooths herself out and regains her composure. Fox-Force 5 continues on their way in a halting, staggering, heads-back-laughing walk. And none of them paid any mind to Jason, who was clearly moved by this gift from the gods.

It's got nothing to do with Jason's dilemma, but suddenly he knows he's made the right decision. Fate just spoke to him through a flashing naked beaver.

So what if he's splitting duties? He's honing his craft, still operating the café, and God and Doyle Brunson willing, he'll make some extra money at the tables. Oh yeah, and for the first time in a long time, he's having some fun, all kinds of fun.

I tease him that he's Forrest Gump's girlfriend, Jenny. Forrest was on leave from the army and he'd heard that Jenny got a job in a theater. Now Jenny had told Forrest that her dream was to become a folk singer, so when he walks into the theater and sees Jenny sitting topless on stage while playing a guitar and singing a Dylan song, he's all choked up:

Her dream had come true. She was a folk sin-ger.

Okay, so maybe it's not the same thing. Singing in front of drunk and horny men who only want to see her tits wasn't exactly what Jenny had in mind when she said she wanted to be a folk singer, and playing part-time poker in Vegas while still putting in 90-plus hours a week baking scones and muffins in San Diego wasn't exactly the way Jason had planned it, but it was good enough... for now.

So, gentle reader (you knew this was going to eventually turn to you, didn't you?), if you're like 99.99999% of the population, you have your ambitions, too, regardless of what they are.

Only you suck.

I suck.

We all suck compared to Jason.

Let me put it this way, are you sacrificing even 10% of what Jason's sacrificed to get what you want?

I doubt it. I rarely meet anyone who gets what they want. Everybody's got plenty of lofty ideas, but I rarely see anyone carry through with them. I run into hundreds of people who want to change careers, but the only effort they expel towards that end is complaining to me or any other poor bastard unlucky enough to be in the way of their lament.

At least 3 times a week, someone asks me what he or she should do to lose weight. I tell them I'll help them, but the first thing they have to do is write down everything they eat over the next three days.

It's not like I ask them to clean out the stables of Zeus, but to this day, only *one person* has ever completed the task. She, however, was highly motivated because she wanted to look good in her wedding dress. After she'd bagged the guy, she reverted to her dumpy self.

I'm usually highly resistant to motivational articles or articles designed to harness the psychology of positive thinking because I'm a motivational reductionist; I tend to break motivation down to the simplest statement -- *If you want to do something bad enough, you'll do it*. Clearly, most people are comfortable with the status quo because they don't do it.

But what the hell, I've come this far so I might as well try to offer a couple of words of advice.

Get off your ass.

For once in your mediocre, lack-luster life, take *one thing*, one goal, to completion; see one thing to fruition. You know how to get the new job. You do. Really. You don't need anyone to tell you about education, certifications, studying, contacts, etc.

Do it or just stop boring the hell out of the rest of us, okay?

And if your ambitions or dreams have to do with your body, my God, what could be easier? If you had Jason's drive for just *two hours a day* and you applied it to your goal, *nothing could stop you.*

But maybe you feel the economy's thrown a foreclosed monkey wrench into your plans and you're not eligible for a bailout.

If you've been hit, then you might think about taking advantage of the circumstances; do what it takes to ride out the storm. Money tight? Gas so expensive you can't make the 30-mile drive to your favorite Ethiopian/Italian fusion restaurant when you're jonesing for some Couscous Diavolo? Finances so tight you can't join your autoerotic asphyxiation club for their annual choke-off in Cancun?

Maybe it's time to go a little Spartan.

Eat smart. One skipped dinner at Ruth's Chris Steak House could buy a week's worth of quality food; a month's worth of protein powder. Take some of that time you might normally spend recreating and get thee to the gym, or the garage, or the track. Use these times to get your body (or your mind) right. Do two-a-days for once in your lousy un-productive life. Sprint. Lunge old ladies across the street. Do hip thrusts using your neighbor's garden gnomes.

It may or not be the best time to invest in the market, but it's sure as hell the best time to invest in you.

-- 2008

Mom Was a Stripper

And for some reason, the girls all smell like vanilla,
probably as the result of a single entrepreneur
having cornered the strip club body lotion market.
I tell you, I can't even open a tub of vanilla protein
powder nowadays without getting a raging hard-on.

M y mother was a stripper.

There. I've said it. After all the years of denial, all the years of lying. All of it, *over*, out in the open.

I don't know why it took me so long to tell you this but believe me, I was in the dark about it for the longest time, too.

Mom and I lived in Windsor, Ontario, in a run down clapboard house near the edge of town. Every evening, just before 9 o'clock, she'd put me to bed before heading off to work. Whenever I asked her what she did she'd say, "I'm the Ambassador to France, Honey."

I always took her at her word because, heck, I was only 18 at the time and didn't know any better. But in retrospect, the fact that she went to work wearing a trench coat and shoes with 7-inch clear plastic heels that had tiny plastic goldfish floating around in them should have been a dead giveaway.

And there were other clues, too, like the fact that she paid for *everything* — groceries, the rent, nipple rings — in dollar bills that were folded lengthwise, plus the 8-foot high metal pole she'd installed in her bedroom. A lot of times I'd walk in on her and catch her hanging upside down from it in her underwear while the stereo was playing *Brick House* by the Commodores.

She'd always say, "I'm just practicing in case I ever want to be a fireman, Honey."

I always believed her.

Then came that fateful day when I heard the ice cream man coming around the corner, the speaker on his truck blaring out that happy *Turkey in the Straw* tune. I wanted a cherry Popsicle but I didn't have any money. I couldn't ask mom because she was at the grocery store, so I ran into her bedroom to search for some loose change.

I started rifling through the drawers of her dresser but the bottom one was stuck. When I managed to yank it open, mounds of sequined G-strings and colorful panties billowed out. There must have been a thousand of them jammed in that drawer.

Suddenly, I started to piece it all together.

When she came home, I confronted her. I sat her down at the kitchen table and asked her flat out, "Bubbles, are you a stripper?" She broke down and started crying, taking some pasties out of her pocket and dabbing her eyes, explaining that she wasn't really the Ambassador to France, but what she did was sorta' the same thing because she was always negotiating deals and maintaining friendly relations.

I forgave her, of course, but tragically she died later on that very evening. She was on stage dancing to her signature song, which was *Footloose* by Kenny Loggins, when her frenetic jiggling shook loose an embolism that bumped and ground its way to her big stripper heart, where it lodged and killed her instantly.

She's buried out back next to the parking lot of the strip club under a big pink tombstone that reads:

> *Here lies Bubbles*
> *Boy could she shake*
> *But you shoulda' seen the girls,*
> *Who came to the wake.*

Given my upbringing, it's no wonder I feel so *at home* in strip clubs.

While there are no cookies baking in the oven, there are always a few HD televisions showing the big game. And then there are the girls, of course.

Girls to satisfy anyone's tastes! Girls dressed in outrageously short schoolgirl outfits! Girls dressed like some frilly Victorian fantasy! Girls wearing little Daisy Duke outfits with tattered shorts that expose more ass than most women *have* ass! Girls dressed like Carmella in accounting...holy shit, that *is* Carmella! Don't worry baby, just keep shaking it and I won't tell!

And there are girls who aren't dressed at all! That's right, naked girls, naked girls dancing to a 5,000-watt sound system!

> *Hey, carrot juice, I wanna squeeze you away until you bleed*
> *(finding out true love is blind)*

And your vanilla friend, well she looks like something I
need
(finding out true love is blind)
I want miss little smart girl with your glasses and all your
books
(finding out true love is blind)
Wind me up and make you crawl to me
Tie me up until you call to me

The bass is turned up so high, it's *whumping* right through me and my balls are swinging and clacking in my pants as though they're part of Newton's Cradle!

And for some reason, the girls all smell like vanilla, probably as the result of a single entrepreneur having cornered the strip club body lotion market. I tell you, I can't even open a tub of vanilla protein powder nowadays without getting a raging hard-on.

Is it any wonder I feel so at home in strip clubs?

Topless bars and strip clubs are universally thought of as disreputable, but I really don't see the problem. No one would give me any guff if I were on, say, a whale watching tour.

Likewise, no one would bat a judgmental eye if I had merely taken my folding chair to the edge of the forest and tossed some corn on the ground in the hopes of catching a glimpse of a fawn, and that's really all I'm doing anyhow, trying to catch a glimpse of a fawn, only I'm using dollar bills as bait and the fawn I'm looking for is wearing a 3-piece chap set made of a stretchy lamé fabric with hard core grommet detail.

And hey! Whadda' ya' know? This fawn's name is Bambie, too! What are the odds? Okay, about one in three, but *still*....

If the visual stimulation of strip club isn't enough, you can even pay one to sit on your lap and grind away! Try getting your wife or girlfriend to put on a skimpy outfit and grind away at your crotch while you're watching *Sports Center* on a big plasma screen. Probably ain't gonna' happen.

Yep, for about 40 bucks, some beautiful girl will put in a workmanlike effort to make you come in your pants in the time it takes to play 4 truncated songs. Actually coming in your pants is an extremely rare occurrence, but some cultures consider it a harbinger of good fortune and a sign from the gods that crops will be abundant that year.

Now if the girl was particularly gifted and the songs were longer, it might just happen; you *could* come in your pants. I once slipped the DJ an extra 20 bucks so he'd play Iron Butterfly's 17-minute long rock classic, *In-A-Gadda-Da-Vida*, as one of the four songs, but it backfired when the friction caused my pants to ignite and Giselle panicked and threw a Mai Tai on my lap.

That only made it worse, of course. They had to call in Red Adair and he managed to extinguish my pants three days later after using some dynamite.

You might have read about it in the papers.

Anyhow, I'm perplexed by the negative stigma associated with strip clubs. And I'm equally perplexed that most married men I know have to *lie* about going to them.

She likes looking at antique furniture and floor tiles. We like breasts.

'Twas always thus and 'twill always be thus. Is that so wrong?

Women are probably worried that hubby is going to actually have sex at a strip club, or enter into some meaningful relationship with someone named Tiffany. Ladies, listen, strippers have to act sexy as part of their job. If there's another group of women more desensitized towards sex then strippers, I can't think of them.

Let's say hubby operates a punch press at work. You think he wants to come home and operate a punch press? Same with strippers. After work, Tiffany doesn't want anything to do with sex, music, or dancing. Instead, Tiffany probably wants to shop for antique furniture or floor tiles.

Let hubby go; he'll adore you for it. He'll adore bragging to his friends how you encourage his strip club excursions, and just between you and me, he'll probably come home so horny and virile that all that dispassionate roll on, roll off sex of the past few weeks, months, or even years will become a thing of the past.

If, however, you're still paranoid over him seeing naked women gyrating their hips, at least put on a schoolgirl outfit once in a while, or maybe one of those 3-piece chap sets made of stretchy lamé fabric with hard core grommet details, complete with some skyscraper heels. Then, screw in a red light bulb, crank up the bass, and swing and clack his balls.

I think even mom would think that's a good idea...at least mine would have.

-- 2009

Generation Dope

Of 1,200 17-year-olds who participated in a phone
survey on knowledge of history and literature,
approximately a quarter were unable to identify
Hitler as the Chancellor of Germany in WWII. Of
that quarter, half thought he worked for the phone
company. Okay, I'm kidding about the latter, but
not the former.

I guess if you need to know anything specific about David, it's that he's a helluva' smart guy. While he appears to have lost a lot of weight lately, I suspect that his high-wattage brain is literally absorbing his body — feeding off it — because really, why's a big brain ike that need all that useless dead weight?

Yep, pretty soon he'll just be one of those giant-head dudes right out of the old *Star Trek* TV series and you'll know the enormity of the problem it's solving by how fast those big blue veins are pulsing.

I have dinner with David whenever I feel like being reminded of what a comparative dope I am and tonight we're having sushi, which of course is good brain food.

As I reach for a piece of yellowtail, I viddy a flash of blond hair from the other side of the restaurant. I turn to see Alexandra, a girl I know from the gym. I smile and do a tight little Miss-America-riding-in-the-parade-style wave and she walks over to our table.

She says she's a bit early for a dinner date so I invite her to sit down and she accepts. Now David's not much for the ladies -- all that sex and the thrusting and sweating and grunting and oh my, the bodily secretions! How distasteful! How... how... *biological!* Besides, sex interferes with the fluidity of his thoughts.

Twenty-year-old Alex, however, is all about sex. She's a "waitress" at a strip club. I suppose it's possible she really just serves drinks, but every strip club employee I've ever met says she's a waitress and really, there must be at least a *couple* of strip club employees who actually dance and get naked on stage.

Oddly enough, David seems kind of interested in Alex. I guess even big brains are powerless against bomb-ass tits. And she seems like she might be at least mildly interested in him, too, even though she's half his age. I can't help conjure up the image of Alex as Marlene Dietrich and David as Emil Jannings in the 1930 classic movie, *The Blue Angel*. Sure, the professor and the nightclub singer who brings him ruin.

Too bad David isn't a genius when it comes to scoring with women. Alex asks him what he's into and I know immediately he's going to blow it, even though we've rehearsed:

21

Stifle your natural instincts. Remember, you're into monster truck rallies and heavy metal. Stuff that intellectual stuff.

But he can't help himself. He answers that his interests include "French film and opera." Oddly enough, that's his idea of a pedestrian response. If he'd given an entirely unguarded answer, he'd probably have said something straight out of *Good Will Hunting* about working on linear algebra problems and debating the viability of agrarian economies.

But no, he went with French film and opera. Too bad these are two of the subjects she's not conversant in, along with, oh, science, politics, geography, art, weather, pencils, aardvarks, battleships, cheese, and just about any subject covered by Wikipedia's entire database.

He loses interest. I guess I can't blame him. Stupidity takes the wind out of my erection, too.

It wouldn't have worked anyhow. The relationship would have been like George and Lenny in *Of Mice and Men* and David would probably have had to put a bullet in the back of Alexandra's head some day after she committed the unspeakable crime of topping off her glass of 1995 Château Margaux with some Snapple.

We soon forget she's even there and David and I resume our conversation. For some reason, our discussion turns to the assassination of John F. Kennedy and one of us, while making some forgotten point, mentioned the year it occurred.

Alex's eyes grew as wide as Jackie's pillbox hat.

"Geez, you guys must be historians or something!"

Now imagine her saying that in a perfect dumb-blonde voice and you've got the flavor of the moment.

Poor Alex. Poor dumb little Alex. We'd only mentioned one of the most rudimentary facts of the assassination, one you'd expect most Americans to know regardless of their age, but she thinks we're professors or something — professors who just might even be brainy enough to have a chance against those kids on *Are you Smarter Than a Fifth Grader*?

But weep not for Alex. It may be that I misjudged her. It could be that I'm stereotyping her profession when I should have been stereotyping her generation. Based on a report conducted by the American Enterprise Institute, she could possibly be her generation's best and brightest.

Of 1,200 17-year-olds who participated in a phone survey on knowledge of history and literature, approximately a quarter were unable to identify Hitler as the Chancellor of Germany in WWII. Of that quarter, half thought he worked for the phone company. Okay, I'm kidding about the latter, but not the former.

Other questions revealed that...

- Less than half (43%) knew the Civil War was fought between 1850 and 1900.

- One in four said Columbus sailed to the New World some time after 1750.

- Only 52% could identify the theme of George Orwell's *1984*.

- Only about half knew that Job from the Bible was known for his patience in suffering.

- Thirty percent didn't know that John F. Kennedy was the one who said, "Ask not what your country can do for you; ask what you can do for your country."

How could you not know that stuff just by *living*? By somewhere along the line mistakenly leaving the television on PBS or the History Channel for a few seconds? By grabbing a copy of *Time Magazine* on the way to the crapper? By overhearing a conversation while in line at the DMV?

More puzzling is how you could not know that stuff after presumably attending school.

Despite "No Child Left Behind," it appears that our educational system is Mr. and Mrs. McCallister and we've left a nation of Kevins home alone, but many of these Kevins aren't smart enough to protect their houses from bumbling thieves without electrocuting themselves, accidentally dropping bowling balls on their own noggins, or somehow ensnaring their genitals in mouse traps.

What gives, President Bush?

Geor-gieeee! You got some 'splaining to do!

On a personal level, the survey reveals a lot. You may have noticed I like to pepper my articles with references to history, literature, poetry, and popular culture. I don't do it out of some pathetic attempt to show off, I simply do it because it amuses the hell out of me.

Anyhow, a lot of those references zing by the younger readers of this column like tennis balls launched at electronic-voiced Stephen Hawking by Roger Federer in their country club tennis match.

ROGER, YOU MISCALCULATED. YOU EXPENDED MORE KILOJOULES THAN THE CURRENT VECTOR REQUIRED. IN OTHER WORDS, YOUR SERVE WAS LONG.

Maybe that's a bad analogy because I picked a smart guy to represent dumb guys. Oh well, you get the picture. Maybe I should scratch the esoteric references, or at least limit them to big, Donnie Darko airplane engine references that are harder to dodge.

Likewise, I often hear that I'm "dating" myself when I reference something that happened BPS, or "Before Play Station." In other words, according to some of these 17-year-olds, if I know about something, I must have been there.

How else could you know about it, dude?

Here's the thing, I know a few things about World War I, but that doesn't mean I was a Doughboy. I know who Benny Goodman was, but that doesn't mean I jammed with the dude. I even know Kurt Cobain shot himself, but that doesn't mean I was in the living room of his house passed out from washing down a half-dozen dope brownies with a bottle of tequila.

It's just stuff me and a lot of sentient dudes absorbed from having senses that are engaged; stuff we absorbed from listening and reading and talking, listening and reading and talking about stuff that's more David than Alexandra.

But the survey conducted by the American Enterprise Institute seems to explain things. The group says the survey demonstrates that a significant portion of teenagers live in "stunning ignorance" of history and literature and probably a whole lot of other things.

The group places much of the blame on the aforementioned "No Child Left Behind" program, which places more emphasis on reading and math at the expense of history, literature, and other subjects.

Of course, that doesn't help explain why U.S. teens rank 24th out of 29 industrialized nations when it comes to math and science scores.

Mark Bauerlein might have a better explanation. Bauerlein, who named his soon-to-be released book *The Dumbest Generation*, perhaps as an homage to Tom Brokaw, believes the rampant dopiness is technology-based.

"When we were 17 years old, social life stopped at the front door," says Bauerlein, 49. Teenagers can continue their blathering online, on Facebook, by instant messaging, or on cell phones in their bedrooms, any time of day or night. "Peer-to-peer contact... has no limitations in space or time."

I think he's got a point. I'm sending a text message to the teens right now:

AYSOS?

Don't answer. We apparently already know many of you *are* stupid or something.

It's interesting that while the Internet is totally spatial — devoid of width, breadth, or dimension — it's created, paradoxically, legions of two-dimensional or even mono-dimensional beings.

If these 17-year-olds exist in cyberspace with the same nitwits they live with in the real world, all the dimensions in the universe aren't going to expand their minds.

In fairness, though, between 5 and 15 percent of 17-year-olds (and presumably younger or older teens) do really well in school and are learning things that would baffle previous generations. Unfortunately, it's the "middle class" of smarts that seems to be on a steep decline.

But that's okay. Society needs its sheep. Sheep are, after all, the backbone of the economy. If we were all as cerebral as David, who'd pick up the trash? Who'd ring up my beef jerky at the 7-11? Who'd take Alex's place in grinding away at a pole while naked?

You only need so many sheep, though. Someone's got to know when to herd them into a pen and close the gate when the wolves come.

The answer of course isn't to ditch the Internet. The answer probably isn't some radical change in the educational system, either. The answer might just be something as simple as placing a *value* on smarts, a society-wide change of perception so that being smart is something we strive for, just as we might strive for popularity, fame, fortune, or having a fit, strong, and esthetic body.

-- 2008

My Speech to the Graduates, 2007

I've got a strong feeling that if Einstein were alive to find his name had been invoked by these hucksters, he'd spit so hard that his loogie would approach the speed of light, reach infinite mass, and wash the offending peckerheads away into a different space/ time continuum.

As I stand here on this lovely spring day looking out over this sunny vista and your bright, smiling faces filled with hope, I can't help but feel depressed as hell.

While I'm often told that your generation is so much smarter and so much more worldly and wise, I think it's a crock. Mankind obviously learns a lot more with each passing day, but I don't know who came up with the notion that you guys absorbed very much of this knowledge.

Nowadays, a general college education is a mighty thin layer of sandwich spread. Sure, they covered all of the bread — tried to expose you to every subject and topic — but the mayo's so sparse you can barely taste it. Of course, there's the old platitude about how the purpose of college is to just teach you how to *think*.

To this — honored students, faculty, and staff — I say horse piss.

Frankly, most of you remind me of the ducks, and for that matter, the beavers, the turtles, and the frogs.

There were 28,800 of them. They left Honk Kong Harbor on a tanker in early January of 1992 en route to Tacoma, Washington. Along the way the ship met 40-foot waves and lost its cargo. More than seven thousand boxes, each one containing a yellow plastic duck, a red plastic beaver, a blue plastic turtle, and a green plastic frog peppered the surface of the turbulent sea.

The rough waves quickly melted away the cardboard containers and the armada of bathtub toys was set free to roam the ocean. Inexplicably, they all seemed to follow diverse courses. Rather than float in one direction, they became victim to some sort of oceanographic chaos theory that sent them to different parts of the world.

Since then, ducks, beavers, turtles, and frogs -- suffering from varying degrees of sun and wave erosion -- have continued to wash up on shores ranging from the Aleutian Islands to Kennebunk Harbor in Maine. Others continue to circle the earth, completing a lap around the Gulf of Alaska to the Bering Sea once every three years.

Like those plastic bathtub toys, I worry that most, if not all of you, will simply hand yourselves over to the capricious currents and trade winds of fate. Rather than take stock of your life and set out on a direct path with grim determination, you'll simply let life make its decisions for you.

It's easier that way.

The trouble is, you'll one day emerge from years of virtual passivity. I say "virtual" because it'll involve a little bit of interaction from you, but no more than a few mouse clicks or abbreviated keystrokes. You'll have spent who knows how long letting songs from iTunes and images from YouTube simply wash over your tree stump of a brain and your only communication with the world will be through abbreviated keystrokes.

You'll have created your own world, all right, but it's just a Myspace world with some really fresh wallpaper. And while it's nice to have a theme song, the recording artist probably didn't have you in mind when he wrote it.

You're bored rats in a lab pressing a lever to get a treat, bored rats that inexplicably have delusions of grandeur.

Unfortunately, for most of you, when you wake up from this electronic torpor, you'll have missed your life. In text messaging language, you'll see that TARFU, 4EAE.

(By the way, I'm NIFOC right now.)

Of course, a lot of you have outs. A lot of you even know "The Secret," so you think you'll be okay. As long as you understand the *laws of attraction*, your imperially slim frame will be draped in Armani and propelled by BMW.

I now ask that those of you who know "The Secret" put on your iPod headphones or text message somebody while I address the others for a minute.

Are you "Secret" believers text messaging? Are you preoccupied? Good.

You see, I don't want to dis "The Secret" in front of the people who believe in it. Like any group that's swallowed any kind of swill-laden dogma, they get awfully defensive when you smite their gods.

"The Secret" started out as a movie, but it's festered and grown into a book, instructional DVDs, and a termite's nest of websites. The premise is that through the centuries, a select group of successful people shared a single belief that was responsible for their success.

The Secret is essentially this: if you *wish* for stuff, you'll get it.

Really. I'm not lying. They invoke metaphysics and science and art and history to back up their assertions. They reason that laws of attraction rule the universe, and that if you simply think positive, you'll attract what you want.

Are you fat? It's all because you think of yourself as a fat person. Are you poor? Negative thinking.

Their team consists of a group of pop-psychologists and general hucksters who spout tidbits like this:

> *Why do you think that 1 percent of the population earns around 96 percent of the money that's being earned? Do you think that's an accident? It's designed that way. They understand something. They understand The Secret, and now you are being introduced to The Secret.*

Apparently, things like drive and intelligence and a whole lot of perspiration have nothing to do with financial success. It was just a case of "the man" withholding information and trying to keep you down.

As evidence, they list a number of Western Civilization's greatest thinkers who supposedly knew "The Secret," men like Plato, Shakespeare, Newton, Hugo, Beethoven, Lincoln, Emerson, Edison, and Einstein. Never mind that we hardly know anything about Shakespeare, these mulyaks believe he was in on "The Secret."

I've got a strong feeling that if Einstein were alive to find his name had been invoked by these hucksters, he'd spit so hard that his loogie would approach the speed of light, reach infinite mass, and wash the offending peckerheads away into a different space/time continuum.

It's *The Da Vinci Code* meets Tony Robbins. The book even includes faux parchment paper, quill and ink fonts, and wax seals. Sure! It's mystical! Written by hobbits or elves or magicians and sealed in a cave for centuries!

Horse piss.

If you flip open any random two pages in their book, they say virtually the same thing: Just think positive! You are a magnet! Think good thoughts and good things will be attracted to you!

Think all his is harmless? I know a college-educated girl who has printed aphorisms from *The Secret* and pasted them to the shaker bottle she carries in the gym. She explains that, "Studies have shown the affirmations cause the molecular structure of the water to change and it becomes a kind of holy water."

Good God woman, if I paste affirmations on the inside of my shorts, it doesn't mean I'm going to pee wine and shit loaves of wholesome multi-grain bread.

I actually know secretaries around town who have, because of "The Secret," tacked up pictures of fancy cars on their cubicle walls. They fully believe that by staring at the picture and thinking good thoughts about it, they'll get the car.

As long as I can remember, I've hung pictures of naked girls on my office wall and thought nothing but really, really, good thoughts, and it's yet to work. Nary a naked woman has plopped her firm buttocks down on my lap. My cousin came in drunk once and relieved himself in my Mexican Hat Plant, but that's as close as anything's come to being naked in my office.

And there are literally millions of these "Secret" people walking among us.

And sure, The Secret "helps" people, but I'm going to quote Karl Marx here and proclaim that The Secret is the opium of the people. People who believe in The Secret surrender responsibility. They don't need hard work or resolve or perspiration, The Secret will provide all. They're all plastic ducks that have cast themselves onto the mercies of the ocean.

If you're vulnerable to every false god that comes along, you're pretty much doomed to be a 7-11 clerk...4EAE. (That's "forever and ever" to you non-texting people.) And not even a dayshift 7-11 clerk. No, you won't be good enough for "the show." You'll work the night shift and when some punk slips a 12-count box of Bud underneath his parka, you'll look the other way lest he use your rectum as a bottle opener.

If you're prone to every false god that comes along, you're emotionally and intellectually weak. You're a plastic duck.

The *real* secret that successful people have known all along is *integrity*. And before you *hrummphh* mightily, let me define the words "successful" and "integrity."

I'm not jaded enough to equate success merely with money. I mean, damn, Paris Hilton gets paid 11 million dollars a year just to show up at parties. If that's your idea of success, by all means practice vapidity and public drunkenness and flash your naughty parts as often as possible. That whorish apple doesn't just fall off the tree; you've got to reach for it.

I define success in the simplest terms: to turn out well, as in your life turning out well — a nice little frappuccino blend of intellectual satisfaction, physical satisfaction, and emotional or spiritual satisfaction. An existence that is, at its end, ultimately free of obsessive *wanting*.

And by integrity I mean adherence to a code, an incorruptible purpose. By and large, those who want something out of life and continue to strive for it against all obstacles, attain it. That's integrity of purpose.

And if by some remote chance college helped you find that integrity of purpose, that was money and time well spent. But I fear that it didn't happen. I worry that many of you are vulnerable to things like The Secret. Unfortunately, it and all other similar "strategies" that involve sitting around and wishing probably aren't going to get you the car, the girl, money, or whatever it is you think the big piece of chicken is on life's platter.

A couple of days ago, I had the macabre pleasure of seeing *Bodies...The Exhibition*. In case you haven't heard of it, it's a traveling exhibition that features more than 250 real human bodies, many of them in athletic poses. There are bodies throwing baseballs and footballs, only the bodies have been stripped of their skin, plasticized, cured, and frozen in a "natural" pose.

When I see or think of the bodies, I can't help but think of this obscure song I used to listen to. The lyrics went something like this:

> *My old friend Trigger up and died, They've got him stuffed and dried, He's staring glassy-eyed out through the parlor door....*

Many of the bodies have been sawed in half so you can see the internal organs. One room even contains plasticized fetuses. In one display case is a complete human skin, a pelt, if you will, including a face. It looks like a rumpled suit someone left on the floor. You can even see the calluses on the bottom of the feet. Another display contains the entire nervous system — and nothing else — spread out on a slab in the shape of a human.

These specimens are prepared in China, and you can clearly see Asian features on the displays. Once the human factory receives the body, they begin processing it. If it's meant to be a display of human musculature, they painstakingly strip off the skin, eyeballs, and all fatty tissue. It's then posed, plasticized, and cured.

(I recently read that the Japanese have invented a robot wine steward that's capable of chemically analyzing and identifying foods. When presented with human flesh, the robot thought it was prosciutto. After seeing the bodies, I realize that human flesh is also *visually* similar to sliced ham.)

If, however, they want to display the vascular system, they inject brightly colored plastic into the blood vessels. Once it hardens, they place the entire body in a vat of acid, which leaves nothing but the veins and arteries.

There's one display that shows the vascular anatomy of a skull. It has the exact *shape* of a skull, only there's no bone or tissue whatsoever. It just looks like a remarkably dense mass of brightly colored blue and red thread floating in solution. You can even see the ghostly imprint of where the eyes should be.

There are also "exploded" versions of various skeletal structures, including more human skulls. As I understand it, the most efficient way to split the skull for display is to take the intact skull and place mung beans into the fissures. The beans in their skull pots are then watered. As the beans sprout and grow, they deftly crack the skull into pieces.

While I was intrigued by the anatomy, I had trouble looking at these pieces as just "specimens." I kept wondering who they were. What did they do? What did they contribute? Were they happy? Did they consent to this? Did they know they'd spend eternity shooting a basketball, their shrunken, plasticized pecker and balls getting dusted by housekeeping once a week?

By policy, all personal records are destroyed. Anonymity is preserved. They lack individuality or distinction. I suppose it's easier for us to deal with the specimens that way. However, dear graduates, it's one thing to lack individuality or distinction when you're stuffed and dried, but it's quite another thing to lack it when you're still alive.

-- 2007

The Pornification of America

You try walking by the average clothing store and see if you don't feel like dropping your pants and rubbing up against the poster of a semi-naked sylph behind the window.

Chicken Bone is on a nut-flush draw, so he checks to see if he can get a free card.

Chicken Bone is called that because he always has a chicken bone jammed behind his right ear whether he's playing poker or not. It's a thighbone by the looks of it, or maybe a wing bone.

To his left is Darryl, a former Marine drill sergeant who's openly gay. Sitting behind Darryl, cooing him on, is his silky-haired Persian boyfriend.

Next to the two lovers is New York Mike, who used to be a columnist for the *New York Daily News* and is currently friend and confidant to Kinky Friedman, the Jewish rock star-turned-gubernatorial candidate for the state of Texas.

Both he and don't-ask-don't-tell fold.

On my immediate right is an almost comatose drunk named Jake who barely knows where he is. Too bad his stack of chips isn't as high as his stack of empties. No matter. Every time he's busted he stumbles around his coat pocket for a roll of hundred dollar bills that's as big as a roll of Charmin squeezably soft toilet paper.

Although he's been playing rags all night, wonder of wonders, he mucks this particular hand.

Occupying the chair on my left is Stuart, a Scotsman who carries around about a dozen business cards, each advertising yet another floundering business enterprise ranging from used car salesman to chauffeur to personal chef. His accent is so goddam thick I hardly ever know what the hell he's talking about.

Every time I bet, he "sneezes" *Ahhh-Bluff!* or *Ahhh-bullshit!*

Funny guy.

He's quiet this time because I fold. So does he.

Alvy is sitting directly in my line of view. She's a short black chick wearing a halter-top that barely restrains her enormous breasts. For some reason, there's a poker chip perched precariously on the left one, threatening at any moment to slide into the dark, bosomy crevice. My God, I bet there are wild pumas hiding down there.

She throws her cards in the pile. Miraculously, the chip stays put.

The rest of the players are equally diverse. There's Alabama Joe who talks like he came straight out of a Faulkner novel, Malcolm, the track athlete who apparently won a gold medal in the Olympics, and Cyber Pimp, the host.

Everybody folds after Chicken Bone except for Alabama Joe, who's the small blind, and Cyber Pimp, the big blind. Chicken Bone's flush doesn't pan out and Cyber Pimp ends up winning the hand with trip Kings.

This is my first time at this local game but everyone else seems to know each other. I'm the new guy — fresh meat — but I'm like, *normal.* I haven't seen such a cast of characters since *Napoleon Dynamite,* but it's okay. I find myself feeling fairly at ease with this group.

About an hour into the game, Alvy excuses herself from the table and says she has to go to work. She picks up her oversized pink leather duffle bag but rather than walk out the door, she ducks behind a 6-foot high partition that's been set up to the right of the poker table.

I'm puzzled but I don't ask any questions. The game continues, but every once in a while I can hear Alvy giggling and this odd *rrrrriiiippppp* sound coming from behind the partition. I swear it's Velcro being torn apart.

Then it dawns on me. Cyber Pimp is called that because, well, *because that's exactly what he is.*

Cyber Pimp's real name is Eric Edmunds and he's one of the pioneers of "chat room modeling." Girls entertain paying customers by performing in front of live video cameras. Alvy is just one of his many "hostesses."

Rrrrriiiiiipppp!

For just $3 a minute, you too can interact with Alvy or any one of scores of other girls that work for Eric, all from the comfort of your jizzum-stained chair. The action ranges from G-rated to Triple XXX, but it's the girls who get nasty that make the most money. Alvy, however, has made quite a bit of money showing off her feet to fetishists who like to watch her massage them or rub them with lotion.

Now show me what the naughty little piggy did, you hot bitch.

At the height of his business, Eric had sultry Brazilian girls showing off their *bundas* in Sao Paulo; Aussies flashing their wallabies in Sydney; and lots and lots of Americans shooting beaver in Miami, Las Vegas, and San Diego.

Many of his offices shut down after competition became fierce, but Eric's business is starting to pick up again since many of his competitors have, because of apparent ineptitude, faded away. Just this week Eric started yet another site, *Bustycam.com.*

Eric finds most of his employees through ads placed in underground or non-mainstream magazines that cater to particular demographics. Most of the time, the ad simply refers them to Covergirlsworldwide.com where they can find out about the company and, should they choose, apply for work.

In the old days, most of his hostesses worked in specially set up offices but with broadband becoming widely available, most of the girls now work from home.

After his contractors are hired, Eric sets them up with as many as 8 different computers so they can sexually multi-task with several customers. Girls pretty much work whatever hours they want and the split with Eric is usually about fifty-fifty.

"The average girl makes about $1,000 a week, but I had one girl here who made almost a million dollars over a four-year period," explained Eric.

Surprisingly, Eric has come to view his business as a little dull. He doesn't date or fraternize with his employees. To him, this is just another business, as the little motivational stickers near Alvy's workstation extolling her to "Do Good Work" suggest.

People occasionally treat him like a pariah, but he doesn't waste time on people whose views are narrow and excessively Puritanical.

Personally, I think it's a totally legitimate business and I think being a chat room hostess is a great job for a student or any female who's struggling to make ends meet. Likewise, I think working as a stripper is a really amazing way for women to make a lot of cash quickly and easily. I've got nothing against porn actresses, either.

If I were female and I had to choose between a lifetime of being a manicurist in Macon, Georgia for my entire life or working as a stripper for a year to earn college money...well, let's just say it wouldn't be a hard decision.

By the way, call me Candy, Candy Kane.

There are those who'd argue that women in the sex industry are being exploited. While that's certainly true of the horrific sex slave industry that plagues Eastern Europe and parts of Asia, it's not generally true of the good ol' American sex industry.

These women aren't being exploited. If anything, they're the ones doing the exploitation. Talk to almost any guy who just left a strip club about $400 lighter while still carrying around an aching erection. Ask him who exactly it was that just got exploited.

With that said, I'm going to make a point that may at first seem contradictory, and that point is this -- I'm worried about the "pornification" of America. I think there's too much porn.

I'm one of the lustiest guys you'll ever meet, but even *I* think that America is overdoing it.

I can't drive to the grocery store without getting a hard-on. How can it be otherwise with all the erotic billboards, sexy bus advertisements, and bosomy store window displays? *You* try walking by the average clothing store and see if you don't feel like dropping your pants and rubbing up against the poster of a semi-naked sylph behind the window.

I can't watch network TV without having my loins get all tingly. I'm not even safe watching the Super Bowl, not with all the up-skirt shots of the cheerleaders and the Bigdaddy.com commercials starring Miss Mammaries. MTV? Forget it! You want T and A? You can't *handle* the T and A!

And please, God, don't lay one of those Victoria's Secret commercials on me; not today, I need to function. Just one glimpse of those silky goddesses in their push-up bras and you'll need to push my office chair into the corner and hang a drool bucket around my neck for the rest of the day.

I'm not talking about the innocent or semi-innocent portrayal of female bodies, per se. I'm talking about the heaving bosoms, moistened crevices, rouged areolae — the stuff that's deliberately loaded, cocked, and pointed right at the neural pathway between your eyes and your throbbing genitals.

At any given moment of the day, I feel extremely agitated, *sexually* agitated.

It's no great revelation that sex sells, but there's got to be something else that sells, doesn't there? *Quality* would be nice, wouldn't it?

I know two brothers who have a huge ocean front house. They made their money selling sandals that aren't that special. They aren't any better than those sold by a dozen other companies.

The secret to their success? Well, according to them, it's women's *asses*. They have a preternaturally round, glistening female butt on every ad.

Do you see the difference here between our mainstream sexual culture and the underground sexual culture? You have to *seek out* an Internet site. You have to *pay* to go into a strip club. You have to *charge* your Visa to get into one of Eric's chat rooms. The porn I'm worried about is the pervasive stuff, the stuff that you can't get away from that's as omnipresent as the sky or the trees or the lovely daffodils.

But I'm not worried about me. I kinda' like being sexually charged all the time. I'm not even that worried about young boys. Nope, it's the little girls I'm worried about.

Have you noticed any of these creatures walking around nowadays? As soon as the slightest trickle of estrogen starts to percolate through their down-covered loins, they turn into tiny whore goddesses. The height of their ambition, their wildest dream, is to appear in a *Girls Gone Wild* video, shaking their butt as violently as a paint can in a hardware store mixer.

Their entire *raison d'être* is to be a sexual creature that stimulates men. Their entire identity is based on sexuality. Do you have a reasonably good-looking teenage son? You can bet he's getting e-mails and text messages filled with provocative sexual language that until recently you'd only hear from a crack whore in need of an angry fix.

Girls as young as 14 are becoming gifted fellatrices, servicing boys underneath school stairwells. Some of them even have contests to see who can get their "man" off first. They put on lesbian shows to entertain enthusiastic crowds of boys.

Don't believe me? Talk to schoolteachers or administrators. Talk to the parents of young boys (not the parents of young girls — they remain, for the most part, blissfully ignorant).

Their clothing is such that they could quite comfortably share a closet with a $500-an-hour whore. They're lined up at the tattoo parlors to get a flamboyant tramp stamp above their heinie so they can better draw attention to their pronounced ass cleavage.

But who can blame them? Look at the ads they see. Look at the TV shows they watch. Look at their role models. Just about every female pop star is a fuck bunny first, a talented entertainer second...or third...or fourth. Where are the actresses that get roles because, well, they can *act*? Acting ability is a nice plus, but *hot* is where it's at.

And if any of thesse actresses are so bold as to temporarily blunt their beauty? Hell, give 'em an Oscar!

Give Nicole one because she put on an unsightly rubber nose and made herself look...shudder...unsexy! Give one to Charlize, too.

My God, the woman didn't wear any make-up and actually gained weight for her role as a homicidal man killer! She temporarily destroyed her fuckability! If that ain't deservin' of an Oscar, then I plum don't know what is!

Where the hell are our female politicians of the future going to come from? Where will the female scientists come from? Thank God I don't have a daughter. I don't know how I'd keep her on track.

Listen, I love hootchie mammas. I love sexual women who can flaunt it and turn it on at will. I have an affinity for strippers and yes, even chat room girls who do what they do as a means to an end. To them, it's just a job. It doesn't necessarily define them. But a woman, especially a young girl, can't be *all about sex*. There's a time and place for everything.

I don't mean to go Old Testament on you, but Ecclesiastes had it right:

> *...a time to weep, and a time to laugh...a time to mourn, and a time to dance...a time to break down, and a time to build up...a time to embrace, and a time to refrain from embracing.*

There's probably also a time to dress and act like a porn star, and a time not to. You ever see Condi Rice wearing those laced up boots with her business suit? Well, I bet when the day's over and the lights are low, Mistress Condi tarts it up and pulls out a nice cat-o-nine tails. Good for her.

Sexuality is a big part of each of us, an important part that I like a whole helluva' lot. I just hope the pornification of America doesn't give us a world where every woman grows up to be as vapid and clueless as Paris Hilton.

-- 2006

Osama and the B-52's

I don't know about that. I just think it's another
biomarker of aging, as concrete as failing eyesight,
droopy testicles, or inelastic arteries. Besides,
what you're familiar with is easier; you don't have
to make up your mind about anything and risk
opening up new mental pathways. It's easier to stick
stuff into old files than open up new ones.

"**T**his is WDOG, Big Dog Radio, blastin' out golden oldies 24 hours a day. We've got Osama on the request line callin' in from the mountains of Pakistan.

What can I spin for ya', Osama Mama?"

"I would very much like to hear 'Rock Lobster' by the B-52's."

"You got it Osama-lama-ding-dong! Woof, woof, woof! What's your favorite radio station?"

"It is, of course, the Big Dog, W-D-O-G. Woof, and death to America."

Man, you think you know a guy! I woulda' guessed Osama Bin Laden's favorite song to be, I don't know, something a little more contemporary, like *Crazy* by Gnarls Barkley or maybe something from *The Pussycat Dolls*, but *Rock Lobster* by the B-52's? Get outta' town!

Of course, that was back in 1996 when he was living with Kola Boof, his Sudanese mistress, so I guess I would have thought he'd be requesting something by R. Kelly or even Coolio — anything but the B-52's.

Call me cynical, but Osama just doesn't seem like a guy who's a sucker for whimsy.

But according to Boof, *Rock Lobster* really was his favorite song. (His other passions allegedly included reruns of the TV show, *The Wonder Years*, and watching Boof "dance like a Caucasoid girl.")

As strange as his music choice might sound, it makes perfect sense to neuroscientist Robert Sapolsky. If you asked him, he'd probably think Osama's choice of music was entirely predictable.

Sapolsky, as explained on a story on National Public Radio, started wondering about music and the brain a few years ago when he hired a young assistant. Sapolsky found his assistant to be extremely annoying. Oh, the assistant did his work just fine, but it was the *music* he played.

One day he'd be tapping his pencil to *Sonic Youth*, and the next day he'd be listening to glorious Ludwig Van. If only the pendulum of his musical tastes swayed from just those two extremes! No, this kid listened to klesmer music, to freakin' Minnie Pearl, even pygmy love songs!

44

Sapolsky, then in his forties, no doubt wanted to shove the kid's forehead through his Bose music system.

He couldn't get over that the kid wasn't stuck in any kind of musical rut, whereas Sapolsky pretty much listened to the same old Bob Marley CD over and over again. Sapolsky could probably karaoke *I Shot the Sheriff* without even looking at the screen. He was disgusted to find he'd turned into one of those guys who pays attention to late-night commercials that advertise anthologies by music dinosaurs.

The greatest hits of Todd Rundgren? Baby, throw me my wallet and the phone and get ready to rock!

Sapolsky kept asking himself, *why*? Is there an age from which a person passes from an open-minded, adventure stage to a close-minded, comfortable stage?

Sapolsky decided to investigate this apparent phenomenon.

He called up 50 radio stations and spoke to the station manager of each. He asked them two questions:

1. What is the average age of the music you play?

2. What is the average age of the people who listen?

Sapolsky found that radio stations use something called the "Breakthrough minus 20" formula. Let's say Billy Joel had his first breakthrough hit in 1976. That means his first fans were born about 20 years earlier.

Breakthrough = 1976, minus 20, or 1956.

In a nutshell, the music you go to high school and college with is the music of your life, and that's the premise commercial radio stations are built on.

From the ages of 14 to 21, you're open to new music. Once you hit about 35, most people won't tap their pencil to anything new, no matter how dynamic. At age 35, your ears, and unfortunately, your mind, close up shop and go to the ranch in Texas to clear out brush...forever.

Let's take a look at my opening example. So party animal Osama allegedly likes *Rock Lobster*, which was a hit in the summer of 1978. Using our "Breakthrough minus 20" formula, we subtract 20 from that and get 1958.

And it turns out Osama was born in 1957.

It looks like those radio stations know what they're talking about. Suddenly, the notion that Osama was rockin' to the B-52's isn't that outlandish, or at least not as outlandish as it might have seemed a minute ago.

So if you're a 25-year-old, 20 years from now you'll be listening to the same crap you're listening to *today*! Your kids will snicker and roll their eyes because the iPod cerebral implant in dad's head, bless his fogey-heart, is playing the "old standards," classics by *DMX, The Killers*, those delightful old crooners from *Slayer*, and Busta Rhymes.

Sweetheart, do you remember where we were the first time we heard 'I Love My Bitch'?

But Sapolsky didn't limit his research to music. He wondered if people are more adventurous regarding *food* when they're younger, so he called up 50 sushi restaurants in the Midwest.

While sushi has been part of the food landscape of the east and west coasts for years, it's still relatively new in the Midwest. According to one restaurant manager in Omaha that Sapolsky called, "uncooked fish wrapped in seaweed still makes a lot of Nebraskans nervous."

While it was difficult to get specific numbers, Sapolsky calculated that first-time sushi eaters were likely to be 26 years old or younger. People from the ages of 26-29 were less likely to eat raw fish, whereas taking anyone over 39 to a sushi restaurant for the first time was a task that only a tag team consisting of Sisyphus and Epicurus might tackle. In fact, only 5% of those over 39 would dare to munch on *maguro*.

After 39, you're stuck with the same old foods you've always eaten. Your window for new foods not only closes, but you pull the drapes down and turn off the lights.

Sapolsky decided to look at one last area that seemed to be the exclusive domain of youth: piercing.

After talking to 50 tattoo parlors and body piercing studios, he determined that the window of tongue piercings is pretty much restricted to ages 16 to 23. Only 5% of tongue-piercing customers are older.

While Sapolsky found the door on belly button piercings isn't as tightly regimented as tongue piercings, it's a pretty safe bet that there aren't too many women over the age of 40 getting them.

What is it about the ageing brain that makes us pass from the novelty stage to the predictable stage? Obviously, there are those who continue to be open to new music, new food, and new circumstances of any kind, but are there any specific characteristics that the stodgy hold in common?

A psychologist named Simington, an expert on ageing, believes those who don't retain their sense of adventure have two characteristics:

1. They stay at the same job for a long time.

2. They become *eminent* or especially successful at that job.

For whatever reasons, this combination ramrods you into a debilitating state. As soon as something new arrives, you're screwed. Your brain short circuits. You spend your free time yelling at kids to get off your lawn.

Well, that's a nice theory, but this transition to fogeydom happens in the animal kingdom, too. When a baby rat reaches puberty, novelty is good — new foods are cool, new haunts are cool — but not quite so cool when they get older.

Similarly, when baboons are moved to a new territory with new plants, the older baboons won't try them. The young ones do, though, while the older baboons sit around and talk about the good ol' days and how you "shoulda' tasted the leaves in the Congo, by gum, because they really knew how to grow them leaves up there...not like these new-fangled leaves, gosh-durn it."

The older baboons are just like the sushi-eaters in Nebraska!

So it must be biological. Robert Sapolsky thinks so. While it apparently can't be explained by an equation or anything chemical, Sapolsky thinks aging creatures all over nature are often drawn towards repetition because, "...you get to a time in life where, by definition, stuff's turning to quicksand and wherever you can get some solid footing, the familiar becomes real comforting."

Similarly, Chris Miller, one of the station programmers interviewed for the National Public Radio piece, says that his listeners can hear an old song and see what they saw, hear what they heard, feel what they felt those many years ago when they first listened to the song.

In effect, it becomes a form of time travel, something permanent in an ever-changing world.

I don't know about that. I just think it's another biomarker of aging, as concrete as failing eyesight, droopy testicles, or inelastic arteries. Besides, what you're familiar with is *easier*; you don't have to make up your mind about anything and risk opening up new mental pathways. It's easier to stick stuff into old files than open up new ones.

I can understand that type of thinking...but it's *wrong*. You have to fight it. The thing is, when you try new things, new adventures, or open yourself up to new experiences, you grow.

And that was a good thing 20 years ago and it's a good thing today, too.

-- 2006

An Inconvenient Truth About Your Balls

Specifically, why are our balls perched right in front in harm's way? They're like twin piñatas hanging off a tree, just begging to be whacked by someone or something (wayward toddlers, exuberant dogs, kitchen chairs, etc.).

With apologies to the forces that created the universe, I'd like to file a complaint. Oh, don't worry, it's not about starvation or war or poverty or any of the usual stuff.

Nor am I bellyaching about personal situations. Sure I wouldn't mind if you sent some money to my Aunt Ludmilla, who's hugely embarrassed because the tragic grocery cart collision at the Piggly Wiggly ruptured her gall bladder and — much to the malicious glee of her daycare workers — caused her to pee day-glo green, but I'm sure you'll help her if you see fit.

Nah. Rather, my complaint has to do with engineering, human engineering.

You see, I'm puzzled by our balls. I'm not talking about how they work, because I'd be a fool not to recognize that they're technical marvels. I mean, who came up with that thing where they rise or drop based on freakin' ambient temperature? Brilliant!

It makes me wonder why GM doesn't do that with their cars. Instead of radiators filled with stuff that looks like Ludmilla's pee, they could have the engine rise and drop to control overheating.

Anyhow, what I'm puzzled by is the *location* of our balls. I started thinking about it after reading an article in *Discover* magazine. The author couldn't figure out, evolutionarily speaking, why our balls are where they are.

Don't get me wrong, I think they're definitely in the right area. I mean it wouldn't make any sense if they were by, say, our ears. Why, that'd require a whole lot more tubing and might make using one of those 1500-watt blowtorch hairdryers problematical.

To be more specific, I'm talking more about *placement*. Specifically, why are our balls perched right in front in harm's way? They're like twin piñatas hanging off a tree, just begging to be whacked by someone or something (wayward toddlers, exuberant dogs, kitchen chairs, etc.).

The balls are the repositories of sperm, which carry our genetic compliment! Excuse me, but putting them in front is like Fed-Ex carrying its birthday presents and important contracts in a flimsy plastic grocery store sack that's strapped to the front bumper, where it can be assailed by the elements or hit by a Toyota or plain stolen by street punks.

Isn't their current placement a huge freakin' gamble? Why, every time we get up we're inviting the whole damn world to play Whac-a-Mole with our balls!

Now why can't the testicles be housed internally? After all, the female of the species doesn't wear her ovaries outside her body. Think how problematic that would be! Just accessorizing them or finding shoes to match would be a nightmare.

I know what some of you are saying. You're thinking that all the other mammals wear their balls outside, so why should it be a problem with humans? Well, I'll tell you, smarty-pants. The other mammals are quadrupeds and as such have thickly muscled hind legs to protect their testicles.

How often do you see a wolverine rolling on the ground holding its balls, moaning *fuh...fuh...fuh...*because it ran into a tree branch and it hurts so bad it can't even finish the swear word? Not often, I bet.

You might also counter with something I already pointed out, that our balls need to be outside so they're better able to regulate temperature. Or the more sexually attuned of you might like the balls just where they are, thank you, because they allow easy access to the nimble hands of off-duty Hooter's waitresses.

But why didn't they just evolve *inside* the body, deeply encased in bone — preferably the same amount of bone a rhino has in its skull? To ensure proper air-cooling and to continue to allow access to friendly waitresses, you'd need some well-placed ventilation holes.

So what if we looked a little like bowling balls? The testicles would be safe! Our DNA would be safe! And think, with all that bone, we could ram Jeeps filled with poachers! Furthermore, Johnny Knoxville would never have been able to make movies that were based on hapless guys getting hit in the nuts.

Maybe you're turning a deaf ear on all this anyhow, because it seems fewer and fewer of us have much use for our testicles.

Just as the Arctic ice packs are diminishing, so it seems are our balls. Maybe we should call it Global Testicular Climate Change. Maybe our balls, because of infrequent use, were so cold that they were pulled completely into our body cavities where they've been slowly sautéed into obsolescence.

And that, buddy boy, is really an inconvenient truth, doubly so if you're my friend Angela.

She's a lawyer. Does well, too. Only she can't find herself anybody worth dating. She belongs to this club, or service, whatever you want to call it, named *It's Just Lunch*.

The company matches supposedly like-minded men and women so they can have lunch, which is historically a low-stress, benign encounter where the woman can have a nice sandwich without having to worry about putting out. If she and her date are compatible, they'll presumably have a second date, go to the movies, and screw politely.

Unfortunately, the hamsters she's met have amounted to a long string of bad beef. The last guy she met seemed to have promise, until, that is, he stood up and said, "Excuse me, I have to go tee-tee."

Believe it or not, this is some hellish euphemism for taking a piss. Angela nearly aspirated her ice tea. In her mind, the date was over.

And the guy before tee-tee boy? Kept talking about how he loves cuddling better than sex. She blew him off, too. By last count, she's had nearly 30 failed lunches.

It's clear that Angela's what I call a T-Vixen – short for Testosterone Vixen. Likes her whiskey and her men straight up. She'd much prefer that tee-tee boy would have said, "Scuze me, but I gotta' go fire-hose some cockroaches off the porcelain." Personally, I would have said, "I have to micturate," cuz' I'm brainy and some girls like us brainy types who use big words.

Regardless, Angela doesn't want a girlfriend with a dick — she wants a lover. But she can't find one.

Frankly, I'm having trouble comprehending the guys she's been meeting. Are they sad examples of Global Testicular Climate Change, or are they so misguided, they're acting how they think women *expect* them to act?

If it's an act, let me tell you, the girls most of us want won't fall for this guff, don't appreciate this guff, and the women we ultimately don't want — the ones that deem our testicles a character flaw — actually *like* expressions like "tee-tee" and the idea of cuddling instead of sex.

But let's say these poor bastards manage to find women who prefer a lack of testicularity. Let's say they end up in relationships with these women. By acting like dickless wonders from the get-go, they're stuck in hamster mode for the rest of their life. Their character has been typecast and there's no way the wife-director is going to let him get out of that role.

If, eventually, Harry Potter decided to revert to Dirty Harry, wifey would spank his hairless butt. I bet you know lots of these guys. Hell, based on what I can see, most of America is comprised of these ball-less wonders. They're these dutiful little husbands that tsk-tsk the shameful world along with wifey every time some movie, television show, magazine, play, song, or person doesn't match up to their tight-assed standards.

But get Harry away from wifey for a minute and he reverts to a frat boy. He's like a dog who's been chained to the tree in his backyard for weeks and the joy of being free for a few minutes causes him to pee on every begonia in sight, dig up the entire neighborhood, and mount every poodle he can find while slapping its fuzzy ass and howling at the moon.

Of course, it doesn't say much for the size of his balls in the first place if he let himself be pigeonholed into this sham of a life.

Hey! I just figured out why the balls are in front! It makes it easier for wifey to remove them and stash them in an old coffee can with the expired coupons, extra house keys, and other non-essential household detritus.

-- 2007

Slay the Dragon

If you're the average person, chances are your job is too small for you, too small for your spirit, too small for your soul. I don't think it used to be that way, at least to the degree it is now.

Oh man, that Ernie leads some great life!

He's always got his suitcase with him, one of those numbers with a collapsible handle and tiny polyurethane wheels. Who knows what exotic places he's off to? Too bad he's closemouthed about his travels. Whenever you ask him where he's going he says, "Life is one big trip, buddy."

I've never met anyone whose life is so full of leisure activities. One night he's off to a Cheryl Crow concert and the next morning he's off to some concert downtown or some new art exhibition. It's the same day after day. Granted it's not shit I want to do, but his life, at least to him, is full.

People in town don't know what he did for a living (he clearly retired early, what with all that free time), but they know he travels a lot and just yesterday they saw him driving a brand new Lexus.

Most people figure he was a stockbroker; one of those Masters of the Universe who got out while the getting was good.

I know Ernie's secret, though.

Ernie is *homeless*. The ever-present suitcase? It contains everything he owns. The constant activities? The guy is a master of *free* — he knows every no-charge event in the tri-county area. And the Cheryl Crow Concert? He simply took advantage of "Dollar Day" at the county fair and she was the featured has-been performer.

The Lexus was just part of a promotion by the local car dealer: "Take a Test Drive and Lunch is on us!" Sure, for driving a new car around the block a few times, he got a 20-dollar gift certificate for a much-appreciated lunch.

Ernie "passes" because he doesn't look like a homeless guy. His clothes are always clean and pressed, but that's just part of another one of Ernie's survival tactics -- he sleeps outside the public library, but every third day or so he scrounges up enough money to spend a night in a cheap hotel where he takes advantage of the free soap and water to clean up.

Tragically, pathetically, whatever synonym of *sadly* you want to throw in, Ernie is almost universally envied by the real stockbrokers in town. They don't know he's homeless. All they see is a seemingly happy guy who doesn't live by the clock or kiss someone's ass all day long.

"That guy sure knows how to live," is the usual sentiment, followed by "I can't wait until I'm retired, man."

A homeless guy is leading a better life than they are!

Despite their trappings of wealth — their restored Jaguars, the enormous "chronometers" on their wrists, their bleached blonde, augmented wives with puffy bovine connective-tissue injected cock-nibbling lips — they're envious of a guy with zero possessions.

Somewhere the demons are laughing.

Now I'm not sure what happened to Ernie, why he dropped out of the workforce, but I don't think it was a pathological aversion to work. I think it's because work sucks. Oh, I'm not talking about my job, I'm talking about Ernie's former job and just maybe, *yours*.

If you're the average person, chances are your job is too small for you, too small for your spirit, too small for your *soul*. I don't think it used to be that way, at least to the degree it is now.

Author and historian Studs Terkel wrote a book named *Working* about 35 years ago. In it he detailed the working lives of regular folks, people who were rarely heard from like gravediggers, construction workers, and waitresses.

Despite the relatively mundane nature of their work, a good percentage of them took immense pride in their work. The supermarket checker had elevated her job into practically an art form, hitting the keys with one hand and pushing the food along with another while periodically whacking the conveyor button with her hip. She knew what everything costs, and when she was away from her job more than a day or two, she missed it.

Likewise, the gravedigger was proud of his neat lines and square edges, explaining that, "A human body is goin' into this grave. That's why you need skill when you're gonna' dig a grave."

The waitress bragged about how when she put a plate down, it didn't make a sound, and how there was a certain delicate way to pick up a dropped fork. She reasoned that every time she served a meal, "she was on stage."

A hospital billing-agent talked about looking in on a patient who'd lost his leg. A flight attendant talked about how she was supposed to spend at least 30 minutes of every flight socializing with passengers.

Terkel found that even for the lowliest laborer, work was a search "for daily meaning as well as daily bread."

But you don't need me to tell you that situations like this are becoming increasingly rare. Competence is rare. Enthusiasm is rare. Giving a shit is rare.

And I'm hardly the only one lamenting this change of atmosphere.

Even Presidential candidate Barack Obama wrote about this problem in his book, *The Audacity of Hope*:

> *Nothing brightens my day more than dealing with somebody, anybody, who takes pride in their work and goes the extra mile — an accountant, a plumber, a three-star general, the person on the other end of the phone who actually seems to want to solve your problem. My encounters with such competence seem more and more sporadic lately; I seem to spend more time looking for somebody in the store to help me or waiting for my deliveryman to show. Other people must notice this; it makes us all cranky, and those of us in government, no less than in business, ignore such perceptions at their own peril.*

Part of what's changed is that just about everyone under 30 carries around a big emotional *grande* frappe contaminated with feelings of entitlement, over-inflated feelings of self-worth, and a residual sense of twisted reality caused by watching too many beer commercials showing people with no visible means of support having tons of consequence-free sex.

How can they help but feel that work isn't necessarily connected to *living*?

"Work" is an intangible, something you occasionally have to do to earn some scratch on your way to finding that thing that allows you to make tons of money for just being you, wonderful you.

But I don't think that's the burr that was up Ernie's butt, nor do I think it's the reason most grounded types are fed up with their jobs. I think it's the changing face of the legal system and evolving business philosophies that play a bigger part of this "quality drought."

Specifically, according to an article in *The New York Times*, new technologies and new management styles have put workers on "digital assembly lines" with "little room for creativity or independent thought."

A sizeable amount of the work force is now employed in call centers where they follow canned scripts and are supervised by a method called "management by stress." Store clerks are paralyzed from making any decision on their own, no matter how fair it might seem, because the entire nation has its balls wrapped tightly in "company policy."

"We're sorry that your box of granola contained a nipple ring, parts of a human head, and a desiccated pork chop, but our manager's not here, and we're not allowed to offer refunds without his okay. Company policy, you know."

I can't believe any clerk saying such things isn't deeply ashamed; doesn't know that *that's not the way things are supposed to work.*

Physicians and healthcare workers in general tend to patients using a watery blend of medical science, dictums issued by managed-care administrators, and cover-your-ass-from-legal-implications protocols.

So it's probably not hard to understand why a lot of people work in hell. But it's silly to think things are magically going to change overnight. You can assume all the personal responsibility you like, but sometimes it won't make a difference.

Sometimes you just have to bolt.

Oh I know it's not always possible. Maybe you have a wife or 2.2 children and a big fat mortgage. I get it. But sometimes it's fear.

I used to be a cubicle worker; one of those guys who was depressed from Sunday night all the way through Friday afternoon. I had aspirations of writing — writing something other than computer manuals for the government — but somewhere along the way my balls had shrunk.

Looking back, I think it had something to do with my office mate. John fancied himself a science fiction writer and he had a shelf-full of rejected manuscripts. John thought he was a great writer and he couldn't understand why he wasn't sitting behind a desk at Comic-Con signing autographs for guys dressed like space aliens. But I knew why. John's writing *sucked*, really, really, sucked. I could see it, but he couldn't.

In my serotonin-depleted brain, paranoia began to grow. I started to think that maybe I was like John, walking around thinking I could write when the truth was, I really, really sucked. So I didn't do anything about it. For years.

John helped create what mythology professor Joseph Campbell called my *dragon*. Campbell believed the dragon is one's binding of oneself to one's ego. He would have said I was captured in my own dragon cage. Luckily, I was able to disintegrate the dragon by anger, desperation, and sheer will.

For others, it may not be so easy. They might not even know what their dragon is, or what they would do if they could kill their dragon. Campbell had some thoughts on that as well. He often wrote about "following your bliss," that which makes you feel the most happy — "not excited, not just thrilled, but deeply happy."

Once you find it, he advised, stay with it, no matter what people tell you.

If they tell you not to go north, go north. If they tell you to walk, run. If they tell you bow down and curtsy, stand up and stick a fist in their eye. "You can't have creativity unless you leave behind the bounded, the fixed, all the rules."

One of my favorite movie passages, one that makes me practically tear up every time I see it, is from *Good Will Hunting*. The characters played by Matt Damon and Ben Affleck are sucking down a couple of beers on a construction site and they're discussing the future of boy-genius Will (Matt Damon).

Will is a reluctant genius, though. He can pretty much do anything but his complex dragons have him resigned to a lifetime of manual labor. His friend Chuckie, a run of the mill wanker, is still smart enough to recognize Will's talent and he's incensed that Will refuses to "leave behind the bounded":

CHUCKIE: Are they hookin' you up with a job?

WILL: Yeah, sit in a room and do long division for the next fifty years.

CHUCKIE: Yah, but it's better than this shit. At least you'd make some nice bank.

WILL: Yeah, be a fuckin' lab rat.

CHUCKIE: It's a way outta here.

WILL: What do I want a way outta here for? I want to live here the rest of my life. I want to be your next-door neighbor. I want to take our kids to little league together up to Foley Field.

CHUCKIE: Look, you're my best friend, so don't take this the wrong way, but in 20 years, if you're livin' next door to me, comin' over watchin' the fuckin' Patriots' games and still workin' construction, I'll fuckin' kill you. And that's not a threat, that's a fact. I'll fuckin' kill you.

WILL: Chuckie, what are you talkin'...

CHUCKIE: Listen, you got somethin' that none of us have.

WILL: Why is it always this? I owe it to myself? What if I don't want to?

CHUCKIE: Fuck you. You owe it to me. Tomorrow I'm gonna wake up and I'll be fifty and I'll still be doin' this. And that's all right 'cause I'm gonna make a run at it. But you, you're sittin' on a winning lottery ticket and you're too much of a pussy to cash it in. And that's bullshit 'cause I'd do anything to have what you got! And so would any of these guys. It'd be a fuckin' insult to us if you're still here in twenty years.

WILL: You don't know that.

CHUCKIE: Let me tell you what I do know. Every day I come by to pick you up, and we go out drinkin' or whatever and we have a few laughs. But you know what the best part of my day is? The ten seconds before I knock on the door 'cause I let myself think I might get there, and you'd be gone. I'd knock on the door and you wouldn't be there. You just left.

Now, I don't know much. But I know that.

If your job's not big enough for your spirit, you have a few choices, clench your teeth and bear it until you die, drop out like Ernie, or find a job big enough for your spirit.

Now. I don't know much. But I know that.

-- 2008

She Wants Me!

I don't blame women for taking advantage of men.
The wonder is that we continue to fall for it. You'd
think that after the thousandth time that Lucy
pulled the football away and we fell on our ass, we'd
learn.

So I was outside on the patio sunning my schlong — you know, for the Vitamin D — when the doorbell rang.

I got up and walked back into the house, simultaneously pulling on my pants and doing one of those awkward one-leg-in, one-leg-out hopping motions that are the lifeblood of the sack racer.

As I buttoned up, I peered out the peephole.

Standing on the other side of the door was something delightfully blonde in a tight pink tank top with a neckline so *low,* so expansive that even Shaquille O'Neal could fit his fat head through it.

And speaking of Shaq, my vantage point was kinda' like what he must experience every day, only instead of peering down at other basketball players' heads, I was looking down at the crown of a beautiful milky white Kobe and a beautiful milky white Lebron, each bedecked by a hint of lacy pink bra.

I love this game!

And it got plain silly from there, because I viddied this wide swath of smooth, downy belly, bordered way down South by a pair of low-rider jeans that some clothing designer-slash-engineer-slash-*genius* on the same plane as Da Vinci had sewn together — -figuring out just how much delicate opposing tension the hips and ass would have to exert to keep the whole rig from slipping down and exposing the hoo-hah.

I remember thinking how a doctor could have easily done an appendectomy on this girl without removing any clothing at all.

Wondrous.

Granted, the view was a little disproportionately magnified because of the lense in the peephole — all tits and nose peering back at me — but even the peephole couldn't hide that there was a spectacular ass-bunny on the other side of the door.

I stood up straight, puffed out my chest a bit, brushed my hair back with my hand and opened the door, a somewhat toothy, hopefully not-too-creepy smile on my face.

"Hi, I'm Jennifer," she said.

Jennifer! Of course! Could it be anything else?

"Do I have a booger in my nose?"

That I wasn't expecting.

"Because I feel like I have a booger in my nose. Can I use your bathroom?"

I must have said *sure* because seconds later she was in my bathroom, presumably examining the reflection of her inner nostril.

I'm pretty sure I wouldn't have let a guy into my house if he feared he had a booger in his nose, but I said *sure* to Jennifer because I'm a man and I'm a sucker for anything soft and smooth with a voice like a nightingale and, well, *breasts.*

And I looked, and behold, a pale breast, and her name that it sat on was Jennifer, and hell followed with her.

Jennifer, it turns out, is a member of her high school volley ball team (of course!) and she was trying to earn money to send her team God-knows-where because I'm not hearing any of the yammering; I'm in the Testosterone grips of *plak tow,* and like Spock, if I don't mate or at least whack off furiously very soon, I will surely die.

All I was thinking was *Penthouse letter, Penthouse letter...* well, that and *I'm going to jail... I'm going to jail....*

Jennifer talked and talked and talked, not coming up for air even once. In between pleas for money and promises of a tactile reward *("I'll give you a hug"),* the little vixen even asked if she could move in with me because, you know, "living with your parents is such a drag."

But nothing happened. Except that somehow, I gave her alleged volleyball team 80 dollars. I was left with nothing but a signed receipt (she dots the "i" in her name with a heart!) and a rapidly receding hard-on.

Even so, I kept reliving the moment for hours if not days, thinking how, for sad words of tongue and pen, the saddest are these, "It might have been." Oh yeah, she *might have been* bent over my vintage naugahyde couch grunting like she'd just hit a succession of jump serves; she *might have been* in the bathroom clearing something out of her nose other than boogers.

I don't know exactly when it happened, during her short visit or afterwards, but a certain delusion began to form and solidify in my mind: *Jennifer wanted me.* Sure she wanted money, but that was purely incidental. Yep, she wanted *me.*

The truth, of course, is that Jennifer didn't want me. She knew that I, along with every other heterosexual male on the block and in fact, the entire tri-county area, would end up falling prey to her bubbly flirtations and give her money, if not the Amex card or the deed to the house.

I don't blame women for taking advantage of men. The wonder is that we continue to fall for it. You'd think that after the thousandth time that Lucy pulled the football away and we fell on our ass, we'd learn.

Of course, we always think women are coming on to us, even if they aren't. The most innocent remark or gesture from an attractive woman is interpreted as flirtation.

We ask her to pass the ketchup, and if she so much as smiles while doing so, we think it's as clear a sign of her sexual receptiveness as if she had stripped naked and writhed around on the floor of the diner while squeezing her breasts together and moaning our name.

I can't tell you how many ordinary looking friends I have who suffer repeated and extreme bouts of this delusion. Mark tells me, eyes afire, that today, two women, on separate occasions, smiled at him!

He can't accept that it's courtesy or that it's a nice day and they're glad to be alive or even the possibility that they're smiling because of his ridiculous Icelandic turtleneck sweater that looks like it was made out of navel lint.

Noooo. They want him. Sexually.

I'm sitting down at a cafe having a coffee with a friend when a girl I know stops to talk to me. She doesn't say so much as a word to my friend, but when she leaves he says, "You see that? She ignored me. I think she likes me."

Where in the hell does this type of misguided self-esteem come from!?!

If you're a woman, you can have a casual conversation with a guy and mention your fiancé, Lorenzo, a full dozen times and it's a pretty safe bet the guy you're talking to *still* thinks you're coming on to him.

I have other friends who, while working out, can't accept the notion that a woman is stretching or doing leg curls for any other purpose than to send them a sexual signal. Heaven forbid they work the seated hip abduction machine:

See my hoo-hah? Now you don't. See my hoo-hah? Now you don't.

"Dude! Could she be any more obvious?"

Sheesh. No wonder women join *Curves*.

The most pathetic delusions take place at the strip club. It almost never fails. A man emerges from the back room after having his first ever two hundred dollar lap dance and he's convinced his girl was turned on; that she liked him!

"No, no, she's different! I've got tickets to the RV show at the coliseum this weekend. I think I'll ask her to go with me."

He won't listen to reason.

God help him. God help *us*.

Listen, the only place where women truly flirt is at the bar on half-price tequila shooter night, or on the Internet. The rest is our imagination.

Speaking of the latter, I've gotten emails from women over the years that would scorch Larry Flynt's soiled paraplegic shorts. A lot of men I know have received similar emails. While they're fun to read and they often cause Jedidiah to rouse from his flaccid nap, I'm pretty sure it's just how women have fun with us.

Sadistic men pull wings off flies; sadistic women send dirty emails.

If I ever met one of these women in person, I'm sure she'd claim identity theft while mentioning the name of her fiancé, Lorenzo, over and over again.

I wonder if women truly realize what suckers we are. It's a wonder any of us have any money at all. If women really knew how pathetic we are, they'd simply line up outside the banks on the 1st and 15th of every month holding grocery bags open with outstretched hands. All they'd have to do is wear something a little sexy and say, "You're cuuuute!" to every schlub that walked out of the bank.

Of course, with our predilection for self delusion, all they'd have to say is, "Hello, it's a bit humid today, isn't it?" and we'd empty our wallets all the same while extracting megabytes of innuendo from their remark.

The women would go home, empty the money on to their bed, strip, and roll around naked on all that cash. I'm pretty damn sure Jennifer is doing the same thing right now.

You know, I betcha' she started thinking about me as soon as she got naked. Oh yeah, she wants me.

-- 2006

The Wedding Crasher

They used to throw rice after American weddings, which at least paid lip service to the notion of fertility, but now they often blow soap bubbles at the just-married lovebirds. It's an apt metaphor, I think, for your balls — each floats away, lingers briefly in the air, and then pops into nothingness.

Another bride, another June, another sunny honeymoon, another season, another reason, for makin' whoopee.

— Makin' Whoopee, lyrics by Walter Donaldson and Gus Kahn, 1928

I went to a wedding last week. The hall was festooned with flower petals and colorful seashells. There were giant posters of the bride and groom in various stages of their life affixed to the walls.

Look, it's Chad at his high school graduation! There's Jessica at a children's beauty pageant! Aren't they cute? Who'd have thought they'd lived such fascinating lives?

Octogenarians, accompanied by screaming, sugar-fueled children, stumbled and swayed to the saccharin music of Mike Calhoun and his Mobile Music Machine.

There were even complimentary beverages.

It was every woman's dream.

It was every man's freaking nightmare.

Don't worry, I've no intention of ragging on the institution of marriage itself. Nor do I have a beef with religious ceremonies that are, in some cases, as old as civilization itself.

It's what happens immediately *after* the ceremony that freaks me out, and I'm not talking about the whoopee. Hell, in America, a wedding seems to be about everything *but* the whoopee, which is supposedly the point of the whole thing.

It's true that every culture has its strange wedding customs. Lovers in ancient Persia declared their love by publicly drinking each other's blood. The Masai of East Africa wear their wife's clothing for one month after marriage. In ancient Britain, wives wore their finest clothing to the wedding ceremony, but grooms wed *skyclad* — in the nude.

Tibetans splashed newlyweds with Yak grease. In central Europe, Teutonic women proved their worth as presumptive wives by standing on the battlefield with their husbands and killing one of his enemies, should the opportunity arise.

Certain unlucky Polynesians were killed right after saying their vows. As soon as they said, "I do," they were sacrificed; pelted with an avalanche of rocks and wooden debris instead of rice. The best man, no doubt, good naturedly affixed empty cans of poi to their cart or canopy, along with a sign that read, "Just Buried."

But all those customs had some meaning. All those customs, whether it was readily apparent or not, had to do in some way with ensuring *fertility*.

What, tell me, does registering at *Bed, Bath, and Beyond* have to do with fertility?

What does wearing a lame champagne-colored tuxedo and dropping 4 month's salary on some arbitrarily priced wedding ring have to do with fertility? What does dropping 27K (the average price of an American wedding) have to do with ensuring that your bewildered jiz meets up with an egg?

Where's the whoopee?

The irony of the typical American wedding is that, despite being the modern-day equivalent of what started out as a fertility ritual, it's the most emasculating thing imaginable.

Enduring what is now an entirely feminine ritual is like a fraternity hazing. It's like Werner Eckhard's EST, where instructors psychologically broke down disciples by emotional and physical abuse. Both the frat hazing and EST are trial by ordeal. So is a wedding.

You've heard of the bends, right? It's what happens when a scuba diver comes up too fast, or when a passenger is in a plane that loses pressure as it ascends. Tiny nitrogen bubbles form in the blood. You experience a rash and joint pain. Your brain goes squirrelly. Paralysis can set in, sometimes followed by death.

Well, the bends are nothing compared to what happens when you propose marriage. You go from playing poker and dirt biking and staying up all night gaming to shopping for dust ruffles, and it happens at warp speed. You don't know what hit you! To make it worse, the dust ruffles you're shopping for aren't even NASCAR or Star Trek dust ruffles but some pastel bullshit with a daffodil pattern.

You've used the same nappy towel to dry every part of your body for about ten years, but now you've got to feign interest in finger towels! Monogrammed finger towels! You now have to give a damn about washers, dryers, and all sorts of *appliances.*

Talk about your brain going squirrelly!

But forget all that, the real ball buster is the wedding itself. You've got to listen to John Denver and Celine Dion songs, courtesy of Mike Calhoun and his Mobile Music Machine!

John Denver and Celine Dion?

Sperm killers!

You've even got to take ballroom dance lessons to prepare for the big day when you get to take turns dancing with your mother, your mother-in-law, your sister-in-law, your sister-in-law's podiatrist, and so on, ad nauseam.

Dancing with your mother-in-law, her aging bosom pressed against your perspiring chest? Your loins swaying gently in sync with hers?

Testicle destroyer!

Then you've got to listen to semi-sincere toasts and speeches, all accompanied by varying degrees of blubbering. You've got to perform like a trained monkey and kiss your bride — who you're already starting to despise for subjecting you to all this humiliation — whenever some jackass dings his bottle of Bud with a utensil.

Do that one more time, Uncle Bob, and I'll jam that fork into your cirrhotic liver...

Don't forget to get down on one knee in front of all those leering fossils that are somebody's uncles or grandfathers or whatever, who are no doubt hoping for a peek at your new wife's upper thigh as you feign being shy and excited while you pull off her garter and touch her firm flesh for presumably the very first time.

You'd best keep to yourself the fact that the darling virgin wanted butt love and made little barking sounds like a Pekinese the night before.

Then you've got to stand motionless with your eyes wide open Amos and Andy style while your wife pretends to feed you a big slab of wedding cake while some loser photographer who's Monday through Friday job is shooting pictorials for Milfhunter.com captures the moment for posterity.

I ask you again, where's the whoopee?

Only your balls are now dead. They've been baked in schmaltz, so whoopee is probably out of the question, anyhow. You might be able to get a hard-on out of something related to muscle memory, but you're probably shooting blanks.

They used to throw rice after American weddings, which at least paid lip service to the notion of fertility, but now they often blow soap bubbles at the just-married lovebirds. It's an apt metaphor, I think, for your balls — each floats away, lingers briefly in the air, and then pops into nothingness.

I think the only people who came close to doing a wedding celebration right were the Vikings. Their rowdy feasting, music, and drunkenness lasted up to a month and the celebrations were refreshingly free of the Hokey Pokey. Guests didn't have to shop at *Bed, Bath, and Beyond*. In fact, *guests* got a gift, no reciprocation required! When things got dull, someone got an axe in the chest and got an all-expenses paid trip to Valhalla.

If I had my druthers, the modern American post-wedding ceremony would be a bit more pagan, a bit more like the Vikings, a bit more *Testosteronish*.

First of all, Mike Calhoun would be stripped naked, tied, and dropped into the fondue pot before being thrown stickily into the street. Anyone who made a ludicrous toast that explained how the bride and groom were made for each other and would grow old together would join Mike Calhoun amid the molten cheese.

Only women would be allowed to dance, and it would be customary for the hot ones to undulate provocatively like Roman slave women while men sipped whisky and nodded approvingly.

Late in the evening, everyone would gather in the middle of the dance floor and watch as the bridal party ceremoniously removed the bride and groom's clothing, followed by the husband and wife coupling on the floor like wild animals while the men — in the manner of Viking oarsmen in their long ships — rhythmically shouted, Stroke! Stroke! Stroke!"

Afterwards, the bridal party would bring in a steaming cauldron that contained soup made from the brides' panties, topped off with some porcini mushrooms and some lemon zest. Eating the soup would, of course, ensure *fertility*.

Ah, who am I kidding? My ideas won't catch on. They're way too radical, but it's nice to dream, don't you think? Maybe a compromise would work, something that left out the stupid mandatory dances, the bad music, the horrible obligatory speeches, and the silly, emasculating rituals involving the garter belt and the wedding cake and all the wretched rest.

After all, the man's got to have his balls intact afterwards, right? That's presumably the point of the whole thing.

I say we push for the Yak grease.

-- 2007

A Sinful Taste for Tiny Waists

Estrogen means smoother skin, pert breasts, pouty lips, and yes, fertility. If you want to spread your seed, you're generally going to take aim at the curvy thing and not the one who looks like it works on the docks hauling freezers off a Hungarian freighter.

According to anthropologist Elizabeth Cashdan, I've been wrong about women. Or rather, wrong about which ones I'm attracted to.

You know those curvy, tiny-waisted ones you see sashaying down the street? The ones that cause a surge of blood to our nether regions, cause our breath to quicken and our heart to race, bring a flush to our skin, and cause our synapses to start bouncing chemical signals off the nooks and crannies of our brain like the ping pong balls in the Saturday night million dollar megabucks lottery drawing machine?

Apparently, we don't really care for those creatures as much as we thought we did. Instead, Cashdan insists what we truly want is women who are shaped like knackwurst.

Her beef, or sausage, as described on the *LiveScience* website, has to do with past medical studies that suggest that a roller-coasterish swimsuit model waist-to-hip ratio of 0.7 or lower is associated with a higher fertility rate and lower rates of chronic disease, thus sending out a silent biological signal to men that says, "Hellooo, sailor!"

(Just to give you a visual, the average Playboy centerfold has a .68 ratio. The average member of Oprah's audience probably has a 1.0, 1.1, or 1.2 ratio. You get the picture.)

Cashdan doesn't buy the small waist/fertility thing, instead believing that "an imperfect body might be just what the doctor ordered for women and key to their economic success."

And, "while pop culture seems to worship the hourglass figure for females with a tiny waist, big boobs, and curvy hips, this may not be optimal."

Yep, Cashdan thinks what we really want is thicker-waisted (fatter) women because their fatness shows they're stronger, smarter, and healthier than those women we *thought* were desirable.

That longing we feel for those tight-waisted mammalian creatures? It's all because of our exposure to popular culture. Man, I am *so* embarrassed. I don't know about you, but I feel humiliated. I feel *used*.

It must have been those beer commercials. They feature curvy wasp-waisted vixens and naturally, due to all the devious, subconscious psychological programming, we've been hoodwinked into thinking we prefer that type of woman.

There must be a secret cabal of tiny-waisted women somewhere, who, bitter about their tiny waists that no man could love, decided to brainwash us with commercials.

Damn those manipulative bitches! Damn them!

But thanks to Cashdan, both my big head and my little head are starting to clear.

What we've always thought was that no matter where you went in the world, whether you were bird-dogging chicks with the Mauri in New Zealand or members of one of the untouchable castes of India, men seemed drawn to tiny waists.

Cashdan, however, thinks that's all bunk. She compiled data from 33 non-Western populations and four European populations, only to find that the average waist-to-hip ratio was .8.

She wonders if .7 is ideal, why do most women exhibit a higher ratio?

The reason, she maintains, is that women with thicker waists not only demonstrate greater economic success, but their additional body fat makes them physically stronger and better able to deal with stress.

She believes this higher waist-to-hip ratio has to do with androgens, the class of hormones that includes our beloved Testosterone. She asserts that Testosterone "increases waist to hip ratio in women and increases visceral fat, which is carried around the waist."

She adds that cortisol, another androgen that happens to help the body deal with stress, also increases fat around the waist.

Consequently, these high-Test, high-cortisol, relatively straight up and down women could be associated with health advantages that might be particularly useful during times of stress.

As argumentative ammo, she notes that in Japan, Greece, and Portugal, where women supposedly tend to be less economically dependent, men place a higher value on a thin waist. She contrasts this with Denmark and Great Britain, where there tends to be more sexual equality and ipso facto, a longing for tuber-shaped women.

While she concedes that hip ratio may indeed be a useful signal to men, she states that "whether men prefer [a waist to hip ratio] associated with a lower or higher androgen/estrogen ratios (or value them equally) should depend on the degree to which they want their mates to be strong, tough, economically successful, and politically competitive."

Of course. It's all so clear. Women with .7 waists are weak and dumb! Women with .7 waists can't eviscerate cattle or field-dress a moose, and they're so dumb you can easily kidnap them by getting them to stick their fingers in one of those Chinese finger cuffs!

But thicker-waisted women? They're strong. If the tractor ran out of diesel and the horse has colic, you can harness them up and plow the back 40, thereby assuring that the children will eat this winter! And if the crops fail and the bank wants to take the farm, she won't go all squirrely on you. She'll maintain a stoic demeanor, unconsciously run her hands over her ample, gingham draped, cortisol-fueled midriff and say, "You are veak. I am strong. I vill crush you."

Wait... that might have been what Ivan Drago said in *Rocky IV*. Never mind.

And these heftier women are what I was subconsciously sexually attracted to all this time, right Ms. Cashdan? Oh, would that I had emptied my load on the broad torsos of thick-waisted women more often! My seed would have had more canvas with which to paint its erotic message! Less of it would have torrented off their silky sides into the chasms of the rumpled 1200-threadcount sheets below!

Come to me, my stout, knackwurst shaped women!

Phooey.

For an anthropologist, it seems Ms. Cashdan has based her theory on the weakest arguments imaginable. If one were skeptical, one might think she had an agenda, or at the very least some bias against women who possess the physical attributes so highly prized by *most* males.

She wonders why, if .7 is the ideal, so many women have waist to hip ratios of .8 or more?

I'll tell you why, Ms. Cashdan. Doughnuts. And Ho-Ho's. And the Cheesecake Factory. Wretched excess in general, and the resultant insulin resistance that causes their waists to thicken like grandma's goiter ridden neck.

That's often why .7 generally belongs to the young, those that haven't yet born the ravages of years of bad eating, which brings to mind another point. Nowhere in Cashdan's report do we learn if she broke her waist-to-hip studies into age groups, as younger girls would naturally have a better chance of attaining and maintaining the hallowed ratio.

And regarding the point about so few women having the .7 ratio, it's an *ideal*, not the norm. Perfection rarely is. An 8-inch cock might be ideal, but that doesn't mean it's the norm and it explains why Enzyte commercials are so successful.

Cashdan's explanation for the thicker waists, unfortunately, has to do with Testosterone and cortisol. The trouble is, Testosterone rarely leads to an increase in visceral or subcutaneous fat. Instead, it *reduces* body fat in both men and women. And as far as cortisol, it seems she's got it backwards. Cortisol, produced in excess by chronic stress, can lead to fat being preferentially deposited around the waist.

When additional stress is piled on, the energy stored around the waist as fat can be quickly mobilized by newly released cortisol.

One could just as easily make the assumption that .7 women are *resistant* to stress. Cool as cucumbers, they don't release cortisol and therefore, don't deposit fat around the waist.

Lastly, she points out that Danes and Brits seem to be less enamored of .7 than the Japanese, Greeks, or the Portuguese. I could swallow this argument more easily if the Danes weren't one of the leading producers of blond, wasp-waisted porn in the world and one of England's major contributions to recent modern culture wasn't the Page 3 girls.

Take a look at Page 3 girl Keely Hazell, Ms. Cashdan, behold her preternatural waist to hip ratio and tremble before her!

Unfortunately, Cashdan's musings, and they're nothing but musings— are trickling down into mainstream, already being referred to as *fact.*

After reading Cashdan's paper, *Newsweek* journalist Sharon Begley berated her magazine for the "Biology of Beauty" article it ran in 1996, titling her rebuttal, "We Take It All Back."

> *"Finally, more scientists are taking aim at the ludicrous idea that there is a biology of beauty—specifically that men prefer women with an hourglass shape because that is a sign of fertility, and men wired to find fertile women attractive were and are more likely to have descendants, who would carry their gene for that preference. Or so the story has gone."*

Because of Cashdan's article, and because empirical evidence suggests otherwise (she's seen "Barbie" types who can't get pregnant), Begley calls the science of beauty "claptrap."

Then she pulls out the *big* ammo:

"In fact, studies of isolated populations in Peru and Tanzania find that men there find hourglass women sick-looking. They prefer 0.9's—heavier women."

Listen Ms. Begley, some populations eat people, too. It's hardly an argument that *not* eating people is merely a cultural affectation somehow picked up by the 99.999999% of the world population that doesn't share that particular culinary taste. If anything, your example of Peru and Tanzanian populations proves that *their* preference is cultural.

Peru and Tanzania. Christ.

And whether a tiny waist really sends a signal to our reptilian brain that the bearer of such a swell waist to hip ratio really is more fertile is impossible to know.

However, nature usually has a reason for most things. Estrogen emphasizes secondary sexual characteristics by depositing fat on the breasts, hips, and glutes, but *not* the waist, presumably the better to emphasize the relative size of the other things we covet.

Estrogen means smoother skin, pert breasts, pouty lips, and yes, fertility. If you want to spread your seed, you're generally going to take aim at the curvy thing and not the one who looks like it works on the docks hauling freezers off a Hungarian freighter.

And neither Ms. Cashdan nor Ms. Begley should mistake what men marry as *preference*. Most men aren't ideal, either, and they simply marry the most genetically gifted mammal that'll allow him to stick his dick in it. That, for better or for worse, determines a lot of human natural selection.

-- 2008

Yahtzee!

I thought some men were balls/brain polarized
— they were ruled by one or the other; brains
north, and balls, of course, south. They were either
cerebral bastards who made their decisions based on
reason and intellect, or walking penises whose moist
slit of an eye was focused solely on finding another
jiggly girl in a tube top.

I thought I was a student of human nature. I thought I had it all figured out. It was simple!

I didn't need no stinkin' Freud to tell me that it all came down to *balls* and *brains*.

I thought some men were balls/brain polarized — they were ruled by one or the other; brains north, and balls, of course, south. They were either cerebral bastards who made their decisions based on reason and intellect, or walking penises whose moist slit of an eye was focused solely on finding another jiggly girl in a tube top.

Others, like me, were ruled by a combination of the two, each side engaged constantly in a death-struggle with the other, each side trying to gain the upper hand in determining the course of my actions.

If you're so cursed, you could probably relate mightily to Gollum's schizophrenic tendencies:

> *Gollum: Master won't give us what we want. We wants the precious! The one in the Dolce and Gabbana jeans! We ought to wring Master's filthy little neck. Kill him! Kill him. And then maybe we takes the precious out to that hip little jazz club just outside of Mordor!*
>
> *Sméagol: No, noooo, we have to go homses and work on the Willoughby account!*

That's right, your balls are Gollum and your mind is Sméagol, fighting each other for control and to determine priorities.

Jerry Seinfeld thought it was more like a chess game between his brain and his penis; the brain presumably wants to play chess while the penis' pursuits are more pedestrian.

Personally, I likened my internal struggle to a football game.

TC's Half-time score:

Balls 21

Logical Thinking 5

Okay, so it's been a lop-sided battle. Logical Thinking had a bad draft for about 20 years in a row and while it's only been able to muster up a field goal and a safety (accomplished while the Balls team was rubbernecking the cheerleaders), it's currently working on a new hurry-up offense that employs a rarely used single wing formation that will be sure to stymie the powerful but strategically simple-minded Balls team whose game plan is pretty much based on giving the pigskin to their sturdy running back and shouting, "Run Bubba, run!" as he rhythmically plunges straight ahead...again and again and again.

But I've recently learned there's a third player; a third motivating force and it's been there all along!

I've been thinking I've been playing 2-team football when I've really been playing 3-player *Yahtzee*.

I'm sort of dumbfounded that I never even considered the presence of this third player before, especially since it seems to account for so many of my actions, your actions, and the actions of lot of people around the world.

The bizarre thing is there's not even an English word that describes this impulse, but the Greeks sure had a name for it; Plato sure had a name for it.

Plato believed the soul was divided into not only reason and lust (what he called *Eros*), but also something called *thymos*.

Thymos is the part of the soul that comprises pride, indignation, shame, and most importantly, *the need for recognition*. We need people to recognize our worth. If they don't, we feel disrespected and we often erupt in rage.

Man, I tell you, it explains a lot.

World War II? Easy. After the Treaty of Versailles that ended World War I, Germany agreed to eat a lot of shit. They weren't allowed to have an army, they had to give up vast territories, their ships were given to the Allies, and they were stuck with a 33 billion dollar tab for the war, which didn't even include the tip.

This set Germany off on a thymotic crisis (not to mention an economic one) that hit a short little asexual vegetarian named Hitler particularly hard. In order to gain recognition, in order to purge himself and the Germans of all that disrespect, Hitler built up their Army, repopulated the Rhine, and just for the hell of it, marched into Poland.

Hey World, how do you like diese äpfel?

The Middle East? Ha! Give me something tough to explain!

The typical Arab male feels the world is disrespecting him, looking down on him for his economic status, his educational status, and most importantly, his religion.

Let's hear some ululating for those 72 virgins! U-loo-loo-loo-loo-loo-loo-loo-loo!

More locally, W. won't fire anyone, no matter how poorly he or she performs, because of his thymotic nature. Firing someone means he made a mistake in hiring that person in the first place, which conflicts with his need for recognition and approval.

Heckuva job, Brownie!

The Democrats continue to whine at an increasingly shrill pitch because Bush and the Republicans continue to stick it to 'em. If the GOP just threw them a bone once in a while, the Dems' thymotic impulses would be assuaged a bit and maybe we'd see some bipartisanship.

Barry Bonds is a walking poster child for thymos since he allegedly started using steroids and GH because of the adulation that Mark McGuire was getting from the fans in 1998 when he made his run at Roger Maris' homerun record.

I hit lots of home runs now, so love me! Love me!

Thymos explains everything about Arnold Schwarzenegger's life, from bodybuilding to business to marrying a Kennedy to becoming governor.

Men and women sometimes leave their spouses because of thymos. Wife number one, you see, didn't follow Cosmopolitan's Tip #10:

Always see the same tiger in the mirror he does.

So he left her for someone — at least for now — who sees that same tiger.

Why do all those jerks wear sports jerseys with Michael Jordan's or Lebron James' number on them? To bask in the reflective glory of their favorite sports star! To gain recognition from their physical achievements! It's second-hand thymos!

Why is losing an athletic competition so painful? Why is coming in second so bad? Because you don't get recognition for being number two.

What is fashion but thymos on parade?

Probably the main reason guys lift weights is for recognition!

Look at me, I have well-developed pecs and broad shoulders, not to mention some bitchin' rhomboids. Look, I even have that funny little delineating line — the name of which I don't know — which separates my abs from my torso and makes me look kinda like a Gladiator's breast plate! Damn, you know I'm special! Say it. Say I'm special. Go ahead, say it...please?

Thymos!

Work forces go on strike and employees quit, probably not so much because of poor pay or less than perfect working conditions, but because they didn't get...*respect!*

> *Leary: I have a rendezvous with death. And so does the President. So do you, if you get too close to me.*
>
> *Horrigan: You have a rendezvous with my ass, motherfucker!*
>
> *Leary: Frank, Frank, do you know how easily I could kill you? Do you know how many times I've watched you go in and out of that apartment? You're alive because I have allowed you to live. So you show me...some god-damn respect!*

— Clint Eastwood being dangerously dismissive of John Malkovich's thymos in the movie, "In the Line of Fire"

Why do rich people strive endlessly to get richer and richer? Sure, money for money's sake is a logical answer, as is the pursuit of power, but what are money and power but means to get recognition?

I don't mean to portray thymos as purely a negative thing, for in truth, it motivates us to do both the best things and the worst things we do. Jumping into the ocean to save a drowning man is a thymotic response, as is striving to better yourself or the planet around you.

I actually believe that a lot of Americans have a diminished thymos. They're either too self-absorbed or too dull witted or just too plain dead inside to get too fired up about much of anything. These are some of the people who get us thymotic types all worked up, quite willing to stick an axe in the chest of whoever was disrespectful of us.

But I guess we need the people with weak thymos. Who else is going to work at 7-11 or be a greeter at Banana Republic?

What's cool is that if you're cognizant of thymos, you can easily figure out why most men — and quite a few women — act the way they do. Most of the people on the street who get all red and veiny-necked and ready to kill you are simply looking for recognition or respect. Most of the trouble you might have with family members or fellow workers probably has to do with their desire for recognition.

While I now realize that the control of my destiny is a 3-player dice game instead of a football game, the balls, for better or worse, are still winning. The balls, in fact, have just rolled 3 Yahtzees in a row, while logical thinking and thymos can't get the dice to stay on the freakin' table.

C'mon, *Yahtzee!*

Note: Special thanks to David Brooks of "The New York Times" who taught me about thymos in his March 16th op-ed column.

-- 2006

The 7 Cowboy Values

Americans, along the same lines, are afraid of two-bit ideologues half-way across the world who might, without interference, eventually acquire the technology to hit the Virgin Islands with a nuclear missile that wobbles like one of Tim Tebow's passes after he got his melon knocked.

H owdy.

A lot of you don't know this, but this columnist thing? It's not my real job. Shucks no, my real job is helluva' lot more harrowin', excitin', and downright romantic than writin' down words and such.

Truth is, I'm a cowboy of sorts, only instead of roundin' up cattle I round up shopping carts.

Rollin', rollin', rollin'
Though the streams are swollen.
Keep them doggies rollin'
Rawhide!

That's right, I'm a cart wrangler at Costco. When you're done loading your 50-packs of tighty-whitey Hanes underwear, 10-pound cans of olives, and 2-gallon tubs of hemorrhoid cream into your Ford Explorer, I retrieve the cart, or as we boys in the business like to refer to them, the iron horses. We don't try to understand 'em, we just push and shove and roll 'em.

Yep, we're your huckleberries. We're the last American cowboys.

And when nighttime comes, we make ragin' campfires out of discarded Sanyo plasma TV boxes. We cook up some of those big Costco cans of Van Camp Pork 'n Beans and we stare up at the light from the faraway Toyota dealership. We listen to the mournful yelps of the feral poodles, that're no doubt lamentin' their tattered ribbons and their overgrown pom-poms and the regrettable fact that they have to steal water and kibble out of the bowls of domesticated dogs that are labeled "Duke" or "Spot" instead of "Fi-Fi."

And we sing songs, too — all the cowboy favorites like *Home on the Range*, *The Yellow Rose of Texas*, and *Don't Phunk With my Heart*.

It's a tough life, a lonely life, but a man like me wouldn't have it any other way.

Why am I tellin' y'all this after so many years? Well, it's kinda *germane* to my story, you see.

Last week, after a particularly rough day when we herded in over 6,000 carts, I was rummagin' through the remaindered Costco books, lookin' for something that would nourish a cowboy soul, when butter my butt and call me a biscuit, I stumbled on a book full of purty pictures called *Cowboy Values* written by some ol' sod horse by the name of James P. Owens.

Owens was a stockbroker for 35 years, but as the years piled on and his portfolios grew and shrank, he became disenchanted with his profession and disenchanted with America. He saw that where America once evaluated a man's character by his actions and accomplishments, it now evaluated a man by what kind of car he drives and the size of his portfolio.

Owens then realized that his lifetime fascination with the Old West might provide some guidance. He started thinking about all the Westerns he'd enjoyed throughout the years and all the books he'd read on the era and inspiration struck him in the face like a bag of oats thrown off a wagon.

Cowboys weren't just matinee idols; whether in the movies or real life, they stood for something. They had character and they had a clear, unshakeable —albeit unwritten — set of beliefs they lived by each day.

So after a year of studying the subject, he wrote a book called *Cowboy Ethics* that he hoped would serve as an inspiration to Wall Street.

You don't need me to tell you that Wall Street hasn't paid much heed, but Owens hasn't given up. He's since written a follow-up book that I mentioned earlier, *Cowboy Values*, and while he still manages a hedge fund, he travels around the country preaching the ways of the cowboy to any group or company that'll listen.

The book, as well as its predecessor, is simple and straightforward, but complexity isn't the cowboy way. After digesting innumerable movies, textbooks, and first-person accounts, Owens distilled the cowboy way into 7 core values that not only define the cowboy, but America, too.

1. COURAGE

Of course he's willing to die. You think we do this kind of work because we're scared to die?

— Virgil Cole, *Appaloosa*

Talk to any psychologist worth his id-odized salt and he'll tell you that most people are driven by fear. Hell, Americans seem to be afraid of lots of things, mostly the wrong things. They're afraid of two-bit terrorists, terrorists who've lately taken to hiding explosive devices hidden up their ass.

That's right, hidden up their ass. You know, if you're a terrorist who's gone to the excruciating trouble of shoving an IED up your ass, feel free to blow me up; I'll just spend eternity pointing a finger at you and laughing at how I imagine your face looked while you corkscrewed a pound of plastic explosive, some copper wire, and the guts of a cell phone up your ass.

Americans, along the same lines, are afraid of two-bit ideologues half-way across the world who might, without interference, eventually acquire the technology to hit the Virgin Islands with a nuclear missile that wobbles like one of Tim Tebow's passes after he got his melon knocked. Ho-hum. Trust me, if anyone ever gets close to that, we'll light them up like the bonfire after the last Sadie Hawkins dance.

Don't get me wrong, it's potentially a serious problem, but there are thousands of nuclear bombs on the planet and few people seem to worry about them. Worrying about Iran or Korea getting a couple without the means to deploy them efficiently or accurately seems a little disproportionate.

The Justice Department just came out with a report the other day that says *half* of American's children were assaulted in some way last year. Half! That seems to be worth worrying about a little more than a couple of pathetic ideologues.

And we seem to always be afraid of losing things, of people or the Government taking things away from us. We're like little kids worried that some bully is going to take away our tutti-frutti ice cream cone.

If and when it happens is one thing, but paranoia about things that probably won't happen seems to be sapping our collective spirit.

None of this was necessarily the kind of fear Owens was writing about, but nevertheless, he believes, rightly so, that fear is constrictive.

He believes we ought to acknowledge fear and then confront it, that we should accept risk, change, and failure as a way of life, the way the cowboys did. If you accept that some bad shit, along with the good shit, is going to happen, you castrate fear and put a brand on its quivering ass.

Along the same lines, we need to endure hardship and adversity without complaint. That doesn't mean we shouldn't stand up for what we believe in and make tough choices. Quite the contrary. But the cowboy doesn't spend precious time worrying about intangibles, things that he can't see. He's worried about the herd he's responsible for. He worries about his land, his family, and his neighbors.

That's the cowboy way.

2. OPTIMISM

> *Vin: Reminds me of that fellow back home that fell off a ten-story building.*
>
> *Chris: What about him?*
>
> *Vin: Well, as he was falling people on each floor kept hearing him say, "So far, so good...so far, so good!*
>
> — *The Magnificent Seven*

America, lately, seems to be programmed to avoid negatives instead of embracing positives. Look at the scoundrels on cable news (on both sides of the political aisle) decrying the impending falling sky. As a writer, I know instinctually that adversity and conflict and blood make for a good story, but I'm talking about novels; you know, *fiction*.

Broadcasting the news shouldn't be based on the same formula as a best-selling novel. Of course, it shouldn't be based on optimism, either.

Rather, it should be based on truth, which is always a blend of the good and the bad.

As individuals, Owens believes that the cowboys had a faith in the rightness of the natural order of things, and they chose to focus on the good in their lives and had a deep gratitude for any good fortune that came their way.

What's the purpose of this wished-for optimism? It's simple, really. Owens says that you need hope and confidence for anything good to occur. In cowboy terms, you won't drive any fence posts if you automatically assume the wood's infested with termites.

3. SELF RELIANCE

No brag... just fact.

— Will Sonnett, *The Guns of Will Sonnett*

Owens writes about watching video of the aftermath of Katrina and seeing thousands of people standing around doing nothing to help themselves. He was freaked out that so very few seemed to take responsibility for their own well-being and instead chose to wait around for FEMA.

Regardless of how fair or unfair a point that is, it's worth thinking about.

It may be true, and if it is, it's more a reflection of what's happened to us as a society. How many Americans are trained to live without technology, or perhaps more importantly, have the skill or knowledge to find food, shelter, or improvise life-saving strategies in the event of a disaster?

What would you do if the power went out, went out for good? Would you know what to do, how to feed yourself, how to keep yourself warm?

Hell, we've outsourced just about everything. From what I've heard, it's hard to find even a piece of furniture that was entirely built in the U.S. On a more domestic level, how many can even cook a meal or fix a leaky water faucet?

That wouldn't have sat well with the cowboys. They valued competence over convenience and put in the time and effort required to learn a skill. In fact, they found satisfaction in every accomplishment. More importantly, they took responsibility for their own well-being.

4. AUTHENTICITY

If you get to thinkin' you're a person of some influence, try orderin' somebody else's dog around.

— *Cowboy saying*

How many people do you know that aren't full of cow pie? Very few, I'll wager.

How many people really say what they mean? Say things without hypocrisy, pretense, or a self-serving agenda? How many people say things out of conviction rather than a fear of being rejected by the herd?

The cowboys took satisfaction in who they were, and their actions were guided by their coherent set of core beliefs. They recognized their strengths as well as their weaknesses.

Their identity came from personal values expressed not only in words, but deeds too, and not from what kind of car they drive, where they vacation, or their position in their company.

They believed that a rich man isn't the one who has the most, but the one who needs the least.

5. HONOR

It's sad that governments are chiefed by the double tongues. There is iron in your words of death for all Comanche to see, and so there is iron in your words of life. No signed paper can hold the iron. It must come from men. The words of Ten Bears carries the same iron of life and death. It is good that warriors such as we meet in the struggle of life... or death. It shall be life.

— Ten Bears, *The Outlaw Josey Wales*

Cheating, unfortunately, has become an American way of life. The end almost always justifies the means, and too often the end is a bigger bank account.

We expect to be cheated. We expect to be lied to, and this perverse core belief leads to a kind of rudeness and acrimony that poisons the soul of America. It's horribly sad, but we've all collectively brought it on ourselves, whether we're the soulless cheaters or the distrustful cheatees.

Not so with the cowboys. Owens writes that being worthy of trust means everything to a cowboy. If one of his cows strayed into another's herd, he fully expected to be compensated in full when the cow's new owner eventually sold him. It was part of the social structure of the West; without it, the entire system would have collapsed.

Cowboys told the truth and they acted with integrity, no matter what the cost. Furthermore, they knew that just because something was legal didn't make it right.

6. DUTY

From now on I see a red sash, I kill the man wearing it. So run you cur. And tell the other curs the law is coming. You tell 'em I'm coming! And Hell's coming with me, you hear! Hell's coming with me!

— Wyatt Earp, *Tombstone*

The cowboy felt that he had a responsibility to something bigger than himself. He was willing to sacrifice self-interest to protect his family, community, or country.

This kind of thinking was absolutely necessary, writes Owens, "as brave men were the only bulwark against the dangers and lawlessness of the frontier."

Owens believes that nowadays, the "drive for economic and social success have intensified to the point where there is no stigma in neglecting obligations to others; it's simply assumed that 'someone else' will take care of it."

Not so for the cowboy. They did what had to be done.

7. HEART

Well, he sure as hell wasn't one to complain. Woke with a smile, seemed like he could keep it there all day. Kind of a man that'd say 'good morning' and mean it, whether it was or not. Tell you the truth, Lord, if there was two gentler souls in this world, I never seen 'em. Seems like old Tig wouldn't even kill birds in the end. Well, you got yourself a good man and a good dog, and I'm inclined to agree with Boss here about holding a grudge against you for it. I guess that means Amen.

— Charley Waite, *Open Range*

We're turning into a nation of cold-hearted bastards. Sure, we'll pony up when we see a heart-rending video of some kid whose Christmas presents were burned up in a fire, but we'll turn a blind eye to the homeless and needy in our own neighborhoods.

Hell, why not? The latter aren't celebrities; no one will know if you help them. No one will know what a warm-hearted bastard you are if your charitable act isn't done publicly.

The cowboy found rewards in giving because he recognized our shared humanity. His charity wasn't determined by the bottom line, wasn't determined by matters of profit or convenience.

...consider the disgraceful aftermath of Hurricane Katrina...or the shameful treatment of our veterans...or our chronic failure to ease the plight of the homeless or the medically uninsured. It's hard not to believe that heart is a shrinking element of our national character.

Owens doesn't think America is resented just because it's the richest and most powerful country in the world, but because our national priorities are "out of whack." We act out of self-interest, misdirected ideology, and political party loyalty, not heart.

Not so the cowboy. He lived by humanitarian ideals; he lived with heart, which Owens characterized in the following ways:

• Seeing the good in people • Seeing the beauty in life • Finding rewards in giving • Recognizing our shared humanity • Feeling at one with nature • Kindness to all living creatures — including ourselves.

Is all this cowboy stuff corny? Is it just sentimental pabulum, Pollyanna horseshit as anachronistic as the cowboy himself?

Part of me, the jaded part, wants to think so, but the better part of me really does believe in the values espoused, regardless of whether or not they were truly part of the lives of the real cowboys and not just the celluloid ones.

I've often written of rites of passage, advocated that young men, upon achieving adulthood, be given some rules to live by, some code of honor. The damn trouble is that it's hard to advocate the merits of such a code, especially when those who have no code sometimes seem to prosper.

But those of us who do have a code know that it helps us prosper in ways the jaded can't even comprehend. It helps us in forming meaningful and satisfying relationships and meaningful and satisfying friendships. It helps us live fulfilling lives, gives us peace of mind, and gives us, through our efforts, a better community, country, and world in which to live.

And living by such a code doesn't mean that we can't also prosper financially. I don't believe for a second that you have to be ruthless and self-serving to make money. Quite the contrary, I'm quite certain that a personal code like that espoused by Owens, along with a similar business code, will actually further one's chances of being prosperous financially, and of course, spiritually.

-- 2009

Shape of Thighs to Come

But that's not the worst of it. You know those large female breasts many of us are so fond of? They're so last year. Style.com has named legs the new erogenous zone. That's not so bad, but The New York Times gave the title to clavicles. That's right, clavicles.

I'm not sure how to break it to you, so I might as well just lay it on you.

It's over.

The six-pack abs? The rippling muscles? Finished.

They're no longer *fashionable*.

Stop all the clocks, cut off the telephone,

Prevent the dog from barking with a juicy bone,

Silence the pianos and with muffled drum

Bring out the coffin, let the mourners come.

It's true. *Vanity Fair* said so. They just declared that the gym body is yesterday's fashion. The creative director at Barney's in New York supports the assertion, saying that, "Male models have never been so concave. They're on low-carb diets, and they don't work out anymore — they jog. It's a look coming out of Paris..."

The head of Pucci International, a company that makes mannequins for upmarket retailers, says, "The gym body has almost become a cliché."

Feel free to experience your three stages of grief, but please do it quickly as I've got an early lunch meeting.

First, anger: Bastards!

Then, denial: No f-in' way!

Finally, acceptance: I guess I can cancel my gym membership and start collecting stamps; I've always liked stamps.

But that's not the worst of it. You know those large female breasts many of us are so fond of? They're so *last year*. Style.com has named legs the latest erogenous zone. That's not so bad, but *The New York Times* gave the title to clavicles. That's right, clavicles.

Sigh.

The stars are not wanted now; put out every one,

Pack up the moon and dismantle the sun,

Pour away the ocean and sweep up the woods;

For nothing now can ever come to any good.

Yes, bony parts are taking the place of fleshy parts. Pucci International reports the best-selling female mannequins are thin, flat chested, narrow-hipped, and long legged, *with good collarbones.*

Man, I'm gonna' miss those lovely titties.

Sigh.

Please, everyone, hold hands and sway back and forth while I sing:

> *Kumbaya my Lord, kumbaya*
> *Kumbaya my Lord, kumbaya*
> *Kumbaya my Lord, kumbaya*
> *Oh Lord, kumbaya*

Amy Fine Collins, the author of the *Vanity Fair* article that trumpets the extinction of all things abs and tits ("The Shape of Thighs to Come"), posits that bodies have always followed the lead of fashion and then quickly become passé.

Amy, Amy, Amy, you're a fine writer, but I'd like to feign a model-like bulimic episode and vomit on your shoe. Collarbones? You expect us to get off on clavicles!?!

Excuse me, but while deeply hollowed clavicles might be useful in keeping an errant money shot from cascading onto the sheets, they're hardly a body part that's lusted for by the reptilian portion of our brains.

Okay, I'll admit that notions of what constitutes the ideal *female* body have vacillated more erratically than Dick Cheney's EKG, but the essence of what turns us on has always been there. We've always liked breasts and we've always worshipped the .7 hip-to-waist ratio, it's merely our acceptance of body fat levels that fluctuates.

While the original Venus De Milo was a curvy chunk, our modern-day version, Jessica Simpson, is lean and taut, albeit bestowed with so many saliva-inducing parabolas as to induce apoplexy in Euclid himself.

The female breast itself, though, has followed a peculiar path in the last 70 or so years, influenced as much by fashion as by science.

Consider 1940's era actress Jane Russell, who you used as an example in your article. She forced her assets on the movie public through the use of bras that made her breasts look like missiles. Whether she was showing off her angry tits or silently supporting General Patton's tank troops in Europe we'll never know, but it popularized big breasts and made actresses like Marilyn Monroe, Sophia Loren, and Jayne Mansfield possible.

The big-breasted movement suffered a literal recession in the sixties when models like Twiggy defined breast fashion, but that madness ended quickly with the arrival of Raquel Welch.

As you pointed out, Amy, it was about this time that science intervened in the form of breast implants. In a kind of fleshy space race, breasts became larger and larger without concern for the natural teardrop shape preferred by nature. Since the shape was hard to duplicate, medicine stopped trying. The bowling ball look became the norm. It was totally unrealistic, but men folk by and large stopped caring a long time ago. It's almost to the point that the infrequent real breast is the one that catches the puzzled attention of males, if only because of the sheer novelty.

I'll also concede the point that fashion may have affected the kind of butts that women aspire to and men covet.

Back in the 1940's, Betty Grable's no-cleavage mono-butt (as displayed in her iconic one-piece swimsuit photo that was a GI favorite) was in fashion, which was replaced by a boyish butt that was quite fashionable until J-Lo started hauling her junk around. That led to a spate of butt-implant surgeries and hip-hugger jeans that exposed so much ass cleavage that a girl, if so inclined, could catch a Frisbee without using her hands.

And I'll concede how it seems that female fashion seemed to influence automobile designers, at least back in the fifties. I appreciate the notion that the "jutting, red-tipped taillights of a 1958 Chrysler LeBaron could make a grown man blush."

But that's where it ends, Ms. Collins, that's where it ends. Fashion is admittedly a powerful force in shaping our perceptions, but our balls, Amy baby, are immune to the vagaries of fashion. Fill the magazines with all the pictures of clavicles and rib cages and jam the airwaves with ketogenic, sallow skinned models, but it's not gonna' change our preference for curves. Hell, to do that, you'd have to swizzle stick our insulas, which is the part of the brain that allows us to tell fresh food from rotten.

But let's get back to male Homo sapiens. You assert that, "the android-y aesthetic of the pumped-up he-man with washboard abs percolated into mainstream conspicuousness from gay and black subcultures."

You believe the trend has reversed and since fashion is extolling the virtues of the size-zero male, society will follow suit.

Amy, let me puke on your other Jimmy Choo.

From the Farnese Hercules to John L. Sullivan to Sandow to Muscle Beach to comic book superheroes to Arnold Schwarzenegger and Sly Stallone, men have always gravitated towards muscle.

Check out the following quote, Amy:

> The new age of today is at work on a new human type. Men and women are to be more healthy, stronger: there is a new feeling of life, a new joy in life. Never was humanity in its external appearance and in its frame of mind nearer to the ancient world that it is today.

You know who said that, Amy? It wasn't Tom of Finland and it wasn't 50 Cent; it was Adolph Hitler. I'm not ascribing the modern, apparently now passé love of broad shoulders and deep chests and rippling muscle to der Fuehrer, only pointing out that the love of a hyper-masculine esthetic ideal is maybe the product of a lot more than gay or black subculture.

I think the love of a mesomorphic frame is hard wired. Study after study has shown that a muscular form is a cultural ideal. Granted, we're probably not talking about the excess that's seen on the stage of a competitive bodybuilding show, but we're talking about at least NFL running-back muscle.

For better or worse, men attribute positive personality traits to muscle. Men view their bodies as instruments and those with strength or power will be more useful, more likely to be dominant, confident, and independent.

I'll readily admit that there's some minor psychological flaw in just about anybody who starts lifting weights; some insecurity or weakness that requires muscular armor to either hide it, shield it, or cure it, but as therapy it's a hell of a lot more effective and rewarding than a psychologist's couch or a lifetime addiction to smoking, drinking, or eating comfort food.

The end result, aside from hopefully reaching an esthetic ideal, is often a confident, self-actualized being who carries the lessons learned in the weight room into every facet of life.

It all comes down to a love of the heroic, Amy. Muscle, throughout history, has been next of kin to the heroic, and the heroic is eternal. Fashion is just a passing whim, destined to be dumped into the back of the closet with the bell-bottom pants and the platform shoes.

-- 2007

The New Rat Pack

I worry all that beautiful ass cleavage might
exacerbate PTSD in some of the Marines as those
rifts between the girls' delicious butt cheeks might
somehow remind them of the rift between the
Sunni and Shia in the Sandbox, but my lust quells
my concern.

I feel like an absolute sheepdog, and not one of those Westminster Kennel Club sheepdogs, mind you, but one that's been herding farm animals all day and smells of mouse shit from sleeping in the barn.

It's the *incongruity* that's making me feel a little self-conscious.

I've just walked into this beautiful, expansive house and except for my friend, I'm the only one who's not wearing a suit; I'm the only one whose hair isn't Marine issue.

No, I'm wearing ripped jeans, a T-shirt, and my comparatively long hair is lying on top of my head in its normal Dutch Boy paint-can fashion.

"Who invited Bon Jovi?" is what they must be thinking.

Regardless, the 8 men in attendance are all courteous to a fault. Two beautiful young women in cocktail dresses offer me a glass of wine. And there's Sinatra music playing on the stereo, Sinatra!

The truth is that I didn't know what to expect; all I knew is that my friend and I had been invited to this house on top of the hill in La Jolla to teach poker.

But these aren't rich, arrogant fops who've decided it'd be a hoot to rub elbows with the unwashed. No, these men are largely Marine officers and they, along with a couple of Navy men and a few enlightened civilians, constitute the Richardson Society.

It started in Iraq, just north of Fallujah, explained Richardson Society co-founder Lieutenant Alexander Martin. He and three other Marines were sitting down next to a tank in the hot sun and while they didn't exactly complain (it's unseemly for Marines to complain), they *noted* how they missed the amenities of life; you know, the wine, the cigars, and of course, the women.

It was then the four of them vowed that when they got stateside, they'd meet once a month to sample those missing amenities -- the best food, the best cigars, the best wine and scotch, and of course, the best women. And none of this civilian slacker wear crap with butt-crack pants and backwards baseball caps — they'd wear suits, damn it.

Furthermore, they decided their meetings would have some sort of agenda other than just sampling hedonistic delights. They decided they'd learn something every month, invite some expert in some field to teach them something; teach them how to be *better men.*

One month it may be someone teaching them about finance, or clothes, fine watches, wine, ballroom dancing, how to meet and treat a lady, or even poker.

And the name, the Richardson Society? The goddam Aussies get credit for that one. On the way back from Iraq, Lieutenant Martin's ship docked in Perth. He and his friends decided to grab some of those long-missed amenities by staying at the 5-star Richardson Hotel.

Some of the Marines — not Lieutenant Martin or his companions — went *Great Santini* at the hotel with a bit of standard-issue, high-grade, unbridled Marine Testosterone and all its resultant drinking and rambunctiousness. Hotel management expressed its disapproval by deciding to roust not just the individual perps, but every single Marine out of the hotel; dispose of the "riff-raff" in one vile, fell swoop.

So at 2 AM, when Lieutenant Martin and his inner circle were quietly relaxing in their rooms in bathrobes, management knocked on their doors and asked all of them to leave; asked a leader of over 200 men to leave; asked a Marine surgeon to leave; asked a Marine with a law degree to leave!

"You know, we saved Australia from Imperial Japan in World War II..." they reasoned.

"I don't care," sniffed the hotel manager, "I'm German."

The only other hotel in Perth with vacancies was some fleabag dump on the outskirts of town where the Marines were forced to bivouac. "Right then and there," explained Lieutenant Martin, "we decided to name our men's group the 'Richardson Society' as sort of a 'fuck you' to the Richardson Hotel."

So here sits the Richardson Society, an idea made real. Athena popping out of Zeus' head.

We've moved on to Scotch now, and the girls make sure our glasses are never empty. The men are all good students, and they seem to get excited over the idea that Texas Hold 'em has, in a sense, military applications; things like bluffing and the concept of "coming over the top," where you counter an opponent's aggressiveness by coming back at him *twice* as hard.

After poker school, the men invite us to share a good cigar. But you don't just light the thing; you have to *learn* about it; you have to know the cigar so you can appreciate it more. That's Richardson Society dogma.

One of the men, a Marine captain who's a month away from becoming a full-blown major, describes the origins of this particular blend of cigar as the hostesses clip the ends off and hand them out.

The conversation then turns to issues of masculinity, like "When is a man too old to wear a sports jersey?" (The general consensus is high school.) But then it switches to something a bit meatier when I ask them about the war.

"We don't look at it the way most civilians do," is what I'm told. They explain that they played soldier when they were kids, dreamed of being soldiers all their lives, *trained* to be soldiers all their lives. And if they never got to use those skills? Well, they'd be as disappointed as any athlete who never got to run a race, any musical virtuoso who never got to play a concert. So they fight, and for the most part, they don't question.

Similarly, when one of their comrades dies, it's a damn shame, but it's part of the job; it's part of what they signed up for.

And all during these conversations there's Sinatra playing in the background. They relate to him, as he's emblematic of a time when masculinity was more clearly defined.

They dig the suit thing, and seemingly the whole "Rat Pack" philosophy: Treat a dame like a lady and a lady like a dame. Make sure your trousers break just above the shoes. You gotta tip big and tip quietly — fold the bills three times into a small square and pass them in a handshake; never drink a drink immediately after it's poured; better a carton of milk than a serving of warm vodka. Sex is great, but you gotta have style, you gotta have class.

Flash forward three weeks. This new "Rat Pack" is throwing a Valentine's Day party. This time, I'm wearing a jacket and tie and while I'm still a little sheepdoggish, it's okay; I can pass.

As I approach the entrance to the house, there's an enormous ice sculpture on the lawn in the shape of a heart. Nice touch, but that's nothing compared to what's inside.

There are four hostesses at the door in matching black dresses with luscious red pumps and flaming red lips. The dresses are form fitting little numbers that show lots of cleavage, but the hemlines are pure asymmetrical devilry! They're sinfully short, of course, but the designer must be wearing the other half of this amulet I wear around my neck because the hemlines angle up severely in the back so you get an eyeful of panties and ass!

I DON'T KNOW BUT I'VE BEEN TOLD...

HOSTESS PUSSY AIN'T THE LEAST BIT COLD!

I worry all that beautiful ass cleavage might exacerbate PTSD in some of the Marines as those rifts between the girls' delicious butt cheeks might somehow remind them of the rift between the Sunni and Shia in the Sandbox, but my lust quells my concern.

The hostesses have bottles of champagne in one hand and champagne flutes in the other. They're all toothy smiles, cleavage, and loamy loined hospitality! They hand me a glass as soon as I enter.

And then, then, this 6-foot blond vision comes walking towards me carrying a tray of cigars and matches! Did these bastards tap into my subconscious to find my weakness? Her name's Jessica, Jessica Morgan ("Like the rum," she coos), and she is — get this — a model! What are the odds?

I sidle up to her and whisper in her ear, "Excuse me, Jessica, I don't mean to embarrasses you, but I can see your *ass*." She laughs sweetly. Of course she does! I've died and gone straight to hebben where de angels am! I'm a funny fuck! Everything I say is funny! It's almost as if she were being paid or something!

It's all I can do to light the cigar instead of my nose.

And the house is full of these hostesses, along with what must be 80 or 90 non-hostess babes, all wearing cocktail dresses. The Rat Pack is there, of course, along with a number of other Marines and assorted civilians, but there are far more women than men.

The floor is covered with rose petals, as are the beds in the various rooms. The tables and are adorned with huge, ostentatious candelabra filled with oversized red candles that drip gobs of hot, bloody wax impertinently onto the tables and floor.

There's a sushi spread and not one of those lousy beer and cheap wine bars, but a full bar. You want a Manhattan? You want olives in your shaken not stirred martini? You want Stoli instead of Grey Goose? No problem! Ask either one of the two bartenders or their assistants.

And if you meet a girl and want to get away from the pounding music and the dancing? Take her to the hookah room! Push aside the gauze curtains, get comfy on some of the giant pillows, and toke on any one of the five hookahs while you get to know your new friend, who, because of her high heels and short cocktail dress, is made completely vulnerable by the awkwardness of the pillow that's engulfed her. She can't even get up without doing a Britney-getting-out-of-the-limo move! But she doesn't seem to mind, though, because she's buzzing on her 6th glass of champagne.

Not surprisingly, the men of the Richardson Society don't just see this is as a party; it's a *drill*, a war game of a sort where they practice the skills they've learned. Sure, the wine, the scotch, the cigar, the dancing, the women... they've studied it all and trained for it all.

These things can't just be experienced, but *conquered*. But that's how they view everything. It's Thoreau meets the Marines:

> *I went into the woods because I wanted to live deliberately.*
> *I wanted to live deep and suck out all the marrow of life...*

*to put to rout all that was not life; and not, when I came
to die, discover that I had not lived.*

So raise a glass to the Richardson society, but do them the courtesy
of learning a little something about that scotch you're drinking,
okay?

-- 2008

Top Ten Testosterone Facts

Beowulf wouldn't have fought the dragon without Testosterone; Helen of Troy wouldn't have launched a dingy, let alone a thousand ships. Without Testosterone, there'd have been no exploration; everyone would have stayed home to hang drapes. No conquest! No invention! And definitely no whoopie!

The other kids spent most of their time outside playing street baseball, but 11-year-old TC — nerdy, bespectacled 11-year-old TC — was usually down in the basement tending to his beloved plants.

Yep, I fancied myself a botanist. The years of study and the resultant degrees awaiting me were just a formality.

I read all I could about plants. I even stole botany textbooks from the library. I was obsessed with making them grow faster and I ran experiments using different fertilizers and even different wavelengths of light. One side of my pasty basement-white face was usually bathed in red light and the other blue. My imaginary friend had a hunchback and called me *Master*.

Then I learned about auxins — plant hormones. You rub one type of auxin on one side of the stem, and the stem bends and grows in the opposite direction! Yes, yes! That's how plants bend towards the sun! It's elementary, elementary, you other 11-year-old fools! Can't you see it, or do you have the minds of mere *10-year-olds*?!?

But then, as is the norm for mad scientists of any age, came the discovery that ultimately spelled doom for my plants and my aspirations. I found something that had the potential of giving me control over all mankind! My fiendish laughter was interrupted only by my asthma attacks.

You see, dear reader, I stumbled onto something in a long forgotten, dusty text no doubt written by alchemists of a long ago age...okay, I read it in *Science News*. Anyhow, what I read about — eyes wide open and breath quick and shallow — was a super plant hormone called *gibberellic acid* that had been used in Vietnam to make crops grow at an incredible rate.

Oh-momma-oh-momma-oh-momma.

Big hand-rubbing plans!

So I got some -- well, stole some -- of the hormone (anything in the name of science), but I was an undisciplined young scientist. Rather than using small amounts on a select number of plants, I applied it to all of them! Dr. Frankenstein, wherever you are, you understand, don't you?!?

111

That night, I slept fitfully, fully expecting that when I awoke, I'd be greeted by dozens of man-eating Audreys populating my personal *Little Shop of Horrors*, all screaming *"Feed me, TC! Feeeeeed meeeeee!"*

But instead, I woke up to the *killing fields*. The plants were dead or dying, the victims of youthful exuberance.

That pretty much ended my botany phase, but the experience didn't end my fascination with growth factors and hormones. Rather, my fascination just transitioned from plants to *humans* and instead of courting gibberellic acid, I fell in love with Testosterone.

Testosterone, for being a relatively simple molecule, is at the root of human desire, human ambition, and even human history itself. Its effects are part biology, part psychology, and part mythology. Beowulf wouldn't have fought the dragon without Testosterone; Helen of Troy wouldn't have launched a dingy, let alone a thousand ships. Without Testosterone, there'd have been no exploration; everyone would have stayed home to hang drapes. No conquest! No invention! And definitely no whoopie!

And, of course, to an athlete, Testosterone is what stirs the competitive drink. It's what makes us win, and more importantly, makes us *want* to win. It is also what makes men look like men and the more you have, chances are the more *man* you are. It's the ultimate recreational drug; it's the nectar of the gods.

So, in honor of my love affair with Testosterone, I'd like to present my 10 favorite little-known Testosterone facts, some having to do with Testosterone history and others having to do with its chemistry and effect on human physiology. Here they are, in no particular order:

1. Testosterone and Estrogen: So alike and yet so different.

Testosterone and estrogen — miles apart, the yin and yang of human behavior and development, right? Well, they may have different effects, but they sure don't look much different.

If you compared the Testosterone molecule to the estrogen molecule, you'd find they're so similar that they could be merged into one three-dimensional figure! Virtually the only thing that's different is that the Testosterone molecule has one extra, solitary hard-on of a carbon atom in the top-center that stands straight up.

Doesn't it seem appropriate that Testosterone itself would have a penis?

Science writer James McBride Dabbs describes the similarity between the two molecules as a metaphor for the similarity of men and women:

"Men and women are similar in many ways — in their bodies, their minds, their hopes and fears. We should remember this underlying similarity when thinking about the ways in which they differ."

2. "Spermatic Economy"

Prior to the isolation of Testosterone in the 1930's, maleness was thought to be represented by that which was visible; in other words, sperm and seminal fluid.

It was commonly believed that male secondary sexual characteristics — like muscle mass and genital growth — were associated with the production of sperm.

This led to the predictable but horribly sad notion that sperm shouldn't be squandered. The medical profession warned men to not have excessive sexual intercourse or heaven forbid, masturbate, lest they deprive the body of this vital substance. Furthermore, sperm was thought to exist in a limited supply. Your tank supposedly only had so much gas, and you'd best not be riding around on the sexual Autobahn burning up that precious bodily fluid and, along with it, your masculinity.

Pity the poor skinny, sickly men who were assumed by every sniggering onlooker to be chronic masturbators who had discharged all their masculinity into their sister's bloomers.

Of course, that's pretty much what we think today when we look at some of the specimens of manhood walking around campuses.

3. The Primitive Beginnings of Testosterone Therapy

In 1869, a French physiologist named Charles Edouard Brown-Séquard theorized that injecting the sperm of a healthy young animal into the veins of an old man would produce vitality. Twenty years later at the age of roughly 72, the crazy old coot *tried it.*

Brown-Sequard revealed to a startled audience at the Société de Biologie in Paris that he had reversed his physical decline by injecting himself with the liquid extract derived from the testicles of a dog and a guinea pig. He insisted the injections had increased his strength, improved his mental acuity, and even lengthened the arc of his urine stream by 25 percent so he could blast cockroaches off *le toilette* wall.

The procedure caught on in France and soon spread to the United States, where William Hammond, a former surgeon general, reported that the preparation reduced pain, improved cardiac function, and restored potency.

Meanwhile, Brown-Séquard continued to "refine" his formulas:

"Cut bull testicles into four or five slices, mix with one liter of glycerine, store for twenty-four hours turning frequently, wash in boiling water, pass the liquid through a paper filter, and then sterilize at 104 degrees."

We now know that Brown-Séquard's formulations relied heavily on the placebo effect. Regardless, he inspired laboratory research and clinical applications that led to the discovery of Testosterone.

4. Testicle Transplants

In 1913, a professor of surgery at the University of Chicago performed the first testicle transplant on a twice-cursed 33-year old man who had lost one testicle through an accident and the other through a botched hernia surgery. It's believed that the donor testicle was purchased from a 3rd party who didn't have the balls to say no.

Four days after the operation, the patient insisted on leaving the hospital so that he could "satisfy his desire."

Amazingly, testicle transplants became relatively common place soon after. In 1918, the chief surgeon at California's San Quentin Prison began "engrafting human testicles from recently executed prisoners to senile recipients."

Soon after, he switched to using animal testicles.

The physician, L.L. Stanley, ended up doing 21 transplants with human testicles and over 300 with animal testicles. San Quentin inmates were literally lining up to get the procedure and recipients reported "a feeling of buoyancy, a joy of living...."

About the same time, and inspired by Stanley's work, a French physician began transplanting monkey testicles into patients who complained of loss of sexual drive. He declared that the procedure promoted physical and mental prowess and advocated that it be performed on children to create a "new super-race of men of genius."

While that never happened, reports appearing much later in 1949 showed that doctors gave oral and injectable forms of Testosterone to premature infants, both male and female. A year later, a study found that methyl Testosterone made babies grow faster with no apparent ill effects.

Probably as a result of the aforementioned study, docs began giving Testosterone to anorexic and underweight children as a "general growth stimulant." This occurred as late as 1961, but luckily, the practice didn't last much longer as scientists became aware of the side effects of relatively indiscriminate use of Testosterone on prepubescents.

5. Gonad Tablets

The Testosterone craze of the early 20th century led to the development of several over-the-counter formulations of dubious effectiveness. Among the most popular — often prescribed by physicians of the day — was *Henry Harrower's Gonad Tablet*. It contained 0.25 grams of adrenal; 0.50 grams of thyroid; 1 gram of pituitary, and 1.5 grams of prostate and Leydig cell extracts. The label said it was to be taken 3 to 8 times a day.

Also popular were "Ovacoids" and "Testacoids" (that "curiously strong" bulge in your pants lets you know it's working!), along with "Concentrated Orchitic Solution" that contained tissue from the "small, hard testicular gland of the healthy young, live goat, ram, or monkey," dissolved in alcohol and water.

6. The Discovery of Testosterone

In 1929, researchers discovered that male urine contained the mysterious male hormone. Two years later, a professor at the University of Gottinggen named Adolf Butenandt, in conjunction with the Schering pharmaceutical company, isolated minute amounts of the substance and named it *androsterone*.

In 1934, another researcher purified the hormone from cholesterol, and he and Butenandt were later named co-winners of 1938 Nobel Prize in chemistry for their work.

In-between those events, in 1935, a professor named Ernst Laquer, with his colleagues and the Dutch pharmaceutical company, Organon, purified the hormone even further from bull testes and gave it the name — *queue up sound of heavenly choir* — Testosterone!

7. Horny Baby Boys?

So innocent the baby boy!

We like to think so, but during the first 4-6 months of a male baby's life, his Testosterone levels are almost at pubertal levels! While we're not sure why this occurs, some scientists think that the high levels have something to do with "brain masculinization."

Oh, the baby's crying! He's hungry! Maybe, maybe not. Could be that he just wants to grab some tit. Fortunately, nature, in her wisdom, has designed it so that infants of this age can't walk; otherwise, they'd be humping the family schnauzer and walkin' up to assorted MILF's -- tiny, engorged penis in hand--and sayin' "Hey, how ya' doin'?"

Luckily, Testosterone levels decline to normal childhood levels after these first few hormonally tumultuous months.

8. Athletes and Low Testosterone

It seems counterintuitive, but male athletes typically have lower Testosterone levels than couch potatoes!

Comparative studies have shown again and again that free and total T concentrations in chronically trained athletes (runners, weight lifters, rowers, cyclists, and swimmers) are surprisingly low. In fact, the Testosterone levels of trained subjects were only 60-85% of untrained men.

While FSH and LH levels of trained men didn't differ from untrained men, T levels were significantly affected. Some researchers attribute the discrepancy to alterations in hepatic and extrahepatic (muscles, skin) metabolism of Testosterone, which can't be compensated for by the athletes' gonads.

And, while exercise of any kind for as little as 5-30 minutes results in a significant increase in Testosterone, levels *decline* below baseline 15-60 minute later. What's more, this reduction below baseline can last up to three days, depending on the duration and intensity of the exercise!

So does this mean that fat bastards are more virile than rock-hard athletes? God I hope not.

9. Testosterone Levels and Sex Ratios of Children

A student at Georgia State University named Jonathan Bassett had read implications in the scientific literature that indicated that females with higher Testosterone levels gave birth to more boys than girls.

While this doesn't make much sense off-hand, high levels of Testosterone in fertile females might affect the viability of male and female zygotes after conception.

In any event, Bassett decided to do a study of female trial lawyers — a field typically populated by high-Testosterone females — and beauty queens. Using waist-to-hip ratios, Bassett figured that curvaceous figures might correlate with low levels of Testosterone, and that the sex ratio of their children might differ significantly from that of female trial lawyers.

He was right. Fifty-eight percent of the children of female trial lawyers were boys, while former Miss America's had *twice* as many daughters than sons.

Want some sons to help you with the farm work? Marry the girl on the next farm who looks like Warren Sapp.

10. Testosterone, Finger Length, and the Isle of Lesbos

Look at your hands. Hold them up in front of you as if you were trying to catch a stripper's just-flung panties. Is your ring finger (the fourth finger, counting the thumb) longer that the index finger (the second finger)?

If it is, and you're male, good for you. In the first trimester of pregnancy, when you were firmly entrenched in momma's womb, male hormones started to roll up their sleeves to help build your body. It's this early exposure to Testosterone that seems to make a difference between the lengths of those two fingers.

Biologists call this the 2D:4D ratio.

No one really knows why this happens, but it's been known for a long time that some bone growth is determined by Testosterone.

Researcher John Manning of the University of Liverpool has even done studies that indicate that exceptional athletes and math whizzes have extra long ring fingers, perhaps suggesting that they might haven gotten extra doses of Testosterone when they were in the womb.

Equally amazing and downright compelling about this whole 2D:4D discussion is the fact that women generally have digits of similar length, with the notable exception of *lesbians.* They tend to have ratios that are similar to those of men.

It's certainly not foolproof, though. Don't look at your girlfriend's hands, discover that she's got a conspicuous 2D:4D ratio and automatically start rifling through the drawers of her nightstand in a frantic search for a box that contains sexy pictures of J-Lo and a Martina Navratilova signature-model vibrator.

What researchers have found, though, is that when they look at hundreds of straight women and hundreds of lesbians, many more lesbians had ring fingers that were longer than their index fingers.

Somehow, these women, like men with similar dynamic digits, might have gotten an extra dose of Testosterone during their first trimester in the womb. As a result (and this is just one theory), their sexual preferences leaned strongly toward other women. Were it not for their lack of penises and an affinity for LPGA-sponsored events, they might as well have been men.

You know, I probably could go on all day about what I think are interesting facts about my favorite hormone, but I've got to go downstairs and check on my latest experiment, which involves giving inordinate amounts of Testosterone to a troop of Boy Scouts. I only hope I learned some restraint from my ill-fated plant experiments.

REFERENCES:

Dabbs, James McBride, *Heroes, Rogues and Lovers*, McGraw-Hill, 2000.

Griffin, James, and Ojeda, Sergio, Textbook of Endocrine Physiology, Oxford Press, 1996.

Hoberman, John, *Testosterone Dreams: Rejuvenation, Aphrodisia, Doping*. University of California Press, 2005.

Luoma, TC, Luoma's Big Damn Book of Knowledge, Oxford Press, 2005.

Nieschlag, E., et al, *Testosterone: Action, Deficiency, Substitution*. Springer, 1998.

Rothman, Sheila and David J, *The Pursuit of Perfection*, Pantheon Books, 2003.

-- 2007

A Harpoon Through the Heart

It's funny that people always talk about how mental illness is closely related to talent and success. I don't necessarily buy it. Look at sheep woman. She's plenty mentally ill, but just because she flings her feces against the wall doesn't mean she's Jackson Pollock.

Baahhh! Baahhh!

The bleating of the sheep! Nothing like a farm. Nothing like growing things. And you should see the winter wheat. Greenest stuff you ever saw.

Only I'm not on a farm.

I'm standing in line at the goddam *post office* and there's an Asian woman directly in front of me with her adult daughter and the daughter is picking her nose and inexplicably making sheep noises, *loud* sheep noises.

Baahhh! Baahhh!

Rather than endure this uncomfortable situation with some polite indifference, nearly everyone in the post office is staring at the faux sheep. Probably the rudest is the old coot standing directly in front of the two-legged Dolly.

He's made no attempt to mask his rubbernecking. In fact, he's done a full 180-degree turnaround and his face is only inches away from barnyard girl. He looks almost exactly like Droopy Dog, only his mouth is wide open-- either out of sheer astonishment or the inability of his aged facial muscles to keep his gaping pie hole shut.

Dolly is oblivious. She scoops a bugger out of her nose, examines it with all the wonder of a child watching *Winnie the Pooh* for the first time, *eats it*, and then continues her bleating.

Baahhh! Baahhh!

I figure she's making like a sheep for one of four reasons:

1. She got a chopstick in the ear when she was a child and it egg fu yunged her brains.

2. She's plain bat-shit loopy.

3. She's making a shrewd social commentary on how modern man has been reduced to sheep.

    4.   She's mocking me.

Given my present state of mind, I'm inclined to choose door number 4.

Sure, why not? The whole world is mocking me anyhow.

It has to do with what's in the box I'm holding and why I'm standing in line at the Post Office alongside what looks like the cast of *Twin Peaks*.

Three weeks ago, on Ground Hog's Day, my first book was released. I've written several, but this was the first to see print. For a writer, having your first book published is a big deal. It's like the feeling an athlete gets when he signs a pro contract, or like Olive felt when she learned she'd get to compete in her first Little Miss Sunshine pageant.

I absolutely thought the world would change after my book was published. There'd be women! I'd autograph their breasts with Sharpie permanent ink laundry markers! There'd be moolah! And finally, after all these years, recognition!

In between entertaining the adoring women, I'd answer congratulatory notes from friends, colleagues, and family. I'd get to choose between talk shows. Leno? Sure! Letterman? Absolutely. Oprah? Sorry, but TC is booked solid for the next 6 months.

And then there'd be the men's magazines begging me to write a column.

"TC, there's a Mr. Hefner on line 3. Can you take the call?"

It'd just be a matter of picking through the offerings.

But the world didn't change. Not one lick. No chicks. And the congratulatory notes from friends and colleagues? I got one from my attorney and from the Danish stoner who cuts my hair. That's it. No one in my family even bothered to acknowledge the book.

And as far as interview shows and columns in men's magazines, someone would have to *read* the book first before I got any offers, but judging by the way the book has sold on Amazon, only a paltry few have read it. Mock on, sheep woman, mock on.

Hannibal Lecter: "Well, TC, have the lambs stopped screaming?"

TC: "Hell no! There's one right there and it won't shut up!"

So yeah, I'm feeling a little deflated and my literary output has been reduced to a few seafood recipes, bitter and angry seafood recipes:

Crab Bisque

2 damn cans of mushroom soup

2/3 cup...fuck it, make it 4 cups, sherry

1 cup sour cream

2 cups spoiled milk

7 ounces lobster, but shit, lobster's expensive and your friends sure don't deserve anything expensive, so eat the lobster yourself and feed the SOBs some canned tuna

Serves 4 bastards.

Maybe it's the writing equivalent of post-partum depression -- post-printum depression.

But rather than give up, I'm standing in line at the post office with sheep woman to send another copy of the book to yet another magazine editor. Of course, being that I'm likely the Charlie Brown of authors, any editor who contacts me will probably want to globally replace all references to my penis with, I don't know, *gummy bear*. "You know, so we don't offend the children":

> *"While the female psychologist asserts that sex gets better as a man gets older, I doubt very much that an old man taking his semi-erect **Gummy bear** out of his pants and screaming, 'Oh my God, it's orange! It's orange!' after failing to remember that he spilled Metamucil on it earlier that day, constitutes 'better' sex."*

Kill me now. Or jam a pen in my brain and let me become a ruminant like sheep woman so we can blissfully bleat at the world and spend the evenings bathing each other with Woolite.

Maybe I should take comfort in the story of Philo T. Farnsworth. Most people don't know that Farnsworth invented modern television in 1928. He toiled in obscurity for years and then RCA and the fledgling National Broadcasting Corporation (NBC) copied his invention and stole the patents through legal maneuvering. Farnsworth died drunk, obscure, and broke in 1971, even though he might have been the greatest inventor of the 20th century.

Wait a minute...maybe he's not such a comforting role model, after all.

How about Franz Kafka? Dude wrote some awesome short stories and books, many of which are still analyzed in Freshman Lit classes. Of course, Kafka didn't get anything published until after he died. You can't get chicks after you're dead!

I guess neither are examples of how perseverance pays off. Besides, it's probably a little silly to compare my little odes to hoo-hah with Kafka. Maybe I'd best compare myself with semi-failures a few rungs lower, somebody like Anna Kournikova. Sure, we're both tall, blond, have a hellacious body, and love to eat pussy. Okay, I don't know if she shares that particular passion with me but my goodness, isn't it pleasant to think so?

Regardless, neither of us has fulfilled our expectations. She never won a big tournament and I never wrote the Great American Novel.

It's funny that people always talk about how mental illness is closely related to talent and success. I don't necessarily buy it. Look at sheep woman. She's plenty mentally ill, but just because she flings her feces against the wall doesn't mean she's Jackson Pollock. No, I think success has more to do with tenacity and the ability to survive your heart being harpooned over and over again.

Just about every success story, whether in writing, the arts in general, sports, bodybuilding, business, relationships, you name it, is all about perseverance.

In the movie *Cool Hand Luke*, George Kennedy beats the living hell out of fellow work-farm inmate Paul Newman, knocking him down again and again. But Luke doesn't stay down. He gets up out of the dirt over and over again, albeit a little more slowly each time.

"Just stay down, Luke. He's just gonna knock ya down again, buddy...It's not your fault. He's just too big...Let him hit you in the nose and get some blood flowing. Maybe the bosses will stop it before he kills you."

Even Kennedy ("Dragline") begs him to stay down:

Dragline: "Stay down. You're beat."

Luke: "You're gonna have to kill me."

Finally, Dragline is so damn in awe of Luke that the last thing he wants to do is hit him again. Luke ends up "winning" by earning the respect of every last inmate.

Maybe that's a good model for all of us, regardless of our goal.

Of course, the guards shoot Luke in the throat at the end of the movie, but hey, I prefer to cherry pick my life lessons, discarding the bad fruit.

I'm really not all that downtrodden about my book. For one thing, I haven't done a lick of marketing, and I doubt much that the world is going to beat down my door unless I take the initiative and promote the damn thing. I was, however, puzzled by the indifference of friends and colleagues until I had one of those Wolf Hour epiphanies.

I realized that we've all got a "book," that one thing we take pride in that, for whatever reason, doesn't get too many other people excited. It could be getting a degree, a promotion, or even something so alien to other people as developing a new variety of flower. Maybe we're all so interested in our own book that it's hard to get excited about anybody else's.

I guess the only difference is that some people keep pushing their book, or keep writing new ones, never giving up, until they get what they want.

-- 2007

Drunken Girls

Obviously, we're not talking about girls who've fallen
into garbage cans and look like 60's icon Joe
Cocker as they try, with fingers stiff and splayed,
to dislodge the chicken bones from their long
hair, or who, in an effort to reapply their lipstick,
have inadvertently smeared their faces to look like
Cleveland Indians' mascot, Chief Wahoo.

Zzzzzzzzzziiiiiiinnnnnnnkkkkkkkkk.....

Good God, what is that noise? Am I at the quarter carwash?

Sure, I'm using a high-powered wand to spray the soapsuds off my SUV.

Zzzzzzzzzziiiiiiinnnnnnnkkkkkkkkk.....

Only I'm not at the carwash. It's 2:30 in the morning and I'm standing outside a nightclub while Miranda--crouched down with spandex and Lycra slacks pulled down around her ankles--*pisses* on the front right hubcap of my vehicle.

She's completely out of it, of course, loopy on about what must have been a dozen Mojitos. We've just left the bar and Miranda has suddenly decided she desperately has to pee. The bladder must have spent the last hour or so trying desperately to send a signal up the spinal cord to the micturition center in her brain, but the signal itself was late because it too got wasted on all that alcohol and had to pull over to sleep it off.

But rather than try to go back in the bar to use the bathroom, she decides to use the long blacktopped urinal trough that's known to some people as Girard Avenue. My assignment is to stand guard on the opposite side of the car while she lets loose with a Katrina-like flood of urine.

Why she's chosen to pee on my *car* instead of the actual street is a mystery. I'd also like to see *how* she managed it, as I've assumed the only way women could direct their stream *up* was the same way a guy takes a gushing garden hose and turns it into a powerful jet stream by putting his thumb over the nozzle.

While I'm briefly tempted to walk around and see this wonder of nature — along with seeing if she'd managed to write her name in the dirt on my hubcap--I steadfastly hold my urinary sentry position, partly out of chivalry and partly because I'm sort of afraid she'd do one of those crowd control numbers where they hose the rioters back.

The metallic noise stops. Miranda pulls up her slacks and starts with the drunken chick theme song, which generally consists of shrieking the words, "OH MY GOD!" over and over while convulsing in laughter.

She's decided to add an instrument to her litany, so she lays her torso on the hood of my abused SUV and starts pounding on the hood with her fists.

There's clearly nothing more for us to accomplish here so I walk over to her side of the car, gingerly step over an astonishingly large puddle, and open the door. I deposit her in the passenger seat using the same technique policemen use with apprehended perps -- one hand firmly on the shoulder, the other forcing her head down so it won't put a dent in the door frame.

I lean over her to snap the seatbelt shut, and my face is tantalizingly close to her breasts, which are half-cradled by, half-perched atop, the built-in bra cups of a midnight black, boned, corset-type number that's held together by tiny silver clasps.

But I don't linger and I don't touch. This, after all, is a drunk chick who's all too vulnerable. I dutifully drive the delicate little flower home, incident free...except for the few times she gave other motorists the finger.

Oddly enough, up until the car-washing incident, Miranda had been incredibly lucid. We'd spent about an hour having a really, great, substantive conversation. But in seconds, she went from debutante to drunken frat boy. It was like one of those hypnotist acts you see on cruise ships:

> HYPNOTIST: *When I snap my fingers, you will turn into a world-class drunk.*
>
> AUDIENCE VOLUNTEER: *I am highly skeptical of hypnotism in general and...SNAP!...Hey, d'ya think I'm like, pretty? Why iz it so bright in here? You're kinda' cute! Hey, you're not one of those phonies are ya? Cuz' I hate phonies...but you know, I kinda' like ponies! I hate phonies but like ponies. Hey, I made a poem!*

I saw Miranda the next morning. She'd managed to make it to work, albeit two hours late. As I talked to her it became clear that she didn't remember a thing! Sure, she remembered seeing me at the nightclub, but she didn't remember the conversation, the drive home, or the peeing.

My God, she's Guy Pearce in *Memento*! She's had a head injury and she has no short-term memory. The only way she can piece together the past is by tattooing notes on her body and taking pictures of things with a Polaroid camera!

So we're one-sided virtual strangers again; I know her, but she doesn't know me. I actually feel kind of bad about this. I mean, I opened up my soul to her, told her my secrets! Told her about the state-appointed psychiatrist, my fear of clowns, and how that guy who did the crying Britney video was like, so right on, but she doesn't remember — not any of it!

I tell you, though, I keep thinking about her. I keep thinking about that night. I keep thinking how *vulnerable* she was, and now, with the added info that she has no memory, the bad boy part of my brain keeps thinking about how I missed a free pass, how I could have checked that beautiful body for those memory-stirring tattoos, if you catch my drift.

It's only a fantasy, though. I'd no sooner have sex with a completely drunk woman than I would a coma victim, but I have to tell you, there's something about schnockered girls that's exciting.

From what I can tell, it's not only me who finds the idea...well, arousing.

I told a friend about it and he got really animated as it reminded him of something he'd noticed himself. He sometimes hangs out on RedTube, which is the naked equivalent of YouTube. Like YouTube, RedTube has a "Most Viewed" section and coincidentally, many of the favorite videos are often of drunk girls entertaining frat boys.

Obviously, we're not talking about girls who've fallen into garbage cans and look like 60's icon Joe Cocker as they try, with fingers stiff and splayed, to dislodge the chicken bones from their long hair, or who, in an effort to reapply their lipstick, have inadvertently smeared their faces to look like Cleveland Indians' mascot, Chief Wahoo.

No, we're talking about sexy girls who are all touchy-feely and aching to get out of their oh-so-restrictive clothes! Libidinous trollops whose sexual appetites rival the gastronomic appetites of famed hotdog eater Joey "Jaws" Chestnut.

I asked a few women if they were aware of this rarely spoken of turn-on, and nearly none of them were. Their initial reaction — not entirely unwarranted, I guess — was one of disgust. They assumed that the allure of drunken women was exactly because they were vulnerable; that men could exert "power" over these women.

This is, of course, the same motivation attributed to rapists; that it's not about sex, it's about power.

I beg to differ. While sex with drunken girls can be, at some point, indistinguishable from rape, the allure is not about power. It's about unbridled passion.

Your honor, if I may, I'd like to present my case.

If you're like most men, "first-time" sex, i.e., the first time you have sex with someone, is generally the worst kind of sex there is. It's polite sex. It's boring sex. You don't want to push the envelope. It's missionary all the way, but even your pelvic thrusting is inhibited. You might as well be fucking to the metronome your sister uses for violin practice.

With first-time sex, you worry about whether you'll pop too soon. You feel like an idiot asking whether she came yet. You worry about whether she'll be taken aback if you do anything outside the kind of sex your parents have; if you dare to use any gymnastic positions; whether she'll freak if you stick it in her ear; whether she'll be taken aback if, in a fit of sheer animal joy, you briefly pull it out and start playing an "air guitar" version of the Ramones, "I Wanna Be Sedated" on your angry faux-Fender cock; whether you'll make a really stupid orgasm face; whether you'll let loose a sizzling hot stream of errant jism that gets into her eyes and ears and momentarily turns her into a naked, gooey Helen Keller and you have to run naked out into the garage to get your Shop Vac!

Anything could happen!

But drunk sex? Drunken sex is often unbridled sex. All those apprehensions? You rolled them up into a ball and shoved them up her butt and by golly, she liked it. Drunken sex is Nine-Inch Nails sex;

animal sex, like those cute little guys on *Meerkat Mansion* have, but without the droppings and small lizard skeletons and stuff.

Still, drunken sex, in addition to all the pitfalls I just described, just ain't right. Women get drunker a lot faster than men do, and the line between rape and consensual sex is way too fine.

Maybe the thing to do is find a girl who's willing but sober and throw your inhibitions out the window. Hell, pretend she's drunk! If she liked it, you'll get another shot. If she didn't, she'll probably get disgusted and throw you out and tell all her friends and they'll point at you and snicker every time you leave the house until you eventually have to move to another town, but at least you'll have gotten some decent sex out of it and you won't have to get your car washed.

-- 2008

Get Bent, Beckham

I don't think David Beckham will popularize soccer in America, but I worry that he'll popularize American self-love; take it to a whole new scary level, one that we could well do without, thank you. Legions of young wanna-be fops will receive, through their new role model, tacit approval to express their inner sissy.

The three Irishmen and I were playing pool in a bar in downtown Detroit. I'd met them in college and I liked them. They told good, funny stories and that, from what I can tell, is pretty much the national sport of Ireland.

Shane and Tom were in particularly good raconteurial form that night so me and Patrick — the other, uncharacteristically quiet Irishmen — just played pool and listened to them spin their yarns.

Several people around us listened, too, as bringing the Irish together with beer pretty much guarantees a good time.

Just before closing time, a tasty Motor City morsel approached Patrick, who was probably by far the best looking Irishman she, or likely anyone else, had ever seen. She backed him up against the wall and trapped him in-between her outstretched arms.

She leaned in very close, looking him straight in the eyes, and proclaimed, "I'm American and I like to fuck."

Patrick, despite his handsome looks, was terrifically shy. His eyelids fluttered and he pulled in his chin and looked at the ground in embarrassment while he fidgeted with his pool cue. Still he rose to the occasion, sort of, and responded, "As...as do *I*."

Suddenly it became apparent to onlookers why Patrick didn't talk much. He had a voice that's best described as a blend between a leprechaun and Jennifer Tilly. It was high. It was feminine. And the fact that it was also *Oirish* seemed to compound the problem.

The tasty morsel recoiled slightly, her lust apparently shillelaghlied by Patrick's pitchy pipes.

Her arms fell to her sides. She stood looking at him for a moment before walking back to her table. I never told Patrick this, but I'm pretty sure she mouthed/whispered something like, "I just propositioned a *hamster*," to her friends.

That was Patrick's curse. He'd been given the face of a god but the voice of a doggy squeak toy. He never overcame it and it's handicapped him socially and professionally to this day.

And this is exactly what I suspect will curtail David Beckham's success in the United States. Excuse me, but have you adoring females out there heard this guy talk? I hear his voice and I hear a little bit of Patrick.

But if only that were just the one yellow flag against Beckham, the only thing preventing him from making soccer as popular in America as it is in most of the rest of the world.

America has more than its share of metrosexuals, but they ain't seen nothing like what they're about to see. Next to the way he bends traditional and even not-so traditional concepts of maleness, his much-vaunted kick is ramrod straight.

Make no mistake about it, this is a genuine sissy we're talking about.

The crying jags after he fails to perform to expectations on the soccer pitch are one thing, but his flamboyance off the field would make a drag queen blush.

He has a different haircut or hairstyle nearly every week. The skinhead look gives way to cornrows that give way to a retro Billy Idol bad-boy 'do. He uses pink nail polish. He wears sarongs. He even wears his pop-star wife's panties.

Of course, that's what we're *supposed* to think, that they're *her* panties, which is kind of kinky and perverted in a way that I can sort of appreciate, but I suspect they're actually *his* panties because there's no way the prissy Beckham would put on someone else's stanky danky pretties.

It's much easier to imagine him crying out in his soft voice:

> *"Posh luv, where are my pink silkies? I hope that tart of a maid didn't bugger them up with the bloody fabric softener!"*

Then there's the photo spread in the gay British magazine just before the English troops left to do battle in Iraq and Afghanistan. One British journalist questioned Beckham's decision this way:

> *"Handing our enemies such an embarrassing pink stick to hit us with when the nation is girding its manly loins?"*

Then there's the one unfortunate tattoo. He's the first man I've seen that actually has a tramp stamp. There, just above his arse, is the word *Brooklyn*.

Sure, Becks loves New York! Pull down his pants and you might see the Lincoln Tunnel, too! Now don't go in there unless you want to end up in Jersey! Maybe you prefer instead to meander a bit south and catch a glimpse of Lady Liberty's erect torch.

But no, Brooklyn is actually the name of one of his sons. We can only guess where the names of his other two children are tattooed. I hope he and his children never experience in real life the same rift, the same deep yawning chasm, that no doubt separates the boys' names on Beck's behind.

It's a pretty safe bet that the Beckham children will have to undergo years of therapy to wash the butt ink off their psyches.

But despite all this, his new team, the LA Galaxy, thinks Beckham will take the country by storm. They've given him a 5-year contract that, with a percentage of merchandizing sales included, might amount to 250 million dollars. They hope that because of him, American soccer will soon rival American football in popularity.

Excuse me, but when average American *Maxim*-reading males learn all this stuff about Beckham the man, who among them is going to wear this *pooftah's* jersey on his back? What mid-American farm-raised hottie is going to lipstick the name "Becks" on a de-husked ear of corn and sneak it into bed with her and turn it into creamed corn while staring at this soy boy's poster?

Granted, he's a handsome bastard, but won't that physique put the kibosh on some of the female lust he's expected to attract from American females? Beckham is a male, soccer-playing version of sometime anorexic Lara Flynn Boyle. Nice face, but get thee to a gym.

It boggles the bollocks to think of the female lust Beckham has generated in other countries. According to *Japan Today*, some Japanese women have even dumped their fiancés and become *hookers* so they can pay for trips to England (and now, presumably, America) to follow their idol.

One Japanese woman even checked into hotels where Beckham stayed during the last World Cup and licked *toilets* that he might have used.

Oh Lordy, Lordy, Lordy.

So it's quite possible he'll generate some female lust in this country. Our females haven't been too discriminating in the past. After all, Pam Anderson married Kid Rock.

But popularizing soccer might be a little tougher.

Back in 1947, Brooklyn Dodger General Manager Branch Rickey was determined to integrate baseball. He thought long and hard about what type of man the first black player should be. Granted, his candidate had to be extraordinarily talented, but he also needed to be courageous and able to withstand humiliation and abuse without retaliating. He had to win the hearts of racist America. He had to pave the way for others.

Jackie Robinson fit the bill perfectly and performed his role beyond expectations.

So Beckham isn't being brought to America to right any societal wrongs, but he's presumably being brought over to transform soccer. They hope he'll take it from a ho-hum sport that's mainly the domain of European and South American transplants and young American girls who don't have much else to choose from in the way of team sports, and turn it into a national pastime.

In my mind, this is equivalent to Branch Rickey having picked Snoop Dog as the first black man to play Major League baseball, or Chris Tucker's character from *The Fifth Element*.

I'm well aware that Beckham has lots of adoring fans here already who think he's the perfect choice to popularize soccer in America. His defenders might argue that I'm just jealous of his success. Damn right I'm jealous. I'm jealous of the throngs of adoring women and all that money's a little irksome, but that's about where it stops.

I really don't like what I see of the guy. And it's not the way he dresses, his hair, the nail polish, his silly tattoos, or his unremarkable physique. All of that's irrelevant to me.

It's the sheer vanity of the guy that strikes me like a Zidane head butt to the stomach. And this comes from someone who makes his living off an activity that *wallows* in vanity. Beckham, though, makes a body shaving, tanning, flexing bodybuilder look like an Amish person in comparison.

I don't think David Beckham will popularize soccer in America, but I worry that he'll popularize American *self-love*; take it to a whole new scary level, one that we could well do without, thank you. Legions of young wanna-be fops will receive, through their new role model, tacit approval to express their inner sissy.

You know, one preening Beckham is quite tolerable. Millions of them are quite another matter.

-- 2007

Teabagging

Anyhow, F invariably fumbles around to unbutton R's tattered flannel nightgown, probes around to find the right hole, and then slaps down that KY jelly like Boo Radley's dad filling up a knothole with cement.

The following is what I hope to be presenting to the Academy next year in Sweden. (It involves some high-level math, but you should be able to stay with me if you're at least somewhat well-versed in Boolean algebra or calculus):

$$S=k/T$$

Let me elucidate.

> *The number of soufflés (S) your wife or girlfriend bakes is inversely related to the times you teabag (T) her.*
>
> *(k is the mathematical constant, which is either Pi, or the number of testicles represented by the starting front offensive line of the Nittany Lions football team. Either works.)*

Okay, so there isn't a Nobel Prize in mathematics, but I'm hoping the sheer genius of my equation will make them reconsider. You see, I really believe there's an inverse correlation between your wife or girlfriend's cooking and the amount of action you get.

I'll get to my reasoning in a second, but you and the Academy should realize I didn't come by this equation easily. It took half a cigar and a whole glass of scotch's worth of contemplation. It came to me while I was pondering *fat people.*

I have nothing against fat people. They're hardly my esthetic cup of tea (or anybody else's for that matter), but I don't care. As long as fat doesn't become the "in" thing for women, I'm the ultimate lifestyle Libertarian; do what the hell you want to do. Everybody has his or her preferred drug and food is the oldest.

Still, I'm somewhat puzzled by the sheer number and sheer bulk of the fat people in these here United States.

I realize that it's partly a cause of poverty: poor people eat cheap food, and cheap food is calorically dense and nutritionally poor — a bad combination.

But there are also psychological reasons. I have a good friend who's a clinical psychologist involved in obesity studies. He's found nearly a one-to-one relationship between clinical obesity and sexual abuse.

In other words, obese people for whom food is an addiction were almost universally abused sexually as children. They simply ate — and ate and ate and ate — to become less sexually attractive to creepy Uncle Bob who was always more than happy to tuck the little ones in at night. Their fat became their squishy armor.

That's pretty damn depressing, but that observation has to do with *really* obese people, the kind of fat people that you see on FOX news being fork-lifted off their couches and carted to the hospital in creaky-springed ambulances while small children point and puff out their cheeks and bellies in cruel mockery of the fat bastard swaying precariously over their heads.

That's not the direction I want to go in, but it did ping-pong my thoughts towards the conventional fatties who are still ambulatory enough to go to the grocery store, the Pizza Hut, or the all-you-can-eat buffet and don't have to rely on a Boy Scout troop to lever them out of bed with some old wooden oars.

I started thinking about a couple I know. R sends me emails all the time lamenting the demise of her sex life with F.

They only "do it" about once a month, and it's always in total darkness and it usually consists of F squeezing out a dog-poo sized dollop of KY Jelly onto his hand because his woman ain't known no natural lubrication for a long piece now. They closed up the place. Put up signs for the kids to stay away. Once in a while, though, at night, you can hear the coyotes singing their lonely song.

Anyhow, F invariably fumbles around to unbutton R's tattered flannel nightgown, probes around to find the right hole, and then slaps down that KY jelly like Boo Radley's dad filling up a knothole with cement.

He then climbs aboard, makes a few semi-coordinated thrusts that are more like an epileptic seizure than fucking, and then literally rolls off her ponderous body and falls asleep before he hits the Serta mattress.

So R's not too thrilled with her sex life because F is as skillful and attentive in bed as a drunken John and F isn't too enthused either, probably because he's sleeping with some fat toad of an alien who obviously kidnapped his real wife, the svelte one he married. Never mind that he's also a fat toad.

But R and F don't discuss their boring, lackluster, somewhat repugnant sex life with each other. Instead, they eat. She has index card boxes full of recipes. The middle shelf in the kitchen cupboard is sagging under the weight of all those damn cook books.

Every activity is based around food. Saturday mornings are for pancakes and sausages. Sunday afternoons are for all-you-can-eat brunches. Monday is Chinese buffet day, and Wednesday is for fried chicken and pie and the quality of each day is determined more by cream, sugar, butter, and crispy golden-brown batter than it is by sunshine, human interaction, mental stimulation, or sex.

I swear they wait for friends and acquaintances to die so they can go to the wake and gorge on casseroles and those Jell-O dishes with the marshmallows and bananas and other crap floating around in them.

Birthdays, anniversaries, and every Hallmark-card invented holiday are a regular Roman orgy of culinary delights, and hey, R, you'd better start picking out the cookies and pastries and candies and snicker-doodles because the holidays are just around the corner and you don't want to be caught with your elasti-band pants down when Jesus' birthday rolls around.

So K and F get fatter and fatter, and their sex life gets less and less satisfying because, frankly, they turn each other's blubbery stomachs.

But that's okay, they've always got the food; the food makes them forget about the frustration, the guilt, the rotten sex.

And that's where I think America is with their food and their fat. Rodney Dangerfield even touched on this once:

> I'm at the age where food has taken the place of sex in my life.
> In fact, I've just had a mirror put over my kitchen table.

Only Rodney was talking about old age. Nowadays, food is taking the place of sex in Americans in their twenties, thirties, and forties.

Sure, there's "sex" all around us, but it's like those damn commercials for beer and Pepsi and even Wrigley's gum -- those people in the commercials are always having fun on the beach and at wild parties and doubling their pleasure with beautiful twins, but the truth is the rest of us are sitting at home on weekends watching them piano-cart that fat bastard out his picture window while we're munching on Cheetohs.

It's the same with sex. It's more elusive than popular culture would suggest. That juicy fruit is hanging low on the branch, but it's just a little higher than most can jump.

So they're frustrated. Their sex life is nothing like what they see on TV. They become acutely aware of what they're missing so the disappointment grows.

But fat Americans don't discuss sex. They're too shy, or they have Puritanical sex that's a real snore.

And so they eat. And eat, and eat, and eat. And then they have less sex, because I swear, that leather outfit I bought you from the Adam and Eve website makes you look like an unfortunate feral pig that got caught in a discarded plastic six-pack holder when it was a piglet and then grew up around it so that its body is grossly malformed into a forced hourglass shape.

But other than that, it makes you look hot, honey. Honest. Cross my heart and hope to die (soon).

My psychologist friend, while he doesn't have any solid data to support it, notes that the Catholic-church functions he attends have a disproportionately higher number of fat people in attendance.

Does religion make you fat? No, but religious *guilt* might, especially if sexual urges are redirected towards food.

But it's all part of the same psychosexual baggage. Frustration, guilt, boredom, bad communication skills, it all leads to bad sex and I believe that a lot of that bad sex leads to good eating, a whole lot of good eating.

So if you're married, I contend that the amount you're getting is inversely related to the number of cookbooks your wife has in the cupboard. The more obsessed your wife is with cooking and food — and the more obsessed you are with eating what she cooks — the less satisfying your sex life.

And if she has a subscription to *Gourmet* or *Bon Appetit*? Brother, you'd best join the Vienna Boys Choir because you're a virtual castrati. But that's as much your fault as it is wifey's.

Hence my elegant equation:

$S = k/T$

Hence my eloquent theory:

The number of soufflés your wife or girlfriend bakes is inversely related to the times you teabag her.

I'm sure there are plenty of exceptions to the rule where people are slim despite being good in the kitchen and good in bed. And then, of course, there are the couples who actually incorporate food in their lovemaking, like Kim Basinger and Mickey Rourke in *9 1/2 Weeks*, or maybe George Costanza, who considered pastrami to be the most sensual of the all the salted, cured lunchmeats.

Neither can I forget my beloved sushi restaurants where you eat raw fish off a naked babe acting as a platter, but I can see how that might lead to more frustration and ergo, more maguro.

Oh, I don't know. All my psychological theorizing is probably just a bunch of horseshit *paté*. Maybe people are fat because they just like to eat. It might just be that simple, but that equation just doesn't seem to add up.

-- 2006

My Speech to the Graduates, 2009

You ever hear of the Greatest Generation? They grew up during the Great Depression, contributed to the war effort either by fighting in it or making materiel contributions to it, and then went on to build America. You guys? Hell, you might well prove to be the worstest generation.

T hank you, parents, distinguished faculty members, and students of Notorious B.I.G. University. I'm truly honored that you've asked me to give the commencement address to this year's graduating class...

Long uncomfortable pause. The speaker looks disgusted. He looks around with a contemptuous smirk on his face, crumples up his notes, and then shoots them into the audience, making a three-pointer into the pronounced cleavage of Miss Weatherby, the shocked glee club director who's sitting in the front row.

Screw this. I was going to make some high-falutin' speech about achievement and bright promise and all the wonderful opportunities in your life, but let's get real. Most of you are sitting out there Twittering and Tweeting and texting and OMG'ing and it's doubtful you'd even hear one word, so I'll just go ahead and say what I feel like.

Gawd, where do I start? I guess I'm going to address only the males out there because they're far worse off than you ladies. You, I'm not worried about too much. All the same, you're welcome to listen in.

Hrrrum (clearing throat).

Good afternoon losers.

If I had my druthers, I'd have you graduates come up here one by one, but instead of giving you your sheepskin, I'd bitchslap your rosy red cheeks so hard and loud that it would sound like I was playing Heigh-Ho Silver horsie in my hotel room with a stable of naked co-eds.

Hell, I'd go *Moe* on you.

The thing is, just about all of you are going to be dead in 60 years or so, assuming, among other unforeseeable events, that the Swine Flu doesn't mutate into Captain Tripps and wipe you all out cuz, the thing is, the younger and healthier you are, the more robust your immune system, the better your chance of drowning in your vomit and assorted bodily fluids.

How's that for a kick in the crotch?

And I don't know if this will bug you or not, but when you go? Nobody will give a shit.

Oh, and one more thing: you're going to be dead a very long time.

You ever hear of the Greatest Generation? They grew up during the Great Depression, contributed to the war effort either by fighting in it or making materiel contributions to it, and then went on to build America. You guys? Hell, you might well prove to be the *worstest* generation.

Here's what your future likely holds:

You're going to drift from job to job because you have bizarrely high expectations for your salary, benefits, responsibilities, and vacation time, while having little concern about doing a good job or showing any loyalty at all to the company that was stupid enough to hire you.

Amazingly, though, you'll continue to have grandiose but highly unrealistic expectations for your future. Sure, you're just treading water until you get a Tweet from some company that wants you to write television shows or design games or do the graphics on a new line of snowboards. It's just a matter of time.

And if, by some small chance none of that works, you've got your secret weapon -- you'll design iPhone apps! Sure, you've got one in mind that makes your screen turn into a virtual flickering Zippo lighter so that after Slipknot has just played their last set, you can wave it in the air and people will say, "That's just stupid cool."

You'll make millions.

Too late, app-boy, they've already done it.

But your parents promised you that you'd be successful, right? They said you were special, that you were all little Bill Gates or Stephen Hawkings—minus the talent, genius, or wheelchair, of course. How could you not succeed? It's only a matter of time!

In the meantime, you'll continue living with a bunch of guys, just like you did in college, because you don't want to give up that dorm life; you want your video buddies and drinking buddies and gambling buddies nearby because they're your smelly, toe-jam, hair-clogged-drain security blanket, and you take inestimable pleasure in waiting for them to pass out after drinking a dozen tall boys and then super gluing elbow macaroni to their faces to see how closely you can get them to resemble the thing Arnold fought in that *Predator* movie.

Besides, you can't afford to live on your own...at least not until you get the call from the gaming company that wants to buy the video game concept that exists only on some ephemeral to-do list in your muddled head.

But still you strut around...

...my God do you strut. You're so full of false bravado and machismo that anybody with half a credit in psychology could see that it's compensation, compensation for fear and feelings of inadequacy.

You don't know what life is about, and you have all these gosh-darn feelings that you suppress on 8 cylinders because you learned that men aren't supposed to have feelings and if people found out that you did, you wouldn't fit in; you wouldn't be allowed to play in all the reindeer games.

And you can't talk to your parents because they won't get it. And you can't confide in your friends because that would reveal you as the weak sissy boy you are.

So you couch yourself in bravado. After all, you have to be a *guy*; you have to be accepted by the other guys.

So you follow the guy rules, the ones that say you have to act tough, not to impress women, but to impress other guys! Walk with a kyphotic slouch, talk without a hint of diction. To do otherwise might make your peeps think you're a homo!

Don't show any emotion other than anger, of course. Don't show interest in art or any music that isn't metal or rap and dress crappy because to do otherwise is so *ghey*! And by God if you get that bitch in your car, push her head down towards your lap until she gets busy. Make sure you get it on video, too. Hell, showing your friends you got a blowjob is better than the blowjob itself!

Trouble is, you can't even see that the heroes you idolize in the movies usually stand alone; are usually ostacized by others for having independent thoughts, but what you idolize and how you act are completely at odds; there's absolutely no congruency.

But go ahead and follow the herd; it's safer. And go ahead and be angry, because that's the only acceptable emotion.

And you deserve to be mad, don't you?

The world is filled with all these beautiful women that you can't have. They dress all sexy, showing their cleavage and neathage and buttage and flashing their underwear and just taunting you, dude. Those...those bitches!

So you listen to angry music. Four out of five gangsta rap CD's are bought by you angry white boys because by God, the black men on those CD's are angry and you can relate! Of course you can! Like that time your dad gave you the old family Volvo for your birthday instead of the new baby Beemer you wanted. That's anger man. It's almost-sorta-kinda like being raised in the Projects, isn't it?

Sure! You can relate to the black rapper!

And you listen to the old guys on talk radio and hate TV that are angry. They're fuming over the lost privileges of other white men! Those problems you're having? Not your fault! You're constantly being emasculated and humiliated by the government and the gays and liberal sissies and it's not your fault!

The angry guys know it's easy to justify any prejudice by exaggerating real or imagined differences with the thing or person or people or institution they've targeted. That's how they play you. Man, you are so easy to manipulate!

But all you know is that you're angry.

That's okay, because there are video games, video games and porn.

The video games allow you to live in a world where you're constantly in control. You never have to show weakness, never have to show indecision or cowardice or insecurity! In real life, everyone tells you what to do, your parents, your teachers, your bosses, but in *Grand Theft Auto*, you're the meanest SOB around!

In fact, the experiences you have in your video games are often more authentic than the ones you have in the real world because, really, if you had sex with a hooker and then killed her and robbed her, that would be like, *bad*. Ask Philip Markoff.

And the porn? It's because you're confused. Those damn bitches on the streets and in the clubs and in the Starbucks keep sending out mixed signals and you can't even scan some girl without being tagged as a stalker or a pervert, so you rely on porn for your "inter-gender" encounters.

No wonder you freaked out that one time you hooked up with a real flesh and blood girl. Man, her asshole wasn't even bleached! What a colossal turn-off!

Luckily your life is all about endless entertainment. Keep busy doing something, *anything*, so you can pass through life as distracted as possible. The only activities that matter are sex (real or electronic), money, power, drinking, and video games. Everything else, all the ordinary activities of life, have no value. They're nothing but a drag.

Trouble is, that's the majority of life. Once you devalue the ordinary activities, your mind sleeps through most of the rest of your life. You need to value everything you do, do everything in earnest, realize the potential for learning in any event, no matter how mundane it may seem.

Oh oh, I accidentally just gave some advice there. Not sure I meant to do that.

But what the hell, I'll see, for my own amusement since no one's listening, if I can offer up some more wisdom. I guess that's what they're paying me for.

Let's try to figure out why a lot of you 16 to 26 year olds are the way you are.

Now I can understand that real masculinity, real notions of manhood like responsibility, caring, discipline, and integrity, are hard to come by.

Young men used to know they'd eventually find value in their work, but now that we're largely a service economy that doesn't produce squat and we're a culture of consumption instead of production, pride in accomplishment is rare; experiencing masculinity as a provider and protector is rare.

Likewise every male schmuck has told you that men don't cry, as if that's the sole trait essential to being a man. As a result, you strive desperately to shut off emotions. You saw your mother as one big matzo ball of emotions, so you started shutting her out of your life as you neared adolescence because you thought being too close to your mother might make you catch gay.

And since your dad was taught not to have emotions, he didn't talk to you about important stuff either. So you never really got to talk about any important stuff with anybody, because important stuff is often feelings-based and again, feelings, as I mentioned above, might make you catch gay.

So you were forced to get your definition of manhood, and life for that matter, from the poor schlubs on TV sitcoms.

Oh sure, you want to grow up to be the henpecked doofus in *Everyone Loves Raymond.*

No wonder no one wants to get married or grow up. Hell, that's a drag. TV adulthood, ergo real adulthood, is a drag. It's all about paying bills, car payments, buying fucking appliances. Who wants that crap?

Years ago, guys used to leave home, complete their educations, start work, get married, and have kids all pretty much at the same time, which, for self-respecting guys, was at the ripe old age of about 20 or 21.

They got married—and bought into all the crap that came with it back then because that meant you could get all the nookie you wanted, any time you wanted. (Girls usually didn't just give it away back then.)

"Honey, I'm home! Now drop the panties and bend over cuz I'm gonna make one deposit I don't need a receipt for."

But there's usually some free nookie around nowadays, which means you don't have to grow up for a long time. Granted, it's generally not the stuff you see on *Girls Gone Wild* DVDs or beer commercials or Bebe ads, but some nookie is better than no nookie.

But if you don't even have Grade B nookie, you've got *Internet* nookie, and that's nothing to shake a stick...well, you know what I mean.

So the nookie factor is all but removed as a reason to grow up and get married.

Likewise, you never learned about feelings and emotional development and real manliness, but you did get all the other supposed answers from parents, teachers, peers, religion, and popular culture that explain what life's all about, but they never asked you any follow-up questions.

So you naturally become punk-ass smarty-pants know-it-alls, who are hugely retarded in that your mind is completely closed by the time you hit...well, your age.

So you use these immutable opinions to put a spin on everything. Despite your relatively young age, you pretty much can't learn anything of value on your own and certainly can't be taught anything.

Well it's time to stop laying blame.

Granted, all those people I mentioned earlier—your parents, teachers, peers, etc.—deserve a lot of the blame. Forgive them, for they know not what they do or did. But that's as far as the blame game goes. Time to man up. Time to fix yourself, because no one else gives a shit.

First, I want you to forget just about everything you ever learned.

I'd like you to be *innocent* again. I want you to be open to experience. It's the only way out.

Start asking questions. Look at everything as a possible learning experience. How does what I'm seeing relate to me? How can I learn from this?

Look for a grain—or a sackful—of truth in what I said at the beginning of the speech. If you know why you act the way you do, know the source of your actions and reactions, you're halfway there in becoming a real human being.

Second, stop being normal.

Normal people are the guys I was talking to in the beginning of this speech. Normal, as it's defined nowadays, ain't good. I'm not saying to get married or not to get married, not saying to find a respectable career or not to find a respectable career; not saying to buy a house and Maytag appliances or not to. That's all up to you.

What I'm asking is that you define your purpose in life—whatever it is—and set about achieving it. Things just start to click after that. You start to separate the bullshit from the non-bullshit, the essential from the non-essential.

Once you start doing that, you may find that the people you hang around with start to look like children to you, and rightly so.

And that's not normal, at least not nowadays.

There's still plenty of time for "normal" things like video games and beer and porn, but let's try to achieve some balance, shall we? Give your inner self as much attention as you give your outer self.

Really, it's the right thing to do. It'll ultimately be a lot more satisfying than the alternative.

As I said, you're going to be dead for a very long time.

Special thanks to the book "Guyland: The Perilous World Where Boys Become Men," by Michael Kimmel, and Dr. Paul Hatherley, author of "The Awareness and Skills Necessary for Enduring Happiness."

-- 2009

Why-Oh-Why Aren't You Hot?

He's not insisting you develop a passion for midget wrestling or that you give up meat. He's not asking you to give up your religious beliefs and instead worship the Rutabaga god that commands his faith. And neither is he asking you to submit to his sexual perversion, which involves nipple clamps, a bucket of canned meat, and a 15-horsepower leaf blower.

In the beginning, there was Abby.

Abby begat Ann, and Ann begat Judith, and Judith begat Amy, and Amy begat a whole slew of other advice columnists.

One of the latest to be begotten is Carolyn Hax, who shovels out advice on relationships three days a week in newspapers across the country.

To her credit, Carolyn doesn't pretend to have any special training in psychology. Instead, she says she has a liberal arts degree and "a lot of opinions and that's about it."

Since I don't have any special training or a degree in psychology either, I'm eminently qualified to squelch her advice, which is best described as Pollyanna pie-in-the-sky idealism soaked in a high-octane estrogen, with just an occasional smidgeon of in-your-face sassiness thrown in for spice.

This recent column in particular caught my eye and fueled my ire:

> *Dear Carolyn,*
>
> *I am 25 and have been with Dave, 30, for almost three years. We live together and plan to get married and have kids. One thing that repeatedly comes up, though, is my body, and my failure to go to the gym or eat right. This has been our only real disagreement. He thinks I would be perfect if I dropped 15 pounds. I am stubborn and prideful and any requests for me to change have been met with anger and tears.*
>
> *After I recently complained about the burden of school loans, Dave said he would give me money toward my bills if I could lose 15 pounds in two months. I have told my friends about it, and some say I should kick him to the curb and the others think it's a good idea. The latter are all gym-going people. They tell me if I let myself go it will be harder to get in shape later.*
>
> *I have always been uncomfortable about my body. I think I can lose a few pounds but I don't think I am grotesque*

enough or that my health is in jeopardy. I need an unbiased opinion.

— G.

Carolyn's answer lets us know she doesn't think much of Dave:

"Whatever gave this guy the idea that he was entitled to 'perfect'? That he had any right to 'improve' you to suit his own needs — especially since he apparently met you as is?"

She continued to berate Dave:

"You're also ready to believe, enabled by friends, that his offer is about your health. It's not. It's about a guy making his love for you conditional.

"He'll only get harder to satisfy, as your body ages and stretches from having kids. Are you ready to spend the rest of your life fighting for the love of the person whose love you want most?"

Her final advice to "G" is to "Run, run, run. And not in the exercise sense."

Carolyn, Carolyn, Carolyn, you're absolutely right. Twenty-first century man has totally subjugated 4 billion years of evolution and now, whenever he looks at a woman, sees only her inner beauty.

Dave is obviously some throwback to a more primitive, superficial time.

In fact, Carolyn, while I've never seen a picture of you, I already know that I love you. Our minds are *simpatico*. Let us grow old together, ignoring your physical trappings, regardless of how repugnant they may be. Rather than resort to odious physical procreation, let us place our foreheads together — let us mind fuck — and from our pure loving thoughts there shall arise a supernatural child born of such love and noble intent that nature itself will burp forth from the ground millions of celebratory puppy dogs that will lick the faces of every man, woman, and child on earth in a slobber fest of love, an act which will vanquish war and hate and poverty and pestilence and nourish and preserve each of us until we die blissfully in each other's arms and Lawdy, Lawdy, rise clear up to hebben where de angels am!

For chrissake, Carolyn, get real.

Here's how I might have answered G's letter:

> Dear G,
>
> So you met someone. In this bizarre, cold, lonely world, you somehow bucked the odds and found someone to love you.
>
> He overlooked your physical flaws and fell in love with you.
>
> That's pretty amazing. You know how many people get engaged on looks alone, only to eventually find out they've married the intellectual equivalent of a tree stump — one with lovely tits, but a tree stump nonetheless?
>
> But still you're unhappy because he doesn't think you're perfect.
>
> Personally, I think he's doing it the right way -- he's found someone who he liked for non-physical reasons; somehow noticed the chubby girl standing in the corner with a Mai Tai and for some reason actually approached her while every fiber of his loins told him to instead saunter up to the moist mammal in the tube top whose ass is such an example of geometric perfection that Archimedes himself would have shouted Eureka at its sight.
>
> He somehow saw the diamond in the rough that is you and is willing to help you hack at the overgrowth to get to the jewel.
>
> He's not insisting you develop a passion for midget wrestling or that you give up meat. He's not asking you to give up your religious beliefs and instead worship the Rutabaga god that commands his faith. And neither is he asking you to submit

to his sexual perversion, which involves nipple clamps, a bucket of canned meat, and a 15-horsepower leaf blower.

All he's asking is that you lose 15 pounds. He's not demanding it, nor is he making your nuptials conditional on it. In fact, it sounds like he's given you a very nice incentive.

You say you're stubborn and prideful, but I think you're guiltier of another one of the seven sins: sloth. Your entire letter reeks of it. I've no doubt you're one of those women who, once they get married, let themselves turn into a toad. Of course, chances are if Dave says you'd be perfect if you lost 15 pounds, he's being charitable. You probably need to lose 30.

It looks like you spent a lot of energy in finding someone to agree with you; to tell you that you're right and that Dave is soooo unfair. You probably had yourself a lot of comfort food, too, to nurture your damaged pride.

Listen, Tubby, in the time it took you to seek out the advice of numerable friends and write your letter to Carolyn, you could have been well on your way to losing the 15 pounds.

Let me tell you a deep dark secret that most men know but never admit. Despite the love they might have for their tubby women, the one thought that keeps going through their heads upon rising and seeing that hulking, amorphous shape beneath the covers is, "Why-oh-why aren't you hot?"

Every time a group of friends talks about someone's sexy wife, there's that little knife prick to his heart because they sure wouldn't talk about you that way.

Yes, it's superficial. Yes, it shouldn't be that way. But it is that way. I promise you, once we get around to eradicating pride, jealousy, anger, and envy, we'll dump superficiality, too. But you better be prepared for a long wait. Man covets beauty. It thrills him. It makes his life worthwhile.

Telling him to cut off these primeval likes and yearnings is akin to telling him to chop off his fingers, which he would gladly do, along with drinking raw sewage or being chained to a rock and having vultures chew at his liver for a solid month, if it meant you'd devote a little time to cultivating your personal beauty.

You want a happy marriage? You want hubby to stay blissful, lower the odds of him straying, and ensure a satisfying sex life for yourself — the kind of sex life where you're in such a perpetual chemical euphoria that you can't even get out of your bed and that it's all you can do to brush your teeth, turn your head, and spit at the trash basket? Hell, that kind of sex burns fat and keeps the pounds off because there's little interest in eating food.

You want to enjoy an active social life because he's proud to take you out and show you off? Do you want to lose the burden of those college loans?

Lose the 15.

If you had written to Carolyn complaining about how Dave was badgering you to get better with money or pick up after yourself, she would have no doubt sided with Dave, but since you're talking about something that rubs close to the bone of almost every woman — body image — she wants you to kick Dave to the curb.

And don't think for one minute this is a sexist thing. If you had written to Carolyn complaining how Dave wouldn't lose 15 pounds for you, I'd be on your side, just like I'm on Dave's side now. My argument would be a little different, but my advice would be the same.

If you're not willing to make the effort, G, then I have just three words for Dave: Run, run, run. And not in the exercise sense.

-- 2009

Protecting Your Balls

Woe be to the fetus or the just-born baby if he's exposed to these chemicals. During the first 3-4 months of a boy's life, he enters into what's been called "mini puberty" where Testosterone levels rise to approximately half of what they might be at real puberty.

I don't know if you knew this about me, but my mom used to be a hockey player in Canada.

She got pregnant while she was a forward for the Saskatoon Beaver Nuzzlers after a tryst with famed Canadian hockey announcer, Walter "Golden Loon" Chevalier.

Oddly, she didn't even know she was pregnant until the championship game against the Thunder Bay Battlin' Lesbians. The scoreless game had gone into overtime and there were only 20 seconds left in the period when she stole the puck from the Lesbian defenseman and found herself in a breakaway situation.

Just as she was about to slap the puck towards the goal, she felt a sudden, powerful contraction. Seconds later, a 9-pound, blue-eyed baby boy was spit onto the ice like a watermelon seed propelled from Dizzy Gillespie's lips.

Baby, bloody placenta, and puck skidded together across the ice like an out of control Ice Road Trucker, past the glove of the outstretched goalie and into the net.

Despite being momentarily stunned, the goal judge flashed the red light and precipitated a celebration that rivaled that of the Canadian Olympic teams' gold medal victory last Sunday. She named me TC on the spot, which is short for "Terrific Canadian." She held me over her head as if I were Lord Stanley's Cup and skated around the rink for all to adore.

The cheers faded to shocked murmurs a few moments later when the crowd began to notice something terribly wrong with baby TC's genitals. While the penis was large enough to serve as a reasonable facsimile of famed Montreal Canadian Guy Lafleur's stick, the nutsack fluttered in the breeze like the Canadian flags that festooned the outdoor rink.

Something was wrong. Something was terribly wrong.

One of baby TC's testicles appeared to undescended, prompting the cruel Canadian sportscasters to call the infant TC, not for "Terrific Canadian," but for "Testicle Conspicuouslyabsent."

My mother's shame was so great that we had to move to the States. She got a job as a stripper and the only time she ever "played" hockey was on stage. She had this act where she'd "skate" around naked and body check the other dancers off the stage. She got great tips, but they didn't even make a dent in the occasional lawsuit.

Me? I grew up ridiculed by the other children. They called me "Uniball," "Cy-nut," and their favorite, "Vinnie Testi-lonely," after the NFL quarterback.

Oh, there were times when the handicap came in handy. For instance, when other kids put a baseball card in their spokes to make their bike sound like a motorcycle, all I had to do was slip off my underwear and wear loose shorts and the winds would buffet my partially empty nutsack and make pretty much the same noise.

Other than that, though, it was pretty miserable.

I eventually got the condition surgically repaired and it left me no worse for wear, psychologically, biologically, or even functionally. Still, I have a certain affinity for stories about testicles.

Case in point, a study was just printed in *The Journal of Clinical Endocrinology and Metabolism* that showed Finns had larger testicles than Danes. This wasn't the finding of some impromptu barroom bet between Scandinavian rivals Olli and Sven, but a genuine study involving 1,600 babies born between 1997 and 2001.

It seems that at birth, Finns have slightly larger testes than Danes, but in the subsequent 3 months, the Finnish testicles outpace the Danish testicles by a 3-fold greater increment in size.

The natural instinct would be to assume that Finns, because they have bigger balls, might also have higher Testosterone levels. While that may be true of the men in this study (more on that later), testicle size generally doesn't mean squat when it comes to Testosterone levels.

If it did, the relative testicle size of Asian men, white men, and black men, on average, would show differences in Testosterone levels (on average, Asians have the smallest testicles of the three races listed, with whites next, and blacks sitting atop the big-ball throne), but they don't.

Likewise, consider that adult males with only one testicle still possess normal Testosterone levels. If the size equals T levels were true, a one-testicled man would present with lower Testosterone and that isn't the case.

The size of the testicles is generally indicative of the number of *Sertoli* cells they contain. Sertoli cells are the specialized cells that produce sperm. If you have balls bigger than the average bear, it's more indicative of your baby-making ability than it is your aggressiveness, bravery, or muscle-building ability.

Keep in mind, though, that more sperm doesn't mean you shoot bigger loads, either. Your prostate determines the volume of your ejaculate and bigger balls generally just means your ejaculate has a higher concentration of wrigglers.

Of course, Testosterone, as produced by the Leydig cells in the testes, has a direct correlation on the size and functionality of the Sertoli cells. That's why taking exogenous Testosterone or steroids makes your nuts shrink. When you have excess amounts of androgenic hormone floating around your system, the pituitary doesn't bother to chemically signal the Leydig cells to produce Testosterone, thus "starving" the Sertoli cells.

Consequently, they stop producing sperm and they shrink. They take a vacation in the Hamptons, or set off to New England to see the leaves change. As a result, men who take large amounts of steroids or Testosterone have smallish nuts and are largely infertile, at least for the duration of the steroid cycle.

Once steroid administration stops, the machinery usually revs up again and the balls swell to their former grandeur.

But let's get back to the study on the balls of Finns and Danes. In addition to a significant difference in the "ellipsoidal volume" of their testicles, the study, along with some other related studies, unearthed some other troubling differences that may have some relevance to all males.

Forty percent of young Danish military recruits have suboptimal sperm levels. Seven percent of all live Danish births required "assisted" reproduction (which I presume means some sort of artificial insemination, as opposed to recruiting some Finnish stud to slide the Legos away and plop Ingrid's ass on the coffee table and screw the holy herrings out of her).

And, in a statistic near and dear to my heart, or my heart-on, about 9 percent of Danish schoolboys had an undescended testicle, as opposed to only 2.3 percent in Finland. Oh, if only I'd been raised in Denmark. I'd have had an army of one-nutted blonde-haired companions with which to play reindeer games!

Anyhow, the main problem with having an undescended testicle, aside from the social stigma, is that it doubles the risk for testicular cancer. Case in point, testicular cancer rates among Danes are about three times higher than the Finnish or U.S. rates.

Even though it's a much bigger problem with Danes, consider that testicular cancer is the number one cancer affecting U.S. men. But there's something else troubling in the statistics above. Remember how I said that testicle size doesn't correlate with Testosterone production? Well, it doesn't, normally, but when you look at the Danish birth rates, you see something slightly contradictory and hugely troubling.

In the Danes, something clearly disrupted their hormone levels in the womb. A deficiency in Testosterone, or some disruption in the way hormones bind with receptors, affected the development of their testicles.

And the problem might have continued once they were out of the womb, resulting in adults with smaller sperm counts and possibly lower Testosterone levels, which might explain the Danes' inexplicable love affair with those Legos.

Too bad these studies didn't also measure Testosterone levels; that might have given us some additional insights, but I strongly suspect that their T levels are significantly lower than that of their Finnish or American counterparts.

The educated guess is the developmental problems had environmental origins, and indeed, Danish epidemiologists have found industrial chemicals like polychlorinated biphenols, questionable flame-retardants, dioxins, biphenols, and pesticides in the land, food, and water.

Woe be to the fetus or the just-born baby if he's exposed to these chemicals. During the first 3-4 months of a boy's life, he enters into what's been called "mini puberty" where Testosterone levels rise to approximately half of what they might be at real puberty. Oddly enough, this phase is unique to primates, and its primary role is increasing the number of the aforementioned Sertoli cells and to increase the growth rate of the penis.

Interfere with this period, and you see a cascade of developmental effects that will affect/plague the male for the rest of his life.

American infants are plagued by a similar set of androgenic demons in the form of phthalates (a chemical found in plastics), PFOS and PFOA (compounds used to make nonstick coatings), and all kinds of other hormone disrupters found in hairsprays, room fresheners, plastic food wrappings, insecticides, and detergents.

The number is growing, too. Each year, about 2,000 new chemicals are introduced to the market, and the majority don't go through even the simplest tests to determine toxicity.

What might be even more troubling is that as many as one third of all infants in the U.S. are now fed soy-milk formula. Too bad that soy milk contains high levels of plant estrogens, and it's well known that these chemicals can suppress FSH (follicle stimulating hormone) and subsequently diminish Testosterone production during "mini puberty."

While there's no definitive proof of this specific affect among humans, experiments with marmoset monkeys have shown that soy formula definitely affects Testosterone production during mini puberty and might have long-term consequences for the testis, resulting in adults with impaired fertility and poorly defined secondary male characteristics.

Lest you think that the chemicals listed are only of concern to developing fetuses, you're fooling yourself. These industrial hormonal disrupters, in addition to possibly contributing to the development of different types of cancer, can also lead to infertility, higher body fat, impaired neural function, and either lower Testosterone levels or a diminished response to Testosterone in adults, too.

Similarly, adult males should probably avoid soy milk or soy products as they've been shown to damage or kill testicular cells, in addition to reducing Testosterone levels.

Here are a few things you can do to safeguard you and Junior from chemicals:

- Buy organic meat and vegetables when you can.

- Don't heat or store your food in plastic containers. Use glass instead.

- Don't cover your food with plastic wrap when you heat it. Use a paper towel instead.

- Don't use pesticides in your home. Use baits and traps instead.

- Try not to eat fish that were caught from lakes, rivers, or streams that glow in the dark.

- Don't let Junior gnaw on plastic teethers or toys, lest he grow up to be the next Clay Aiken.

- Avoid soy milk or most soy products.

While I've concentrated on the chemical hazards faced by your balls, I think I should also address some non-environmental dangers that might affect not only your sperm count, but also your testicular health in general, including Testosterone production.

If you're like me, you can't ride a bike or spin for 15 minutes without feeling like your schlong and nutsack have gone to sleep. The fact is, putting all that weight on your taint constricts the blood and nerve impulses, causing that unpleasant numb feeling.

While it usually goes away in a few minutes, repeated exposure to this kind of abuse might lead to erectile dysfunction and an inflamed prostate. While this doesn't usually affect your testicles directly, riding or spinning can reduce your sperm count and give you the inexplicable urge to cover yourself in weird-looking Spandex when you ride.

Coincidentally, those Spandex bike shorts can also be problematic as entombing your balls in polyurethane and smashing them against your body causes a dramatic increase in ball temperature, and the higher the body temp, the lower the sperm count.

(And while fertility lore has often recommended that men wear boxers instead of briefs to increase fertility, it really doesn't seem to matter much either way. However, wearing looser, breathable clothes in general might increase sperm count.)

If you're going to ride a bike, get one of those seats with a hole in it, or at least one with a split in it to distribute the load more evenly.

Drinking, to no one's surprise, has a detrimental effect on Testosterone levels too, along with decreasing sperm count in general. And if your drinking (or eating) makes you fat, you also produce more aromatase enzyme, which converts some of the Testosterone in your body to estrogen.

In short, avoid as many environmental chemicals as you can, ditch the soy milk (especially for Junior), try not to constrict, mash, or bake your nuts, and keep the partying to a respectable minimum.

Aside from affecting your Testosterone levels, you sure wouldn't want to give birth to any one-nutted children or, God forbid, a kid who'd feel at home in the locker room with a bunch of Danes.

(Author's note: The studies about relative testicle size among Finns and Danes don't pertain to any adult Danish readers as the studies examined babies born between 1997 and 2001. This article will be long forgotten by the time they're old enough to beat the tar out of me.)

-- 2010

The Gathering

Anyway you look at it, a book about boys' bodies seems somehow silly. Boys discuss biological functions. They examine their penises daily with the same rapt fascination as a numismatist who just stumbled onto a rare 1909-S VDB Lincoln penny.

Given that those caveman commercials for Geico inspired some genius TV exec to make a TV show about them, I fully expect to see a show featuring Clitface Vulvapants debuting on FOX pretty soon.

Who's Clitface Vulvapants? It's a *vulva* puppet they used to explain female anatomy on the Tyra Banks Show a few weeks ago.

Okay, so they didn't call it Clitface Vulvapants, but they might have, such was the cutesy approach they used.

"So many women think that you pee and have a baby from the same hole," lamented Tyra.

To dispel this notion, Dr. Debbie, full-time doc, part-time puppeteer, presented the satin and velvet vulva puppet and pointed to different parts as she went along.

"If you're checking yourself out for the first time, this area is called the *mons*; it's the triangular area which may or may not have hair."

The vulva then began to sing "I Feel Pretty," from *Westside Story* while swinging its vulval hips provocatively towards a Puerto Rican penis puppet.

Not really. I'm kidding about the singing and dancing, but not the rest of it.

Apparently this ignorance about female anatomy and mechanics is rampant. I'm even led to believe that women never, ever, look down *there*. The approach they take to their private parts must be much the same as the one they take on the subway: Whatever you do, don't make eye contact.

As further evidence of this female unfamiliarity with their vagina area, there's a new book coming out. It's called *Body Drama* and it's advertised as a "photographic body, health, and self-esteem book for young women."

Former beauty queen Nancy Redd wrote the book to answer questions teenage girls had about their own bodies. For example, she tackles the perplexing question, "My vagina smells — what's going on?"

Given this confusion women supposedly have about their va-jay-jays (the latest "in" word for vagina, supposedly popularized by Oprah), I'm wondering if men need a similar book to answer questions they may have about their bodies:

> Chapter 7: Why does my pe-nay-nay get all swole and look like an angry Verne Troyer when I watch Tila Tequila's show?
>
> Chapter 13: Why does my navel sometimes smell like Gorgonzola cheese?

Anyway you look at it, a book about boys' bodies seems somehow silly. Boys discuss biological functions. They examine their penises daily with the same rapt fascination as a numismatist who just stumbled onto a rare 1909-S VDB Lincoln penny.

They know their penises get all swole because they're engorged with blood from sexual excitement. They know their navels sometimes smell for the same reason their wet catcher's mitt smells when they toss it into the closet for a couple of weeks. (Maybe that's why most young women don't know why their vaginas sometimes smell — they never tossed a wet catcher's mitt into the closet.)

No, boys and men usually are pretty comfortable with their anatomy.

There is one area, though, that boys or, more precisely, men, apparently do need a book about; one area that women seem to have covered but where men are ridiculously inept.

It may sound corny at first, but bear with me a bit -- men seem incapable of forming *close friendships* after they leave high school, college, or the service.

Let me ask you a question. How many friends do you know who you can just call up on the phone to talk? If you're like most men, the number resembles the mouth of the dispirited soul in Edvard Munch's most famous painting, *The Scream*.

Once guys leave school or the service, they rarely encounter circumstances where they're thrown in with a bunch of guys and forced to face a common adversary, be that adversary teachers, administrators, Nelson

Muntz, or in the case of the service, commanding officers, or the enemy itself.

No, after school and the service, your friends are generally fished from the work pool or worse yet, your wife or girlfriend picks them for you. Her friends have boyfriends or husbands so you're expected to bond with them and talk about the infinite permutations of leaf blowers or aluminum siding.

As far as work relationships, they're often superficial and most of the discussions pertain to work itself. If the topic of work were removed from the table, most guys would simply stare at the ground and paw the dirt with their tasseled loafers until the trilling of their Blackberry mercifully breaks the tension.

Similarly, hanging around with your wife's friends' mates is often an equally odious construct. You talk to them, but you wonder what gods you angered to have your fate intertwined with these weasels. If you break up with your wife, you breathe a sigh of relief because you'll never have to lay eyes on those sad sack pricks again.

But the nature of male friendships is a strange animal in general and coincidentally, it's more animal than man in a lot of respects. Most male relationships are based on jealousy and competitiveness. When your "friend" finds a hot wife or girlfriend, you're not happy for him; you want to slit his throat, throw his woman over your shoulder, and nail her in his bed, after which you wipe off your dick with his favorite New York Jets jersey.

When he gets a promotion or his fat uncle dies and leaves him some money, you're not happy for him; you wish it had happened to you.

Conversely, female friendships seem largely to be based on mutual support and genuine caring. They talk about things that matter.

Think about it, do you ever talk about anything other than cars, sports, or maybe politics with the guys you know? Probably not. You don't dare mention anything personal. You have to keep your guard up! You don't want to give the other guy any info he can use against you or divulge any weaknesses.

No, the only person most guys open up to is their wife or girlfriend. That's because their wife or girlfriend is their best friend. But what happens when your wife or girlfriend *is* the problem? Who do you open up to then?

Sadly, when a couple breaks up, it's the guy who has the worst time. The girl usually has a huge support system and she's out shopping and having margaritas for lunch with her friends while the guy is at home in a dark room moaning into a wet catcher's mitt while growing a tumor.

He ends up trying to remarry the first thing with tits and a Clitface Vulvapants between her legs.

But men often dismiss the notion of having any genuine close friends. They regard having close friends or buddies as a remnant of immaturity, so they deliberately avoid or even sabotage friendships. Have these same men accidentally bump into an old childhood or school friend, though, and see what happens. The joy is such that it reminds you of a labrador that was suddenly reunited with his master after having been separated by Katrina. Tell me that joy isn't a sign of a latent hunger for friendship.

Dr. Herb Goldberg studied male relationships and he conceptualized four distinct phases in the development of a "buddyship." These four phases include the *manipulative* phase, the *companionship* phase, the *friendship* phase, and finally, the *buddyship* phase.

The first phase is where most male relationships begin and remain. It's best described as kind of a symbiotic relationship where each party feeds off the other. The men come together because one has a skill, talent, or resource the other can use to further himself in business or socially. The other can contribute to the relationship merely by being a sycophant or admirer, or perhaps by contributing something like a good sense of humor.

Once there are no mutual benefits to be gained, the friendship dissolves.

The companionship phase forms when the relationship revolves around some sort of shared activity, whether it be golfing, chasing poon, or even lifting weights. According to Goldberg, this shared activity forms the safe structure or excuse for getting together. "The relationship is limited again because there are no real roots of mutual caring."

In other words, if one of the men punctures a lung and goes to the hospital, they won't see each other until the other is well enough to participate in their mutually shared activity again.

Once the commonly held interest disappears, so does the relationship.

Once in awhile, though, the companionship phase can evolve into a friendship. Goldberg says this can happen when competitiveness dies a bit and neither man feels jealousy or envy towards the other. In other words, you can be beaten in some game of skill by the other and not automatically feel a strong urge to defile his woman and afterwards clean off your dick with his favorite Walter Ray "Deadeye" Williams Jr. bowling shirt.

In general, though, this phase means you take pleasure in each other's company, conversation flows freely, and each knows they have a couch to sleep on when necessary.

The friendship can turn into a buddyship, Goldberg explains, only after some mutual crisis tests the friendship. If the crisis is transcended, vulnerabilities have been revealed and deep trust has presumably been formed. Hence the buddyship phase, which is actually more like a brother-brother phase.

As the saying goes, a friend won't rat you out if you kill somebody, but a buddy? A buddy will help you dispose of the body by feeding it through a mulcher.

Interestingly, this is the phase that's most threatening to some women, as buddies don't allow each other to be exploited and they won't hesitate to tell the other when he's being manipulated or self-destructively controlled by a female. Not only that, but a guy will tell things to his buddy that he won't tell his mate, and that makes it doubly threatening to a woman.

For hubby to have a buddy is almost worse than hubby having a girlfriend! The girlfriend can be righteously attacked as being a betrayal of trust, but alas, the buddyship can't, at least not openly. She may try to undermine the relationship with cutting jabs or dissing the friend, but she can't openly object to the closeness of the brother-brother relationship.

I believe these kinds of brother-brother relationships are extremely valuable. Having a close group of friends or buddies is an incredible creative resource, a "life workshop." I get to talk about the brutal realities of life with my friends and I get to engage in mutually enjoyable banter. And, if life is playing rough, I often get invaluable advice and support.

This kind of thing is worth cultivating so I've created an artificial construct to nurture such relationships, kind of a friendship *reef*, if you will, only without the Moray eels and sharks and stuff.

I call it "The Gathering" as an homage to *The Highlander* movie. Okay, not really, but "The Gathering" sounds a helluva' lot better than a "men's group." I got the idea from a friend's father who's been part of such a group for 35 years. Every couple of months, regardless of where in the country they live, they get together for a weekend just to be men.

So now I do it, too. Every month or two, I climb to the summit of Mount Olympus and let loose with a blast from the ceremonial ram's horn. If it's raining, I use e-mail.

Six of us meet together at a bar, restaurant, or one of our houses or apartments. While there hasn't been any set topical agenda yet, it's not out of the question. We might, in the future, meet to discuss a political issue, a philosophical issue, a problem one of us might be trying to deal with, or even babes. It's wide open.

How, you might ask, is this much different from just deciding to hang out with your buddies? Well, it is and it isn't. Just hanging out doesn't require any commitment; The Gathering does.

In other words, being part of The Gathering requires that you be there. You can't say you've got to mind the kids or you're watching the Fiesta Bowl or that you just don't feel like leaving the house. Granted, it's not exactly a blood oath or anything, but you need to make an effort to be there; you've made a pact. It's not a level of commitment on the same level as having to be at your wife's or girlfriend's birthday party, but it's the same level of commitment as having to be at your *grandma's* birthday party.

If you miss it, it's not the end of the world, but it's pretty bad.

Women don't need this kind of artificial construct. They show up. If their friend is having a freakin' Tupperware party, there's some silent part of them that compels them to go; they wouldn't think of blowing it off.

Men are different. They need the blood oath.

I think it's a great idea. I think it's important for men...rather, *friends*, to get together. In a time where masculinity is at best, ill defined, periodically being in the company of other good men is rejuvenating. It can help redefine yourself or help you reclaim your lost identity; it can fix you up when you need fixing.

-- 2007

How to Pick Up Girls

Men, regardless of what power they might have, regardless of what intelligence they might have, and in stark contrast to their normal acumen, use the same tactics to relate to women when they're 40 as they do when they're in 4th grade, or at best, as when they're 14.

It's sunny and oh-so warm and I'm drinking coffee at an outside café and it's only February, but this is California so the months and seasons don't really mean shit and the girls who walk by are already wearing short-shorts, and their silky legs and the little slices of tantalizing ass that flash a fleshy smile every time they take a step are already starting to take on the color of a Cadbury caramel candy.

I'm sitting there with my friends and we're feeling a potent little buzz from the caffeine, the solar energy, and the libidinous depth charges that every third or fourth girl who sashays by drops onto the submarines in our pants.

It is mighty fine.

But it's all we can do to stay focused on our conversation and for all we know, our level of discourse might be on the same level as a group of guys who've been passing a bong:

> *"You know that cranberry scone you're eating? What if...what if that scone were like another universe, and in that universe there were like, millions of planets and on those planets, there were like billions of guys eating billions of cranberry scones, each with universes inside them!?!? Whoa...I just blew my mind."*

But it at least *seems* like we're having a serious discussion, mostly about economics, believe it or not, which is a subject I'm not well-versed in, so I'm mostly asking questions.

I need to tell you a little about my coffee-shop friends before I go on. Coincidentally, nearly every one of them owns a business. Many of them are highly regarded in their professions and a lot of them make some serious coin, so much coin that they seem to actually be embarrassed about it; actually go to great lengths to hide it and seem at least a little blue collar.

Their education levels range from dropped-out-of-high-school to PhDs, but all are smart and all have been pretty successful in life.

So the conversation is fairly sophisticated and intellectual, but lest you think they're just garden variety stuffed shirts, the conversation is almost always peppered with at least a few jokes and plenty of inappropriate remarks about women.

But this is until Kelsey walks up. Kelsey is in her twenties, blond, and oh-so fine. She's dressed in business-slut wear, which in this case means a tight, black, belted shirt dress that's just long enough to be semi-appropriate for business, but short enough to make you want to bend her over the copier and collate and hole-punch her vagina a couple dozen times.

Likewise, the black stiletto heels are low enough to allow her to navigate the tight corners of an office, but high enough to make you want to throw her on her back, grab those pointy heels, pull her legs apart, and hold onto them as if they were the handlebars of a chopper as you pile drive her across the boardroom table, her peach-fuzz covered ass squeak-squeak-squeaking against the Lemon Pledge shiny finish a half-a-foot per passionate thrust.

So how do these powerful, accomplished men relate to Kelsey, who is obviously drawn to them because of their status, power, and money? Do they include her in the conversation, or do they pepper her with sophisticated flirtations?

Guess again. Alex, captain of industry, a PhD, literally one-degree of separation from anyone in Washington, stands up and proceeds to tell Kelsey a freakin' knock-knock joke:

> ALEX: "Hey Kelsey, knock-knock!"
>
> KELSEY: "Uhh, o-kayyy, 'Who's there?'"
>
> ALEX: Gestapo.
>
> KELSEY: Gesta – .
>
> ALEX: (Blitzkrieg fast, before Kelsey can get "Gestapo who?" out of her mouth, Alex grabs her by the lapels with his left arm, raises his right arm as if to strike her, and shouts the punch line) "THE GESTAPO VILL ASK ZE QUESTIONS, FEMALE SCHWEIN!!!"

Granted, it's a good knock-knock joke, quite possibly the best one of all time – if performed on the right person and in the right manner – but for chrissake, the poor girl flinches and nearly poops her Agent Provocateur panties.

She turns red, regains her composure enough to laugh politely, and then leaves, post-haste.

And therein lies the crux of my lament.

Men, regardless of what power they might have, regardless of what intelligence they might have, and in stark contrast to their normal acumen, use the same tactics to relate to women when they're 40 as they do when they're in 4th grade, or at best, as when they're 14.

You know, the Anglo birth rate in this country is 1.6, which is about 25 to 30% below the number needed for replacement (that number being 2.1). It's no surprise Anglos have stopped breeding since half of us couldn't get to first base without purchasing a "girlfriend experience" from a hooker, let alone find a woman with which to procreate.

Before moving on, I have to offer full disclosure: I've never been particularly gifted at walking up to women and laying a rap on them. There were/are plenty of reasons: I was often overly focused on the goal (pussy), overly conscious of the absurdity of the whole ritual, unable to discuss mundane topics without a glaze forming over my eyes, or lastly, being unable to curb what I call my Trekkie-Tourette's Syndrome.

Trekkie-Tourette's doesn't involve shouting "SPOCK'S A COCKSUCKER!" in the middle of discussing favorite lunch spots. Rather, it's a propensity to start slightly weird, slightly geeky, and usually inappropriate discussions. Think Sheldon from *The Big Bang Theory* meets Chris Rock:

> *"Hey Britney, you know that blue chick in Avatar? Did you ever wonder why she had tits? I mean, it's not like the Na'vi were even mammals! It wasn't expressly discussed, but I suspect they were fuckin' oviparous!"*

You might think that some chicks like that sort of stuff, but they don't. Noooo they don't. Sigh.

Anyhow, let me serve as a cautionary tale to all who might otherwise follow in my footsteps. But despite my lack of high skill in this area, I can at least say that I don't regress to the level of an adolescent when it comes to talking to women.

I'm not sure why this happens to men. Maybe it's because they're used to having discussions where demonstrating power and business acumen is the primary goal and as such they haven't had practice trying to be friendly, vulnerable, sensitive, attentive, and playful at the same time.

So they resort to telling jokes, usually bad ones. Or they resort to bragging, busting the chops of other males that may also be vying for attention, or laughing overly hard at anything the female says.

I'm surprised some of them don't paint a clown face on their dick, drop their pants, and do a blue Henny Youngman imitation:

Take my penis–please!

Or better yet, glue some dog hair on their cock so that it looks like that hunky-hunky werewolf from the *Twilight* sequel.

Trouble is, women are keenly aware of this social ineptitude, causing them to mentally roll their eyes, go home agitated and have sex with a cucumber, that, if not necessarily more entertaining than the schlubs she just encountered, can at least be added to a salad after doing the deed.

Oh, there are plenty of dating gurus out there who suggest all kinds of methods. Most famous, perhaps, is Mystery, who devised all kinds of jargon and tactics for picking up women.

Beautiful women, according to Mystery, rarely travel alone, so you have to target a "set," which is a group of two or more people that the "target" woman travels with. In order to acquire your goal, you have to befriend the entire set.

There's also "the 3-second rule," which states that you have to approach a girl you're interested in within 3 seconds, lest you overanalyze the situation and cause your balls to retreat, frightened turtle like, into the abdominal cavity from where they can't be coaxed from without affixing a bit of worn panty to a fish hook and dangling it in front of them provocatively.

Mystery also advocates using "negs," which are backhanded compliments of a sort that telegraph a supposed lack of interest (supposedly, girls get off on guys who aren't interested in them—how fucked up is that?) and cause a woman to drop her "bitch shield."

It appears, though, that a delicate touch is necessary. For instance, saying something like, "My God, were you the only lesbian to survive the fire?" to your "target" would probably be considered, in Texas Hold Em' terms, as "coming over the top."

Maybe something more subtle would work, maybe something like, "I can tell by your camel toe that your vagina is a little crooked, but then again so was the Mona Lisa's smile, and it was thought that her crooked smile suggested that she was perhaps a bit enigmatic and quirky, and by extrapolation, I can venture a guess that maybe your hoo-hah is a bit enigmatic and quirky."

Okay, that probably wouldn't work either. Like I said, I have Trekkie-Tourette's Syndrome.

It's more likely Mystery had something a little more subtle in mind, like saying, "An attractive girl like you should take better care of her nails."

Supposedly, that would cause her to be confused and wonder why a guy who presumably wanted to bed her would insult her, however mildly.

Dating guru Dave Wygart's approach is a bit more conventional. He lists common sense tips like smiling, positive body language, moving slowly (as not to alarm her), not fidgeting, maintaining eye contact, and perhaps most importantly, observing something in the environment and commenting on it (in lieu of some snappy but ultimately lame line).

While most of his list seems to be a no-brainer, I've observed that the last point deserves some serious thought. Like I said, I was never particularly gifted in approaching beautiful women, but I've observed plenty of guys who were and the one thing—maybe the only thing—they shared in common was that they appeared to have mastered the art of trivial conversation.

It may sound like I'm belittling the concept, but I'm not. Being able to lay an innocent (in tone, at least), semi-engaging, "trivial" rap on women is the Rosetta Stone. All that other stuff doesn't matter. In fact, remembering all that other stuff probably creates anxiety in males, thus causing them to go home alone night after night to make bittersweet video love to Tifa Lockheart from *Final Fantasy VII*.

Being able to converse easily leads to confidence, no matter how delicious your "target" is. Confidence allows you to come across as a sexual being and not an accountant. Confidence creates chemistry, which increases the chances of you combining with her chemistry and acquiring the soft, moist alloy that's the real-life *unobtainium*.

Hell, I recommend practicing trivial conversation, practicing it on the family dog, old people, geeks, corpses, whoever, and then progressing upwards, sexually speaking, to female types, first practicing on women who don't make you sweat like you're a member of the prison work crew in *Cool Hand Luke*.

Once you master that, you'll be ready to kill the lion, fly solo, go on your Walkabout, whatever analogy you prefer to describe your rite of babe passage where you approach a beautiful woman and communicate with her.

Listen, it's the only reason you see all those smarmy, greasy, often goofy-looking guys with good-looking women... well, except that they might have money. Of course, you can see that money hasn't really helped my friends who, because of their inability to carry on trivial conversations, are still making little league plays for major league women.

-- 2010

All Women are Lesbians

So what really does turn women on? From the studies, we'd assume just about everything from aardvarks to toaster ovens get their body revving, even though their minds might not know it.

In 1997, marginally hot moppet-haired actress Anne Heche freaked out the heterosexual world by starting a widely publicized love affair with the equally moppet haired lesbian comedian Ellen DeGeneres.

Bear in mind that Heche hadn't—prior to that point—been involved in any muff-diving relationships.

The affair lasted two years, after which Heche fluffed up her probably likewise moppet-haired vagina and went on to marry a dude.

In a similar situation, non-famous, ordinary person Julie Cypher left a hetero marriage to hook up with Chuckie look-alike Melissa Etheridge. Twelve years later, they separated and Cypher returned to heterosexual relationships.

What in the wide, wide world of pussy is going on? Can't these women, and untold thousands like them, choose between nuts and no-nuts?

Psychologist Lisa Diamond, prominent sexologist at the University of Utah and author of *Sexual Fluidity: Understanding Women's Love and Desire*, figures that in the case of the aforementioned celebrity hook-ups and others like them, female desire is largely dictated by intimacy or emotional connections.

She believes their desire is malleable, so much so that sharing a laugh over lattes or a rerun of *Friends*—whether it be with a compatible male or the comely dental hygienist she met in aerobics class—will do much more to determine lust and sexual proclivity than any sexual orientation.

Others believe it's cultural, as if watching girl-on-girl scenes on *Gossip Girl* or *90210* compels women to imitate the TV images and get naked with their sorority sisters. Most, however, probably believe as psychologist Diamond does, that women get sexual after shared experiences that foster emotional closeness.

I tend to think it has more to do with women being largely blank slates, sexually speaking. While the majority of men have a sexual orientation, women appear to be far less rigid when it comes to penis or vagina.

If you doubt that, consider the experiments conducted by Meredith Chivers, a psychology professor at Queen's University in Kingston,

Ontario. Chivers put together a little porn movie featuring men making love to women, women making love to men, men making love to men, and women making love to women. The film also featured men and women masturbating, a nude well-toned woman doing calisthenics, and a chiseled dude walking naked along the beach. Oh yeah, it also featured clips of bonobo chimps fucking.

While the film might end up getting an award at the next AVN awards, her real intent was to show it to men and women and gauge their arousal, both objectively and subjectively.

Test subjects were individually plopped down into a brown leather La-Z-Boy chair and fitted with a device known as a plethysmograph. The mechanics of the device are sex specific. Men are fitted with a wired little cuff that slips over the penis and detects swelling, while women insert a little plastic probe that sits in the vagina and measures genital blood flow and subsequent moisture by bouncing light off the walls of the vagina. It also causes any Jimi Hendrix posters affixed to those vaginal walls to light up really weird and freaky.

Subjects were also provided a keypad so they could subjectively rate their arousal.

As you might predict, the men responded in what Chivers called "category specific" ways. Straight men bonered up while watching heterosexual sex or lesbian sex. They liked watching women masturbate, and seeing the naked exercising woman do splits and plant fat juicy labial kisses on the yoga mat was downright inspiring.

Straight men obviously didn't care much for the naked guy walking on the beach.

Gay men were aroused in the exact opposite pattern. Neither straights or gays cared much for the bonobo sex scenes, but that might have been because of the poor lighting or the unforgiveable absence of any money shots.

The subjective keypad ratings showed their mind and genitals to be pretty much in agreement.

But the women? Ha! They pretty much lathered up at *all* of it. No matter what their self-proclaimed sexual orientation, they showed strong and swift genital arousal at men on men, women on women, and women with men. They also like watching the naked babe work out.

Their blood flow even rose significantly to the ape sex, although to a lesser degree than all the other situations, except for the scenes of the buff dude walking naked on the beach.

Oddly enough, though, their minds and genitals hardly seemed like they belonged to the same person, particularly in the straight women. Based on their keypad responses, heterosexual women reported less excitement watching lesbian scenes than their vaginas indicated. They reported much less excitement watching gay men than their vaginas let on, and they reported a great deal more excitement than their vaginas showed while watching heterosexual sex.

The lesbians tested slightly differently in that subjective and objective ratings converged while watching lesbian sex. However, while watching heterosexual sex, they reported less excitement than their private parts let on.

Both groups claimed to get no sexual buzz from the ape sex, but as mentioned, they lathered up just a little bit, regardless.

Freaks.

While the results of any one study can be met with skepticism, Chivers has compared 130 such studies and found a similar female mind/vagina disconnect.

So what really does turn women on? From the studies, we'd assume just about everything from aardvarks to toaster ovens get their body revving, even though their minds might not know it.

Another sexologist, Marta Meana of the University of Nevada in Las Vegas, seems to agree with Chivers' findings in asserting that women's arousal has little to do with intimacy. "Really," she explains, "womens' desire is not relational, it's narcissistic; it's dominated by the yearnings of self-love." In other words, women want to be the object of erotic admiration and sexual need.

She admits that women do indeed place a high value on relationships, but it's wrong to think they're the primary source of a woman's desire.

In fact, she suggests that what women really want is to be thrown up against a wall but not truly endangered. "Women want a caveman *and* caring."

This assumption seems to give credence to something Chivers theorized -- that women are most turned on, subjectively at least, by the notion of sex with strangers.

But what of the female sexual malleability thing? Why is it that women seem more open to same-sex dalliances? Richard Lippa, psych professor at California State University at Fullerton, thinks it might be hormonal.

He's tested thousands of men and women over the years and he found that in men, those with the highest sex drives, straight or gay, tended to have a more polarized attraction than most males. That means that if you've got high Testosterone and you're straight, you're even more keenly zeroed in on hootchie mamas. Similarly, if you're gay and you've got high Testosterone, there's little chance that any woman is going to convert you to her team.

But oddly enough, the *opposite* was true with straight women. The higher their sex drive, the greater their attraction to *both* sexes.

I'm puzzled. Puzzled but turned on. As is consistent with Chivers' study involving the bonobo movie, my response to watching or even contemplating girl-on-girl sex is significant, at least as measured by the crude penile plethysmograph represented by the restless bulge in my Hanes.

I'm pretty sure all the researchers are puzzled, too. The research is all over the vaginal board. Hell, there's even a theory that vaginal lubrication is a defense mechanism designed to prevent injury to the vagina. When there's even a hint of sexuality in the air, so the theory goes, women lube up to prevent injury from possible rape.

Gawd, I hope there's more to it than that. That ain't half as sexy as the notion that women are far more sexual and far more open to *paraphilia*—erotic desires that fall outside the norm—than I'd (we'd?) hoped.

Of course, the vast majority of women will probably never explore these alleged erotic desires, largely because—assuming we're not drawing incorrect assumptions about Chivers' bonobo sex film study— they don't even know they have them. That mind/vagina disconnect seems to be huge. Their eyes say no but their vagina says, "Yes! Yes! Yes!"

I suppose the chivalrous thing to do would be to help them explore these desires, to slowly introduce them to all their inherent paraphilic desires the same way one would carefully introduce a piece of chicken skin on a hook to a tasty bluegill.

I am soooo going to Hell.

Note: This column was inspired by an article titled, "What do Women Want?" that was written by Daniel Bergner and appeared in the New York Times Magazine on January 25th, 2009.

-- 2009

The Bikini Contest

You remember that scene in Alien Resurrection when the hybrid Ripley comes across an earlier clone that was ridden with genotypic and phenotypic abnormalities? The misshapen thing begs hybrid Ripley to blowtorch her: Kill...me.... Well that's my soul, and if you've got a blowtorch handy, do me a favor and make me a human s'more, okay?

et me see if I can convey my frustration. Here goes....

Last week this guy I know had a bikini contest/party at his house. I don't know him very well, but nevertheless he invited me. He's supposed to be a major horn dog, so I fully expected there'd be some high-quality mammals prancing and jiggling around his swimming pool.

What's more, he was offering cash prizes to the best bikini and the best body, so you pretty much knew that the scene would be a veritable *Cleavagefield* with giant run-amok breasts that would smash the Brooklyn Bridge, forcing us all to return to Manhattan where we'd get caught in the crossfire between the military and the angry breasts.

And if the girls weren't carnal incentive enough, the host would be grilling up some of the yellowtail he'd caught the previous day. That would be a perfect opening for the old Junior Soprano joke:

> *A blind guys walks by a fish store. He shouts out, "Hel-lo girls!*

Anyhow, most guys would find this scenario at least somewhat appealing, right? Sure, I know it's juvenile and all that, but when two breasts come a' walking, the penis does the talking. Then why the hell couldn't I find a single friend who wanted to go with me?

Kurt couldn't go because he was going to a...a Tracy Chapman concert!

You heard me, a Tracy Chapman concert! Hell, you lose 50 ticks off your Testosterone blood levels for just knowing who she is!

Eddie couldn't go because it was his week to spend with his bratty kid. Jay couldn't go because he was "tired." Rich, hell, Rich blanches when we even *drive* by a topless bar, so strong are his feelings about the "objectification" of women. Brian couldn't even *ask* to go because his wife would padlock his dick and balls in a small wooden keepsake box where they'd eventually get grown over by the green, green heather of his native Ireland and then, when he dies, they'd be given to leprechauns who'd hang them on the rearview mirror of their tiny, fuel efficient Fiats.

I told a Scottish friend about it a few days later and he looked like someone had just peed in his Guinness. "TC, your friends are all homos!" he exclaimed, his Scottish accent somehow making his somewhat crass assertion sound practically Shakespearean in its poignancy.

And this isn't a one-time thing, either. I can't get my friends to do *anything*.

Strip clubs? Forget it! ("What if someone sees us going in?")

The Adult Video News awards in Vegas? They couldn't care less if Jesse Jane won the award for the best double-penetration sex scene. I guess the performing arts don't matter to my friends.

Philistines! That's what they are! Philistines!

Neither could I get anyone to go with me to the World Series of Poker last month.

And lest you think all my interests are sin-driven, I can't even get them to go to a baseball game! They're all European soccer fiends, or they don't care about sports. Tossing a football? Forget it! (You ever see someone from Europe throw something? It's an ugly sight.)

Okay, how about going to nerd-driven activities, like the Comic-Con? Nope. "Popular culture doesn't interest me," they sniff.

So what happens is that I generally go to all these places and events by myself. The guy sitting by himself in the back row of the movie theater at the 11 PM showing of *District 9*? It's probably me, because my friends are over in the next theater watching *The Time Traveler's Wife*, no doubt lactating a watery milk onto their popcorn.

You remember that scene in *Alien Resurrection* when the hybrid Ripley comes across an earlier clone that was ridden with genotypic and phenotypic abnormalities? The misshapen thing begs hybrid Ripley to blowtorch her:

Kill...me....

Well that's my soul, and if you've got a blowtorch handy, do me a favor and make me a human s'more, okay?

It wasn't until I had to retrieve a Nalgene bottle from my dishwasher that the what-should-have-been-obvious answer hit me.

The dishwasher was in mid-cycle, so the temperature of the interior must have been enough to cook cauliflower, but I was going to the gym and I needed the damn thing. I took a breath and sprang the door open. The heat was almost unbearable, and I couldn't see through the steam so I had to feel around, getting scalded first by my special ceramic Brownie the Clownie cereal bowl and then by my special souvenir grizzly bear coffee mug from Alaska before finding the Nalgene bottle.

As I grasped the thing, my face engulfed in steam, I couldn't help but think of the famous scene in *Star Trek II, The Wrath of Khan*, where Spock enters the radiation-filled engine room and fixes the warp drive.

Unfortunately, Spock's been steamed, er, irradiated, to the point of near death:

Kirk: Spock!

Spock: The ship... out of danger?

Kirk: Yes.

Spock: Don't grieve, Admiral. It is logical. The needs of the many outweigh...

Kirk: ...the needs of the few...

Spock: ...Or the one. I never took the Kobayashi Maru test until now. What do you think of my solution?

Kirk: Spock!

Spock: I have been -- and always will be -- your friend.... [Holds up his hand in the Vulcan salute] Live. Long. And prosper.

That's it!

I have been and always shall be your friend.

I need the Spock to my Kirk, the Sam to my Frodo, the Watson to my Holmes, the Butch to my Sundance, the Hooch to my Turner, the Goose to my Maverick, hell, the Thelma to my Louise even, but if he needs to drive over a cliff, I'd prefer he pulled over to discuss it first.

In other words, I need to get a new friend, or new *friends*!

But as you probably know, that ain't easy. Hell, it's easier finding a wife, what with all the matchmaking sites like eHarmony, and it's certainly easier finding a girl friend, or at least a "girlfriend experience," through Craig's List.

But finding a male friend? One with interests similar to you? Not so easy.

There aren't, after all, any classified sections for male friendships, at least not any that don't advertise for a specific type of friend, the kind that might watch *Top Gun* with you but only for the volleyball scene where that hunky Maverick, Ice Man, Goose, and the big dopey guy are all bare-torsoed and oiled up.

Then it occurred to me, why not advertise for new friends through this column? The ad is free and I can go way over 50 words!

How should I begin?

How about:

> *WANTED: WM seeks new friend or friends for moonlit walks on the beach and sunset dinners. Must have balls.*

Uhh, that won't work.

Let me try again:

> *WANTED: WM seeks new friend or friends to engage in occasional debauchery with women folk.*

Me? I'd be a good choice for your lifeline if you go on "Who Wants to be a Millionaire?" I'd also be really good at helping you buy gifts for your wife or girlfriend, especially really cool underwear, and I can tell when meat is done cooking just by looking at it.

I like lifting, reading both fiction and non-fiction, am well-versed on scientific subjects ranging from etymology to entomology to endocrinology, enjoy spicy food, like poker, baseball, bully dogs, whisky, cigars, and women in various states of undress.

You? You're open-minded and definitely not puritanical. You read as much as you lift. You're such a good friend that you send me naked pictures of your girlfriend or wife. You don't know a damn thing about wine, and you won't bellyache about getting cancer if I offer you the occasional cigar.

Unlike most guys, you're able to talk about something other than cars, sports, and women, although we'd certainly spend a good amount of time talking about that last item. You don't condemn my Dakota Fanning fetish, and if I tell you that I just saw Osama Bin Laden having a Pepperoni P'Zone at the Pizza Hut, or that my clothes dryer is a porthole to another dimension where wayward socks go, you'd at least give me the benefit of the doubt until I'm proven wrong.

You've never read a Harry Potter book, don't wear Crocs, and never say things like "beer me." You laugh at my jokes when there's a female within earshot, and you definitely don't interrupt my comic bits until I've played them out.

You think the current *Saturday Night Live*, Top 40 music, and golf all blow, and you think Dane Cook, Twitter, *Family Guy*, Eli Manning, and Gisele Bündchen are all over-rated. You like Pitbull (except for that rotten *Hotel Room Service* song), writer Tom Wolfe, late-night host Craig Ferguson, Jon Stewart, Stephen Colbert, Bill Maher, *Breaking Bad*, *Mad Men*, and *True Blood*, and if you don't, you might as well pack up and go join Al Qaeda, buddy.

I don't expect a kidney or anything, and I don't need you to pick me up from the airport or help me move, but if I'm in jail you're gonna' have to bail me out. Sorry, but that's just the way it is.

You don't hit on my woman until I'm dead or until I've been in a coma for, say, 6 months or so. Oh, and if you can introduce me to Adriana Lima, or someone who looks a lot like her, it trumps all the above requirements.

And lastly, if I ask you to go to a bikini contest, you have to drop what you're doing and go.

-- 2009

20 Layers of Butt Makeup

Police were chasing Ready though Times Square a couple of weeks ago when the wanna-be gangster fired two shots, holding the gun sideways, "like a character out of a rap video." Unfortunately for Ready, the sideways grip caused the gun to jam, enabling the police to shoot and kill him.

I't's happened again.

About a month ago, I was knee deep in possible topics for my column, but I couldn't make up my mind which one I should develop into an article, so I served up short versions of all of them, making sort of an article dim sum, filled with literary rice noodles, prawns, dumplings, and egg tart.

Some people thought it was just the right meal, others were hungry again in a half-hour, and still others kept hitting on the waitress and were thrown out into the alley by the big Chinese guy from chopsocky movies named Chong Li.

Regardless, I'm faced with the same problem again of having too many topics while not being able to decide which, if any, I should develop into a full-length cinemascope article. And my solution is much the same this time, but instead of dim sum, and in honor of the holiday season, I'm serving up an article *turducken*.

So for those of you who don't like de-boned literary turkey, you can nibble on the de-boned duck or the de-boned chicken.

Hasta La Vista, Baby

Automated weapons systems are as entrenched in modern warfare as M-16s, tanks, and MREs.

Every day, thousands of drones deliver their deadly payload to unsuspecting insurgents in Iraq, Afghanistan, and Pakistan, and ground robots are regular companions to foot soldiers on their sojourns into hostile territory.

Sometimes things go wrong, though. A few months ago, an automatic antiaircraft gun malfunctioned during a South African training exercise and killed human soldiers.

Military researchers are having high-level discussions on how these robots and automated weapons are changing the face of warfare, with a lot of discussion centering on safety.

In an effort to coordinate all these drones and other automated assets, and presumably make them safer, Great Britain has established a network of satellites.

The name of his system? *Skynet.* You know, like the *Terminator* movies?

Oh-oh.

You Sure You're not Describing the Jonas Brothers?

A star was recently born at a goat exhibition in India. The goat has six legs, four testicles, and three penises.

"Discharge of urine," explained the owner, "is witnessed after frequent intervals from different penises.

"But still, it is a special goat that attracts attention."

Cockblocked by Geico

If you took out all the commercials, time outs, penalty calls, shoving matches, and referee reviews, a football game would be, according to the Playboy Data Sheet, about 12 minutes long.

Okay, we can accept that.

We can begrudgingly accept that brushing lint off the quarterback or receiver constitutes roughing the passer or defensive interference. We can accept (barely) the stupid rule that displaying any post-touchdown emotion beyond the detached demeanor of Zeno of Citium, the founder of stoicism, will draw a penalty.

We can even understand the ever-so-brief and infrequent shots of the cheerleaders shaking their nonnies. Heavens, we only want the *suggestion* that football's appeal is sex and violence; holding the camera on them for more than a tit-nanosecond would *confirm* it.

But there's one thing we won't stand for, and that's the maddening banner ads that eclipse the views of the cheerleaders when they break to (or come back from) the "real" commercials.

You know the ones I'm talking about, the camera will pan across the undulating midsection of some supernatural mammal in hot pants and devastating halter top when a virtually opaque banner ad for freakin' Geico or Budweiser cockblocks our view of her body.

If I didn't know any better, I'd think the NFL was doing everything it could to kill itself.

VIDEO KILLED THE RADIO STAR

Tony Soprano didn't go for that shit but aspiring rapper Raymond "Ready" Martinez sure did.

I'm referring to the sideways gun pose apparently favored by nouveau gangsters everywhere. Tony thought it was bullshit, but Ready Martinez must have thought it was cool. Too bad it seems to have led to his death.

Police were chasing Ready though Times Square a couple of weeks ago when the wanna-be gangster fired two shots, holding the gun sideways, "like a character out of a rap video." Unfortunately for Ready, the sideways grip caused the gun to jam, enabling the police to shoot and kill him.

Most gun experts and fans of gangster movies credit the sideways gun grip to the 1993 Hughes brothers' film, *Menace II Society.*

Brian Palmer, however, journalist with *Slate*, traces the origin of the sideways grip back to the 1961 Marlon Brando film, *One-Eyed Jacks.* Palmer also points to Eli Wallach using the grip in 1966's *The Good, the Bad, and the Ugly.*

The reason? It allowed the camera to get a better shot of both the gun and the actor's face.

So if someone holding his gun sideways ever threatens you and your friends, calmly explain to the assailant that his stylish gun-grip might cause his gun to jam, which could lead to a very awkward, embarrassing moment, possibly punctuated by snorting laughter where milk comes out of everyone's nose.

The Chicken Ranch, Now With Strutting Cocks

Bobbi Davis, owner of the Shady Lady Ranch, a small brothel near Beatty, Nevada, is very happy.

Davis wanted to add male prostitutes to her stable of sex workers, but until last week a language quirk in the Nevada health code prohibited men from selling their services. The code specifically stated that prostitutes must undergo cervical testing for sexually transmitted diseases, which obviously ruled out men.

Urethral exams have now been added to the code, paving the way for male sex workers.

I'm strongly considering sending in an application, but I haven't decided on a male prostitute name yet. I'm leaning towards either "Beef Flanks" or "Smoky Paprika" (I got the names from one of my mom's recipes for stroganoff).

Main Entry: irony (Noun) ahy-ruh-nee

"I am not a fan of books. I would never want a book's autograph. I am a proud non-reader of books. I like to get information from doing stuff like actually talking to people and living real life."

—Kanye West, promoting his book, "Thank You and You're Welcome"

20 Layers of Butt Makeup

Sammy Sosa corked his bat.

My 7th grade crush, Tammy Newcomb, padded her bra.

My parents lied about Santa.

Given that it's Christmas time, I suppose it's only natural some new Grinch come along and destroy one of my cherished beliefs. This time the Grinch was a Victoria's Secret angel by the name of Selita Ebanks who told the *New York Daily News* that the reason the models look so good on the runway is, *choke*, an *illusion*.

"People don't realize there are about 20 layers of makeup on my butt alone."

Ebanks elaborated further, explaining that the body makeup takes about an hour to apply, plus hair and makeup, which takes another three to five hours. An average of five people worked on each of the 38 models used in the show.

How do I feel about it?

The stars are not wanted now: put out every one;

Pack up the moon and dismantle the sun;

Pour away the ocean and sweep up the wood.

For nothing now can ever come to any good.

A SWATCH OF SNATCH

Most people assume that sexual permissiveness is a modern trait, the sordid affectation of a society on the decline, but even a casual examination of history reveals that sexual permissiveness appears to be cyclical and much more widespread than generally supposed.

Case in point, few people realize that pre-Victorian England, from about 1714 to 1837, was a hotbed of debauchery.

Sex clubs abounded, filled with "posture molls" who posed nude on tables and swung their stuff like current day lap dancers. Pairs or groups could retire at any time to private rooms, and fashionable ladies could make use of "rent boys."

Popular too, was the habit of cutting of swatches of your lovers' pubic hair as tokens of affection. Lovers would exchange them and players of the time would affix the pubic swatches to their hats and display them as symbols of their conquests.

Too bad today's shaved pubes don't allow you to do that. I mean, at best, you might be able to scrape off a little stubble and save it in a Mason jar that you carry around, but it's not nearly as rakish as a hat with wild plumes of pubes.

Jinx! You Owe Me a Couple Thousand Cokes!

Laura Buxton, 10 years old, was bored. There just wasn't much to do in her hometown of Stoke-on-Trent in Staffordshire, England that day. She then got the idea of blowing up a red balloon. She wrote, "Please return to Laura Buxton" on one side of the balloon and she wrote her address on the other.

She released the balloon into the moderate winds, but instead of floating a few feet and impaling itself on a tree branch, the balloon soared high above her until it was just a speck. Then, for some unknown meteorological reason, it started to travel against the prevailing winds.

A few weeks later, a hundred and forty miles later, a man in the town of Milton Lilbourne found the balloon stuck in a hedge that separated his house from his neighbor's.

He noticed the name on the balloon and then took it to his neighbor's house to show it to the 10-year-old girl who lived there.... a girl whose name was also Laura Buxton.

The second Laura Buxton wrote the first one to tell her she'd found the balloon, and because of the extraordinary coincidence, they decided to meet.

Laura of Milton Lilbourne found that Laura Buxton of Stoke-on-Trent had the same color of hair styled in the same way. They were both the same height, which was unusual because they were tall for their age. Coincidently, both were wearing the same *outfit* to the meeting, a pink sweater over jeans!

Both, coincidentally, had brought along their pet guinea pigs, and they too were nearly identical in color and markings! Both confessed to having two other pets, a black Labrador retriever and a grey rabbit!

Because of the freakish similarities, the girls formed a strong bond and remain friends to this day, about 8 years after the balloon was launched and found.

You might be expecting a punch line, but there isn't one. They weren't twins separated at birth; they weren't related in anyway. If you're looking for meaning, it might just be that in a world this big, with this many people, there are bound to be amazing coincidences. It's the old story about a million monkeys sitting at a million typewriters who, eventually, just by chance, recreate the works of Shakespeare.

SURE SHE'S BLIND, BUT MY GOD, THE BITCH CAN GIVE HEAD!

Chinese scientist Libiao Zhang of the Guangdong Entomological Institute found that short-nosed fruit bats spend more time having vaginal intercourse if during copulation the female bat licks the penis of the male bat.

"We did not expect fellatio in fruit bats," said Zhang.

The study was apparently funded by Bruce Wayne, an American, but no one has been able to ascertain his motive.

HEY JOHN CONNOR, GOT ANOTHER JOB FOR YOU.

Opponents of the Hadron Collider in Bern, Switzerland, fear that the machine might inadvertently create a mini black hole that could expand and swallow the Earth.

The machine was built to recreate the immediate after effects of the Big Bang and observe the Higgs bosun, thus giving physicists an inkling to the origins of the universe.

While the collider was set to begin operation over a year ago, it's been beset by inexplicable part failures. Scientists have repaired most of them and succeeded in firing up the mother last week, even though it's operating at a relatively modest 450 billion electron volts instead of the 7 trillion electron volts its capable of.

Why has the project been beset with problems? Two of the prominent physicists argue that it's being sabotaged by the *future*.

The physicists, Holger Bech Nielsen of the Niels Bohr Institute in Copenhagen and Masao Ninomiya of the Yukawa Institute for Theoretical Physics in Kyoto, worry that observing the Higgs bosun might result in calamity, and that agents of the future keep traveling back in time to stop it.

Says Nielsen:

> *"While it is a paradox to go back in time and kill your grandfather, physicists agree there is no paradox if you go back in time and save him from being hit by a bus. In the case of the Higgs and the collider, it is as if something is going back in time to keep the universe from being hit by a bus. Although just why the Higgs would be a catastrophe is not clear. If we knew, presumably, we wouldn't be trying to make one."*

Now if only those time travelers would destroy Skynet too, before the catastrophic world-ending shit really hits the fan.

-- 2009

The Horribleness of High Testosterone

Likewise, cows injected with Testosterone become dominant in the herd, coercing other cows to go into town and tip some people.

If you go canoeing, don't ever, *ever*, paddle ashore to take a whiz.

That's the main lesson you take with you after having watched *Deliverance*.

It's a relatively old movie, but it's been on my mind since I heard the deluxe anniversary edition has just been released on DVD and Blu-ray.

If you've never seen it, it's one of those movies where a particular scene stays in your mind long after you've forgotten the rest of the movie.

Think of the not-cookie-but-cock scene in *The Crying Game*, or Linda Blair puking up green pea soup in *The Exorcist*.

I'll give you an abbreviated Leonard Maltin type synopsis of the famous "love scene" in Deliverance:

Four Atlanta businessmen take a canoe trip down a powerful river that's weeks away from being turned into a hydroelectric dam. Bobby needs to pee so he and Ed paddle to the shore where they're beset upon by gap-toothed, shotgun-wielding mountain men who've got an itch for sodomy. (Hey, it's lonely up in them-there hills and the feral hogs are just too temperamental.)

Ed is belted to the trunk of a tree by his neck. Bobby is forced to take off his pants and tightie whities and bend over a log, his pale white toadstool of an ass looking obscenely out of place and vulnerable in the woods.

As the horrified Ed watches, Bobby is savagely raped, his assailant slapping and grabbing at his ass while urging Bobby to "squeal like a pig." Furthermore, it doesn't appear that the butt-lover had the social grace to use any Vaseline, pig grease, or whatever they use up in the hollers.

The other mountain man then turns his attention to ashen-faced Ed. "You've got a purty mouth," he says, and his intent is sickeningly clear. As the mountain man starts to unbuckle his pants, we see an unfocused image standing near the river that suddenly comes into focus.

It's Lewis. Lewis is the Testosterone man of the group. He's constantly training his body and mind to combat adversity. Lewis has abs. Lewis has biceps. Lewis doesn't believe in insurance because "there's no risk." Lewis also hunts with a bow and arrow, and Ed can see that Lewis has drawn back his bow and is about to let loose with razor-tipped justice.

We hear a *thwip* and a *thwunk* and suddenly the Jeremiah-pulling-out-his-Johnson is wearing an arrow through his heart. A little blood trickles from his mouth and he drops dead. The other sodomite hightails it into the woods.

Rather than paddle the body out of the woods and inform the authorities, Lewis convinces the group to bury the body there. After all, the land's going to be covered by deep water in just a few weeks. Besides, who wants the mess? Bobby sure doesn't want the Rotary Club back in Atlanta to know he's been butt-fucked by a hillbilly. It just ain't something to puff out your chest about.

And that's just where the shit *begins*.

So I never paddle ashore to go pee. I just unzip and fling it over. Every once in awhile I tie a piece of corn on it and catch a bluegill, but that's usually just to impress a girl.

But let's get back to Lewis. Lewis thrived in that environment, but back in the city with normal folk? In a lot of ways it pretty much sucked to be Lewis.

I often write about the good aspects of high Testosterone, but it definitely has a bad side.

I won't compare myself with Lewis, but I know I'm high-Testosterone; my lab tests confirm it and so does some of my behavior.

The high-T explains why I'm in love with so many things physical, but for some reason I'm also equally in love with most things mental. Unfortunately, it's a losing battle. My mind almost always loses out to my balls. My balls have often lead me to make bad decisions, whether they be in love, business, friendships, or even something so simple as what pay-per-movie to buy.

When given the choice of some highly acclaimed drama or the most recent blockbuster with its car chases, gratuitous sex and violence, and sophomoric plot and dialogue, I'll almost always go with the blockbuster; I can't seem to help myself.

Never mind that I'm hugely disappointed almost every time, I never learn. The other night, though, I reluctantly queued up the low-budget feel-good drama, *Akeelah and the Bee*, because there was nothing else on and I was too tired to read. It's about a little girl from Crenshaw High in Los Angeles who overcomes her environment to win the National Spelling Bee.

It was the best thing I've seen in a year. And with nary a car chase, gun battle, or fistfight. Who'd a thunk?

But no matter, the next time the choice arises between action and nuance, my balls will pick the almost-always mediocre action movie.

TC's halftime score: Balls 35, Logical Thinking 7

Not only is that lopsided score daunting, but the balls get to *receive* at the start of the second half and the mind's defense is made up of little guys in short-sleeve button down shirts who wear smudgy glasses and are reluctant to look up from their Blackberries.

Maybe that battle makes me a little different from high-Testosterone men. Maybe most other high-T guys aren't as conflicted. Maybe they are.

Most high-T'ers probably don't agonize about such things because typically, high-T men have blunted feelings — well, the feelings that *aren't* associated with anger are usually blunted. For example, when Tom Cruise did his gopher on the sofa bit with Oprah, most of felt as if we'd just watched Bobby get nailed in the ass again. It was just too much emotion for us to handle. We were disgusted.

That's also why high-T men are often oblivious to problems in their marriage — their feelings are wrapped up in canvas and rusty baling wire. They're also more likely to stray. They're extremely vulnerable to anything in a tube top and high heels, regardless of her personality, disposition, or status. What's more, they think having access to scores of females is their birthright.

Likewise, high-T men often make lousy employees. They don't like subservient roles. They don't like having to take orders. They don't like sharing power. In fact, often the only place where they accept chain of command is in the military, where the rules (and the consequences for breaking them) are clear-cut.

Here's what I presume to be a typical day for a frustrated high-Testosterone guy:

- Wake up with an enormous boner that's turned the sheets into an ersatz pup tent.

- Check under pup tent to see that it hasn't become a temporary shelter for Sherpas.

- Take a piss and try to blast away anything with the temerity to be floating in the toilet bowl, whether it's tissue paper, a used condom, a cigarette butt, or a boatload of Cuban refugees.

- Turn on the news and curse the assholes in the world.

- Get dressed and drive to work, pounding the wheel and tailgating all the way.

- Take orders from the boss while imagining you're giving him a swirlie.

- Dream of the day you'll have your own business.

- Castigate maintenance for keeping it so damn hot in here.

- Alienate your co-workers.

- Cruise Internet porn on company time.

- Whack off in the bathroom.

- Close the door to your office and do push-ups.

- Imagine your female co-workers doing a naked conga down to the snack room.

- Dream of the day you'll have your own business.

- Go to the gym and be distracted because everyone else is doing it wrong.

- Try hitting on the girl at the desk by grabbing your wang and saying, "Hey look, he likes you!"

- Mentally label her a lesbian when she turns you down.

- Leave to drive home, praying that someone will fuck with you.

- Watch all four of the *Die Hard* movies.

Maybe it's not always that bad, but I bet a lot of days are.

It's okay; you're not abnormal. It's the nature of the Testosterone beast, and it doesn't just affect humans.

Inject a male bird with Testosterone and it begins to patrol larger areas and have more fights over mates or territory. Unfortunately, it usually doesn't live as long. Likewise, cows injected with Testosterone become dominant in the herd, coercing other cows to go into town and tip some people. Female hyenas are so highly androgenized that they're the dominant sex with larger bodies and hot, throbbing clitorises.

It usually starts in the womb. Testosterone designs a fetus with huge physical potential and encourages the adult to use this potential. Accordingly, theses high-T children often have learning disorders, at least they're diagnosed as such. Look inside him, though, and you'd just find a kid who's got so much hormone percolating through him that it's all he can do not to grab a stick and play Whac-a-mole with the entire world.

In other words, he's got tendencies that interfere with getting an education, like the aforementioned inability to sit still, along with disrespect for authority.

These kids often get lousy jobs when they grow up because their reluctance to engage in teamwork makes them lousy employees. Somewhat tragically, there's a whole smorgasbord of shit the high-T boy or man just won't eat. They can be stubborn, too, which often costs them their mates, their job, their bank accounts, and their friends.

Interestingly, Testosterone researcher James McBride Dabbs found that unemployed men, depressed or not, seemed to have high Testosterone levels. Did the unemployment itself hoist their levels, or were these men high-T in the first place, and unemployment at the very least put them in charge of their fate and gave them a fight they could sink their worn-away teeth into?

I don't think anyone knows except for the individual high-T guy, but he won't tell you cuz he ain't about to discuss *feelings* with a miserable peckerwood like you.

The high-T men often don't live long, either, because they're unable to run from a fight. It's more painful to walk away than any possible repercussions of staying.

Case in point, there were scores of individuals in San Diego this past week who refused to leave their homes when the fires came. They ignored authorities and stood perched on their roofs, garden hose in one fist and the other clenched and shaking at the heavens.

Top of the world, mom!

Much to the consternation of city officials, most of them succeeded. Sure, they no longer have any neighbors because all *their* houses burned down, but that usually suits a high-T guy just fine. Damn peckerheads made too much noise, anyhow.

To further reduce their already ultimately fated-to-be-short life span, high-T men are hugely reluctant to go to the doctor. It's probably not so much an indifference to illness as it is the unwillingness to put themselves in a position where another man is dominant over them.

Like he wants to listen to some pompous geek lecture at him about his blood pressure. His blood pressure is high *because* he's listening to a pompous geek lecture him about his blood pressure!

Want a high-T man to survive an illness and get out of the hospital? Don't make him wear one of those gowns that tie in back. He'll wither and die; not from staphylococcus but the sheer humiliation of staffcanseeyourcoccus, not to mention your bare ass. Talk the staff into letting him wear a smoking jacket, or at least some pajamas decorated with the mud flap girl.

For you astrology buffs out there, let me put it this way: high-Testosterone dudes have too much Saturn and not enough moon. And all the herbal tea in the world ain't gonna help.

Oddly, though, most of us share this peculiar penchant for what, to the uninitiated eye, passes for altruism or chivalry. We invariably stick up for the poor soul who's being picked on by authority figures. Oh, but it's not so much the poor victim we want to aid; we just want to get in an authority figure's face because it feels good. It's a well-placed loogie in the eye of the bastards who are running things.

Likewise, we'll help the picked on child, the abused woman, and the maligned geek partly because, well, we like confrontation.

I'm a little bit loath to say this, but there are times I really want someone to step out of line. Give me the finger; cut me off; steal my parking space; whistle *Lemon Tree* in the elevator. Please-oh-please.

I've got the makings of a sick bastard. And so, I suspect, do a lot of you.

There's no denying it, the low-T guys generally have happier marriages, higher paying, more satisfying jobs, closer friendships, and longer lives.

Still, I wouldn't trade places with them.

High-T gives you supreme energy, supreme optimism, drive, ambition, an urge to lead and not follow, an incredible zest for life, and the ability to overcome any obstacle. Hell, high-T created our civilization, even though it currently seems like a bit of an anachronism.

And the bit about wanting to help people because we like confrontation? Yeah, that's pretty much true, but despite what I said, I do think high-T makes one want to protect the weak out of pure chivalry.

But in order to reap the benefits of our favorite hormone, you have to take control of your biology. You have to harness and ride that beast known as high Testosterone. I joked about my lopsided half-time score. In reality, it's pretty much a tie and even though my balls get to receive at the beginning of the second half, the defense is quick and cagey and full of strategy.

Having high T is kind of like being a superhero. For instance, Superman could rob banks if he wanted to, but he doesn't. He opts to do good. Sure he occasionally sneaks a peek at Supergirl's underwear with his X-ray vision, but you can't completely suppress your biology, can you?

-- 2007

Vision Quest

I want to be my own hero, be the protagonist in
the book of my life and not just some third-rate
character whose life is notable only for his total lack
of conviction or purpose.

The workout's over. Chalk up another one.

I'm a little too shaky to walk to my car so I stop at the coffee shop to sit down and let my nervous system regain its composure. I've left my wrist straps on because, well, it makes the uninitiated think I just broke out of my restraints and I kinda' like that.

I've also got this giant Rorschach-test of a sweat stain on my green shirt that looks like two poodles doing the Heisman Trophy stance. So the sweaty shirt, combined with my wrist straps, is a pretty fair indicator that I've been working out (or, like I said, just broke out of the psychiatric ward).

As I sip my coffee and pore over my training journal, I note with satisfaction that I just batted a thousand, training wise. In other words, I hit at least *one* more rep or used at least *one* more pound on *everything*.

Aussie, Aussie, Aussie! Oi, oi, oi!

That's when I notice Luigi sitting in the corner looking at me. The pudgeball has this quizzical look on his face. He puts down the textbook he's reading and after exchanging the usual bullshit pleasantries, he asks me if I'm writing down how much weight I lifted.

Warily I say, "Sure," without offering any more of an explanation.

Then he hits me with the question.

"Why do you care how much weight you lifted?"

I'm dumbfounded. My mouth's open and I must look like a pole-axed sheep. Insects fly in to leisurely nibble on a piece of egg salad lodged between my molars.

Then Luigi comes back at me with another:

"Why don't you just train to stay in shape?"

My senses are reeling.

Down goes Frazier! Down goes Frazier!

But I recover. Barely. It wasn't my most articulate moment, but I think I said something like, "Well, for the same reason you're presumably reading that book. I want to better myself. I want to *improve*."

He gives a smug little smile and returns to his book and his soymilk double-frappe-fuckalatte.

Weasel.

But I've been turning Luigi's question around in my head ever since.

Now that I've had some time to think about it, I think this is what I'd say — or what I'd want to say — if asked the same questions again:

"Luigi, when you were a kid, didn't you dream about going off to slay dragons? Didn't you dream about being some kind of hero?

"And as you grew up and realized that you probably wouldn't be slaying any dragons, real or metaphorical, didn't you get tired of just watching *others* do physical things? Didn't you get tired of only being involved in *surrogate* achievement, you know, living vicariously through the basketball players, the soccer players, the Italian bocce ball players, or whoever it is you admire?

"Maybe you actually *were* involved in some organized sport, but if you're like most conventional athletes, you only used weight training as a means to an end. You wanted to be a better tight end or a better power forward, but once you stopped competing in your sport, you stopped weight lifting.

"But you gotta' understand, people like me never stop lifting weights. The part of us that wanted to slay the dragon? It didn't die. It won't.

"We seek to constantly get better, to get the perfect body or set a personal record or just be prepared for all the physical challenges — the *what ifs* the cosmos dumps on us.

"But we know deep down that the perfect body or ultimate personal record can never really be achieved, because our imagination always sets the goal a step or two or three ahead of what we've accomplished. And we also know that the universe is merciless enough to give us a few physical challenges that we won't be, can't be, prepared for.

"So it's not the goal that's important, it's the *journey*. The journey's the thing. The journey's the *reward*.

"There aren't a lot of us in this demographic, Luigi, but *goddam* we've got a powerful lobby.

"People like me are painfully aware of living in a world drained of spiritual values; who feel alienated; who feel impotent. So we try to be a type of hero. Again, we probably won't slay any dragons, but we train *just in case.*

"We not only want to look badass, we want to *be* badass so we can smite evil. And evil has a lot of faces nowadays.

"So we undertake what's much like the classic journey of the hero that Joseph Campbell wrote about: separation from society where we practice denial, endure hardship, experience pain, and ultimately get — or get a part of — what we were seeking.

"The whole training experience is almost like the Vision Quest that was part of the Lakota Indian's life. When the Lakota needed guidance, he'd purify himself in a sweat lodge and forgo food or shelter until he received spiritual guidance — that or a nasty case of heat rash.

"Well, the gym is our sweat lodge and if you don't think a good squat or deadlift workout is purifying, then there are no suitable words to convince you otherwise; you have to experience it yourself. And I tell you, a good workout — no, a great workout, one where you have nothing left and you're sweating and you haven't held back on one rep of one set — *is* spiritual.

"The Hindus speak of the *Kundalini*, the Mother Goddess, the divine power that's asleep at the base of the spine. If you arouse it, the phenomena associated with its awakening range from bizarre physical sensations to pain, visions, brilliant light, ecstasy, bliss, and even transcendence of self.

"This may be hard for you to swallow, but when I do a set of heavy overhead barbell presses and feel that peculiar tension in the base of my spine, I think I know what the Hindus are talking about. At the very least, I've had the pain, the visions, and the brilliant light!

"Sure, this all sounds like I'm comparing weight training to religion, but what is it if it isn't a religion? My best thoughts come to me during a workout, and whatever demons I had plaguing me prior to walking into the gym have been exorcised by my exercise. And what's the gym but a temple and what's the clanging of the weights but the peal of the bells?

"I know it's hard for you to understand Luigi, but people like me practice denial to the point of sometimes being almost monastic. We often avoid people, social events, and rich food, all in the single-minded pursuit of a kind of perfection.

"Yeah, it's sometimes painful, but that's how we achieve heroic status. The more challenging the situation we overcome, the greater our stature. The demon you swallow gives you its power.

"We may never get to fight our dragon, but that's okay. As Joseph Campbell said, the greater life's pain, the greater life's reply.

"And beyond the metaphysical component there's the esthetic component. Sure, most of us want to not only be better, but also look better. We're every bit the sculptors of ancient Greece, only our medium is flesh instead of clay or marble. And if we look better, we might just be worthy of the love of Aphrodite and the pursuit of beauty is a fine and worthy thing.

"But hey, it looks like I've come back the metaphysical, because what's beauty other than the reflection of the divinity of the universe?

"So Luigi, that's why I write down what I lifted and that's why I want to get better. I want to be my own hero, be the protagonist in the book of my life and not just some third-rate character whose life is notable only for his total lack of conviction or purpose.

"So have another soy latte, you uncomprehending, weak kneed, pot-bellied, slack jawed, pseudo intellectual waste of flesh."

That's what I should have said to Luigi, but in retrospect, he isn't really deserving of an answer. Heroes-in-training shouldn't have to answer questions about their convictions. They just do what they have to do.

-- 2006

The Death of Female Sex Drive

A little-known side effect of the pill — one well-known to physicians and the drug companies back then but rarely discussed — is that the pill killed female libidos. Paradoxically, while the pill sexually liberated women, they didn't feel much like taking advantage of that freedom.

I've written about this before, but it's the issue that just won't die.

We're surrounded by male hamsters, men who are weaker in mind, body, and character than they've ever been. The word *fop*, as best represented by Tim Roth in that *Rob Roy* movie, keeps popping up in my mind. Only that fop was good with a sword.

It has nothing to do with sexual preference, but instead a slavish obsession over fashion. But worse than the fops are the plain ol' *effete* — those men lacking in character, vitality, or strength.

Many of these fops flock to yoga classes because the lack of a spine makes you really, really flexible.

Were it not for modern medicine, natural selection would have taken out these hamsters and their crumbling Y-chromosomes years ago. Were it not for Dristan and asthma inhalers, the roadsides would be peppered with their sniffling, honking, wheezing, terminally congested bodies. Without their prescriptions, the landscape would soon be quiet except for all those fatherless Kleenex tissues fluttering in the wind.

Maybe it's the diet. Maybe it's society. Maybe it's the school system. Hell, maybe some xenoestrogens in their Axe Body Spray *axed* their testicles. Hordes of women may be drawn to their spray-on pheromonal scent, but sadly, ironically, the fragrant boys wouldn't know what to do with all that presumably willing flesh. I worry it has something to with all that added *Bom Chica Wah Wah.*

You probably have your own theory. Lord knows I have plenty, but I think I've unearthed a new culprit. Like that TV show, *Bones*, I had to go back pretty far to dig up this corpse, only I had to play both the role of the lonely and cynical forensic anthropologist *and* the cocky FBI agent to figure out what events gave birth to today's lackluster male.

Exhibit A, your honor, is a woman named Margaret Sanger.

In 1950, Sanger was widely known as a warrior for birth control. She saw birth control as the right of a woman to control her body and, consequently, her life, and thus escape the "servitude that came with poverty and unwanted children."

Back in 1950, birth control consisted of little beyond a hastily inserted fizzy bottle of Coke. Sanger, however, dreamed of a drug that would give women total control of the process. She soon teamed up with a wealthy like-minded feminist by the name of Katherine Dexter McCormick. Together they decided to fund the development of such a drug.

In 1952, the two met Gregory Goodwin (Goody) Pincus, who was famous for achieving in vitro fertilization of rabbit eggs in 1934. Pincus was convinced that hormones could be used to control reproduction. So, funded by McCormick, he and his partner, M.C. Chang, began working on the project in 1952.

They tested their pill in 1954 and when given to a group of 50 childless women, it postponed ovulation almost 100 percent.

After more similarly successful studies, the FDA approved *Enovid* as a contraceptive in 1960. Just three years later, over 2.3 million women were using it, and the numbers soared to astronomical proportions in the years that followed. Today, it's estimated that over 100 million women use modern versions of Enovid.

Oddly, not only did the marketing department of the drug company Searle influence the colloquial name of the drug — *the pill* — but also how the pill was to be used.

A month's supply of the oral contraceptive consisted of 20 pills. A woman would then go "off" the pill for a week, during which time she'd experience an artificial period. (Modern versions contain 7 inert "spacer" pills.) The periods were artificial because the user wouldn't actually shed an unfertilized egg along with the uterine lining. She'd just bleed.

There is, however, according to what was known at that time and what is commonly believed today, no medical reason for inducing an artificial period.

So why do it?

Well, the marketing department felt that inducing the women to bleed would reinforce the notion that the pill was working. After all, you don't have a period — if you don't bleed once a month — if you're pregnant.

All that was missing was the catchy Head & Shoulders-style slogan.

That bloody mess lets you know it's working!

All those red corpuscles, mountains of Tampons, and stained white slacks for nothing. All on the whim of a few clever men in suits.

It's only this past year that the drug companies have decided to throw pretense out the window by marketing 3-month pills where the user doesn't experience a period for 3 months. Presumably, this 3-month pill is just a bridge to a perpetual oral contraceptive.

But, your honor, I digress just a tiny bit. The previous point regarding marketing tactics isn't directly related to my argument, so I'll go back to making my point. A little-known side effect of the pill — one well-known to physicians and the drug companies back then but rarely discussed — is that the pill *killed* female libidos. Paradoxically, while the pill sexually liberated women, they didn't feel much like taking advantage of that freedom.

The pill decreases ovarian production of Testosterone, along with increasing levels of Sex Hormone Binding Globulin (SHBG) production up to 10-fold. In turn, the SHBG binds up most of the remaining Testosterone, thereby killing sex drive, muting or nullifying orgasms, and making intercourse all but impossible without petroleum jelly.

So while the affected female might reluctantly acquiesce to sex, she'll first require a dollop of fossil-fuel lubricants and perhaps something entertaining to read over your shoulder while you fulfill your disgusting needs.

I'm really surprised there hasn't been a mass class-action suit against the drug companies and doctors for killing sex for millions of women and their unlucky mates.

To worsen matters, it's recently been discovered that the pill has *long-lasting* effects on female libido. In a study of 125 young women participating in a sexual dysfunction clinic, women who had been off the pill for a year still had SHBG levels 7 times higher than non-users.

The research team's leader, Dr. Claudia Penzer, said the loss of libido might not be reversible.

"There's the possibility it [the pill] is imprinting a woman for the rest of her life," theorized Penzer.

While women with numb vaginas can still reproduce, the lack of fluctuating hormones and libido might have had far-reaching effects on our society.

Consider briefly the female who begins manipulating her hormones at a very early age. Adolescence and the early teen years are when girls (and boys) learn to sexually interact, to pick up on sexual cues and prepare themselves for a normal, healthy sex life, presumably with a well-chosen mate.

Start pumping a girl with estrogen at an early age and it has psychological effects. She's probably immune, blind even, to sexual cues and signals. The red, green, and yellow traffic lights are flashing, but the pill has made her colorblind. She's as handicapped and naive as a female version of Arnold's character in *Twins*. The only sexual cues she knows are the ones she's learned to mimic from watching network television and YouTube videos of celebrities flashing their hoo-hahs.

Consider, too, that women are more sexually receptive during ovulation. While most mammals signal their receptivity during ovulation, human females display no overt biological cues. However, studies show that women usually take it upon themselves, perhaps subconsciously, to dress sexier while they're ovulating.

That tube top on the girl who normally dresses conservatively? That short skirt on the reserved secretary? The flash of laced-bra peeking out from beneath the blouse of the demure waitress? Chances are she's just placed an egg on the launch ramp.

It's also during this time that they're more interested in what we regard as "bad boys," hyper-masculine men who are more interested in mechanical bonding rather than emotional pair bonding. Presumably, these hyper-masculine men are stronger, healthier, and more virile. That, at least, is what their physical presence and confidence levels indicate.

It isn't too far of a stretch to assume that subconscious drives, fueled in part by fluctuating levels of Testosterone, have historically driven females to seek out these more virile men to fertilize their eggs. They want to better the odds of having a healthy child. They want the chromosomal Yin to their Ying-Yang.

Not surprisingly, men are also subconsciously more protective of their mates when they're ovulating, lest some rogue male try to slip a spermatic hockey puck past the husband-slash-goalie.

But with the widespread use of the pill, there's no ovulation. There's no increased sex drive. There's no desire to seek out superior genes. The cuckold rate — the rate at which father's are, unbeknownst to them, raising some other man's child (a product of their wife's infidelity) — has probably plummeted from the estimated 2 to 3 percent.

That, of course, is probably a good thing for potential duped fathers, but it's indicative of a trend. Hormonally skewed women probably aren't looking for superior genes. Their decisions regarding mates and pair bonding are, in technical language, *caca*. They're seeking male roommates instead of bedmates with superior gametes.

Historically, sex-linked traits have allowed males to compete with other males to attract the attention of females. Females affected by the pill are oblivious to the characteristics that might indicate strong, healthy genes.

So it's possible that this lack of sex drive in females — even after they stopped using the pill — and the possible inability to interpret sexual cues and pick good mates, has interfered with natural selection to such a degree that the number of human hamsters has grown by leaps and bounds.

Thus the increased number of male yoga practitioners.

Hence the preponderance of the pasty-faced. Hence the frequency of freaks. Hence the willions of wimps.

And if the psychological/biological argument doesn't cut it for you, perhaps the poetic-romantic version does.

Consider Edmund's soliloquy in *King Lear:*

> *Why bastard? Wherefore base? When my dimensions are as well compact, My mind as generous, and my shape as true, As*

honest madam's issue? Why brand they us With base? with baseness? bastardy? base, base? Who, in the lusty stealth of nature, take More composition and fierce quality Than doth, within a dull, stale, tired bed, Go to the creating a whole tribe of fops, Got 'tween asleep and wake?

For those of you who don't have the patience for the bard, Edmund was essentially saying, why do they treat me, the bastard son, with less respect than the "issue" of "honest" women? A child like Edmund was at least conceived in *passion* rather than sissy kids who were conceived in a dull marriage bed while they parents were half asleep.

Maybe there's something to that. Maybe kids conceived in passion inherited a bit of that coital spark.

Well, it's an interesting thought, but probably not true. An egg probably doesn't know if it was fertilized artificially in a brightly-lit doctor's office or through a satin-sheet clutching, back-clawing romp in the sack.

Still, let's just hope the latter remains the method of choice.

-- 2007

Cool Viking Hats With Big Shiny Horns

The undeniable fact is that most people get involved largely because of their loins. They see something that causes bodily secretions to stain their underwear and they make the tragic mistake of using that as the primary factor in determining whether they should pledge their undying love to that person.

As a writer, I spend a lot of time home alone.

It's not bad except for those times when burglars try to break into my house and I have to rig the house with makeshift booby traps like swinging paint buckets and stuff like that.

The good part is that I get to work in my underwear, the kind with the built-in fly that makes it really easy to scratch myself. Another advantage is that I get to wear cool Viking hats with big shiny horns that I make out of aluminum foil.

Try doing *that* in an office.

I guess the hardest part is the solitude. There are times when I literally don't talk to another soul for an entire day and my voice gets kind of creaky from lack of use, kind of like Tom Hanks in *Castaway*.

Luckily I've got *my* Wilson to talk to, which to you might just look like a blown up condom with a face painted on it tied to the back of my chair, but to me he's a true blue companion, albeit with pleasure-inducing knobs all over his face and a French tickler on top of his head.

When it gets really lonely, I sometimes dress the bull terriers up like people, the male with a bowler hat and a little bow tie and the female with a frilly dress and bonnet. His character is Tuggy McTuggerton and she's Molly Ollyoxenfree and I'm Miles Outlandish and we sit on the porch with our toy teacups and lollygag the afternoon away.

Either that or we play Star Wars where the female, an empty can of Bush's Beans affixed to her head, is R2-D2 and the male, is—no costume needed—the Wookie.

Me? I screw a couple of Danish muffins onto my ears and it makes for a damn convincing Princess Leia.

But sometimes even that doesn't allay the loneliness. Sometimes it gets so bad that I'm tempted to do...well, stuff that would sound plain silly if I told you about it. Thank God I haven't gone there yet.

Still, every once in awhile, just to keep the madness at bay, I have to head out to a coffee shop and just be around some real people.

A good coffee shop is a lot like a bar, except for the noticeable lack of neon lighting, vomit, and ass-baring floozies looking to get laid. The similarity I'm referring to is that coffee shops and bars are great places to listen to people, especially if you're wearing one of those SonicEarz (As Seen on TV!) that allow you to overhear conversations from the next solar system.

The topic that's most often discussed, next to maybe sports, is relationships, as in male and female relationships.

Strangely, almost no one seems happy. It seems every third male and every second female is bitching about his/her girlfriend/boyfriend or wife/husband.

She, invariably, is a castrating bitch, while he's always a selfish prick.

Luckily, she's usually able to numb the pain through distractions like shopping and a vivid fantasy life where her high-powered vibrator is in reality a handsome guy named Roberto who drives a sports car and exists only to fulfill her needs, and he's usually able to numb the pain through distractions like sports and a vivid albeit delusionary fantasy life where he thinks the cashier behind the counter is coming on to him because she smiled at him when he ordered a muffin and who, if only he weren't married or involved in a relationship, would exist only to fulfill his needs.

Oh man, oh man, oh Michael Jackson, ma-ma-se, ma-ma-sa, ma-mah coo-sa, man.

The owner of the coffee shop has, as a result of listening to this type of inter-sex kvetching for several years, vowed never to be involved in a relationship.

Although he hasn't said this, I wouldn't be surprised if his resultant male/female encounters consist of dalliances with hookers; that or using his inestimable baking skills to fashion his dough into enticing anatomically correct female shapes, passionately squeezing and kneading his flour-women's breasts until they squirt a golden shower of California raisins.

It was with these thoughts of relationships that I sat down to dinner the other night. Now I like to watch TV when I eat. I bet you're saying to yourself, "TC likes to watch TV when he eats? You gotta be kidding! Man, you think you know a guy...."

Anyhow, I was channel flipping and I stumbled onto an old episode of *King of Queens*. Doug Heffernan, aka Mall Cop, is afraid to go downstairs for breakfast because family friend and dog walker Holly is temporarily staying in the basement while she looks for an apartment. Doug has no idea what to say to her, so he's reluctant to go downstairs, but his bowl of cereal is calling to him.

Meanwhile, Doug's wife, Carrie, is working non-stop on a project for work and she's pretty much locked herself in her upstairs home office until the job's done.

Doug's stomach wins out and he tiptoes downstairs. Despite his stealth, Holly hears him in the kitchen and joins him. He's frozen. Can't think of a thing to say. He finally mutters, "Cereal...that's what it's all about."

Holly smiles good-naturedly, and she's obviously eager for Doug to say something else. Finally, "IPS" delivery driver Doug tries to tell her about something that happened to him at work the other day, a story his wife had rebuffed hearing because she was too busy.

"I delivered a package to a guy named Bubka Penis the other day," he offers meekly.

Holly does a spit take and spews cereal all over the table.

Doug is thrilled; thrilled that somebody thought his story was funny!

"I bet all kinds of funny things happen to you at work," she says, enthusiastically.

"Yes, yes they do!" exclaims Doug, who's never experienced this before, never had someone in his house listen to him, never had someone in the house who laughed at his stories!

Doug then takes a swig of orange juice directly from the carton, an act for which his wife has scolded him the previous day. Holly sees him and he's embarrassed, saying, "Sorry, I guess that's kind of gross."

Rather than scolding him, Holly bets him five bucks that he can't finish the whole thing in one gulp! He drains the sucker enthusiastically and she pays up with an Arby's coupon, which in Doug's house, "is as good as money."

Has any child's face ever lit up with such happiness, let alone a grown man's? Finally, a woman who appreciates him, who understands him, who doesn't bust his balls!

The next morning Doug bounds out of bed, eager to go downstairs. Meanwhile wife Carrie is still squired away in her upstairs office, still typing away on her work project. As Doug walks into the kitchen, he's greeted with the sight of Holly making pancakes, eggs, and hand cut bacon. His eyes light up.

Someone is making him breakfast! And not just cold cereal!

Holly then asks him if he'd like her to wheel the TV into the kitchen so he can watch while he eats.

The look on his face! The same look he'd have if gold pirate doubloons were issuing forth from her vagina!

Later, he walks back upstairs to dutifully check on Carrie. She's stressed from her work and says to Doug, "I need to unwind. Let's have sex."

He can't f-ing believe it! He got sex from Carrie without having to schmooze her, without having to lie to her that her ass looks good in those God-awful stretch pants, without having to ply her by completing household chores! Did any man ever have it better!?!

Afterwards, smile on his face, he zips up his sweat suit and practically levitates downstairs, where Holly has just finished baking Doug a chocolate cake.

He's buoyant! He's being carried on angel wings! Doug has never been happier

He explains the situation to his friends who've gathered at his house to watch TV:

"If I want someone to laugh at my stories, cook for me, be nice to me, I have Holly on this floor. If I want someone to have sex with, yell at the phone company, tell me when to take a shower, I got Carrie up there. Upstairs wife, downstairs wife, happy."

The next day he has a football party and Holly prepares a taco bar! She walks around with a tray of tequila shooters! All the guys are smoking cigars, which are, in Carrie's world, taboo!

"I just love the smell of cigars," bubbles Holly. "Mmmmm! Something about it just makes me want to bake."

Doug has it great. Unfortunately, like a fat Icarus, he gets cocky and flies too close to the sun. He attempts to juggle a third "wife."

This one's a sister of a friend and she does P.R. for Nassau Coliseum. She tells Doug she can get him tickets to any event. After a few front row seats to hockey games, a locker room meeting with the players, and a chance to ride on the Zamboni, Doug declares to the universe, "Coliseum wife, you're my favorite."

Obviously, this 3rd wife is the comedy crucible in the show. Doug can't handle pleasing all three women and comedy doo-doo hits the fan. He's of course left with one wife, the real one, and he's probably doomed to a life of conflict and dissatisfaction (not that reality would creep into a comedy show).

The weird thing is that I almost got teary eyed over this...this fairly pedestrian television comedy! I saw the pure joy on Doug's face, recognized the feelings of acknowledgement, approval, and pure animal satisfaction he was experiencing, compared it to the relationships I see around me, and I actually felt sad!

Together, Holly and Carrie equaled one decent mate. It wasn't Holly's baking or cooking that would have helped Doug be happy—those acts were incidental. It was Holly's giving nature, her non-judgmental attitude, and her interest in giving rather then receiving.

Granted, Doug is self-absorbed, conniving, slovenly, and selfish, in many ways just the penis-carrying equivalent of Carrie. I get that. Let's ignore that for the sake of argument, though, and assume that maybe

Doug would be a tad more giving and a little less selfish if his mate were a little less selfish and a tad more giving.

But let's forget the Heffernans. The undeniable fact is that most people get involved largely because of their loins. They see something that causes bodily secretions to stain their underwear and they make the tragic mistake of using that as the primary factor in determining whether they should pledge their undying love to that person.

The second factor used to determine the suitably of a potential mate, probably equally unwise to the flow of underwear secretions, is the perceived or hoped for ability of the potential mate to "fill in your gaps" or make you feel secure.

In other words, people usually want something from the other person. They want another person's energy, they want constant attention, they want acknowledgment and understanding.

He wants a whore in the bedroom, a whore who can cook in the kitchen, and maybe a whore-slash-certified public accountant in the home office come tax time. He wants a combination of an underwear model, celebrity chef Rachel Ray, Mother Theresa, and porn star Veronika Zemanova.

She wants...ah, who the hell knows? Let's put it this way, she wants something equally unrealistic, someone who'll fulfill every half-baked need of hers.

Horse piss.

Unfortunately, invariably, the barometric underwear secretions soon become a thing of the past. Unfortunately, invariably, the illusory glow of newfound love soon also becomes a thing of the past and you usually find that your mate isn't filling in your gaps.

You're left with reality. And reality is usually what I see and hear in the coffee shop, not to mention my friends' relationships, the celebrity relationships in the tabloids, *everywhere.*

Granted, it's important for a potential mate to make your underwear crusty and it's nice that your mate will yell at the paperboy when he throws the Sunday paper in the begonias when you lack the courage, but it's not enough.

If you're lacking some essential quality, you ain't gonna get it from someone else. If you're looking for someone to give you things, you ain't gonna get them unless, paradoxically, you forget your own needs and concentrate on the other person's needs.

Unfortunately, the other person in the relationship has to have the same attitude, to give without expectation of receiving anything in return. You and your mate act as energy sources instead of energy drains.

Of course, that kind of attitude is important in all relationships, romantic, personal, or business. It's very Zen. Sorta. At least as interpreted by a guy who works in his underwear and a cool Viking hat with big shiny horns.

-- 2009

Tragic Maturity

Adolescence, while it's a place I like to visit periodically, shouldn't be a lifestyle. Tragic maturity, while appropriate at times, will kill your soul if practiced perpetually.

I don't think I've ever told you this before, but I have the word *Adidas* imprinted on my pecker. No, it's not a tattoo, nor is it some unconventional sponsorship deal arranged by the fine people at Adidas. Rather it's the reminder of an unfortunate accident; a reminder of the first time I met Eduardo.

I was on the soccer pitch, not because I like the game, but because I don't have much choice as most of my damn friends are from Europe and they couldn't throw a baseball or football if you offered them a kilo of Euros.

I'd offered to be the goalie, largely because I refuse to run aimlessly up and down the field in the heat while complaining to God in a foreign language, but also because, as a pure matter of physics, I take up more space in goal than my teammates, thus making it harder, in theory, for the other team to score a goal.

The action was on the other side of the field when one of the opposing team's Brazilian players stole the ball and broke towards the goal — my goal. Tall and graceful, Eduardo artfully dribbled the ball down the field between, around, and even over the defenders. It was if somehow he'd affixed the ball to his shoe with the gum of some sticky Amazonian tree. He was only about ten feet away from me when he blasted the ball as hard as he could.

As it knuckled towards me, he bellowed, "For Brazilllll!"

It hit me right in the crotch. It made a noise like a burly Russian cleaning woman using a baseball bat on a heavy rug to teach it a miserable lesson about her wretched asexual life.

I went down, not slowly, but in a crumpled heap like the victims of the nailgun killer in *No Country for Old Men*. There I lay for 20 minutes in fetal position, hands cradling my nads while the rest of the players either grimaced or chuckled nervously.

While I recovered soon enough, I have the unfortunate aforementioned imprint to remind me of that afternoon. To this day, I can't watch the BBC's *World News* because if I hear the word "Brazil, " I experience a horrific Pavlovian response where, instead of drooling like a dog, my pecker recedes deep into my body like the head of a frightened turtle.

To add insult to injury, Eduardo has since become an unwelcome fixture in my life. It seems everywhere I go, whether it be a bar, restaurant, cafe, or nightclub, the stinking, rotting, soccer-playing albatross around my neck; the Brazilian bringer of testicle death, Eduardo, shows up, giving a whole new meaning to the term, 'cock block.'

He's in his late thirties, amiable, and quite the ladies' man — at least he says he is. He has no discernible job. He gets up when he wants to; does what he wants to. Beyond that, he's a moron. He sucks the life out of me whenever he shows up.

He absolutely murders any conversation I might be having. He lingers and lingers, regaling me in his heavy Portuguese accent with tales of his alleged female conquests.

"Hey TC! I have a new line for the women. They lovvvve it! You want to hear it?"

"Sure, Eduardo, sure," I answer with all the enthusiasm of a weary parent who's been asked yet again to listen to his five-year-old recite *Itsy Bitsy Spider* for the umpteenth fuckin' time.

"I say, 'Hey, I'm a spy. I am James Bond!' Ha!"

Upon saying this, he stands up straight, grins mightily, and literally puffs up, proud as some weird Brazilian bird that's just laid a mangled cricket at a prospective mate's feet. The poor bastard is actually proud of himself! He doesn't realize he's *Forresto Gumpo*, but with an ego!

The oddest, and most difficult thing for me personally, is that he *does* do well with the women! But I have a theory.

It must be because fucking Eduardo, in the female mind, doesn't really count. It must be like those horny female teachers who sleep with their young, underage students, or like Jenny Fields, who fucks brain dead Technical Sergeant Garp in *The World According to Garp*.

Sure, if you fuck something with an I.Q. under a hundred, it's a freebie! There's no walk of shame! You just smooth out your dress and give the thing with a penis a cookie!

Most recently, I was at a local watering hole with my friend Jason and we're having a great wide-ranging conversation when, sure enough, Eduardo walks in to shake our hands and subsequently suck the life out of me.

"Hey TC, I saw your wife running. She has big breasts! Very nice!"

My God, he's the living incarnation of Georg and Yortuk, the two Czechoslovakian "wild and crazy guys" played by Steve Martin and Dan Akroyd on the old SNL!

"Come on, American fox-es, we are hoping it is not long before all our clothes are off and we are holding your big American breasts in our hands!"

Yortuk, a.k.a. Eduardo, even plagues me in the gym. He'll be in the middle of practicing Jiu Jitsu moves against some fearsome imaginary opponent when he'll walk over to fuck-up my deadlift session, even though I'm wearing my headphones and a scowl to ward off humans; even though my timer is beeping impatiently.

I ought to kill him, but I have a morbid curiosity to hear what's going to spill out of this buffoon's head, so I cover up my balls and listen.

Within minutes, I'm bereft of energy and the will to live. I look like one of the people whose blood feeds the vampires night after night. I swear I'd stick a shit-covered stake through his heart if he weren't so damn cartoon-character amiable. You can't kill a Portuguese Scooby Doo can you?

Ruh-row!

Eduardo is just the type of guy I often write about, the boy-man who never grew up, the ubiquitous non-entities who leech off the emotions and finances of others. They contribute nothing. They neither sow nor reap, but yet God — or poor bastards like you and me — feed them (or at least buy them drinks).

Just recently, though, I became re-acquainted with a Universal Law -- every force has an equal and opposing force. This is the way of Newtonian Physics and, apparently, nimrods. I actually met Eduardo's alter ego; his moral Moriarty.

He's roughly 25. His hair is short, perfectly coiffed, and held in place with a dab of mousse or Brylcreem, if they even make that stuff anymore. He's wearing a long-sleeved white shirt with thin blue stripes and a little Polo pony above the breast pocket. The cuffs are not rolled up. His slacks, not pants, *slacks*, are also white, and he's wearing tasseled brown loafers with beige socks.

Of course his name is Andrew! Not Andy, not even Anj, which would probably qualify as Andy of Mayberry cool, but Andrew, which is what they *always* name the clones.

"Andrew 7, report to surgery. We need to remove your liver for transplant into the original Andrew."

Andrew asks me if I've thought about my financial future. He's interning as a broker at Merrill Lynch and he's worried that I'm not investing wisely.

My impulse is to kick the moneychanger in the balls, or at least grab his arm, put his hand down on the table, grab a knife, and Yakuza his finger off.

Instead I listen as uncomfortably as if I'm listening to a ten-year-old tell me how he's just given up breastfeeding. He gives me his lactose-soaked business card and walks over to his 325i Beemer, which is the introductory entry-level car for every wannabe snooty capitalist sonofabitch in training to become a full-fledged self-absorbed asshole.

Obviously, Andrew is the Bizarro version of Eduardo. While Eduardo never grew up, Andrew is an old man at the age of 25. He's tragically mature. He's already heavily invested in a 401K plan. He dresses like the guys in the Father's Day ad for J.C. Penney in the Sunday paper. He campaigned for Ronald Reagan when he was still in his mother's womb. He puts on hypoallergenic latex gloves before he beats off into a zip-loc bag.

Whereas Eduardo sucks the life out of me because of his exasperating slacker lifestyle, Andrew makes me want to take out my dick and stick it in his ear — only because he'd likely find it *appalling*.

When it comes to Andrew, who I've seen numerous times since first meeting him, I almost want to grab him by the lapels and scream at him, *beg* him, "C'mon, I ask you as a man, you straight-laced bastard, at *least* say something about my wife's tits!" That, or proclaim through clenched teeth, "Tassels...belong on...a...stripper! Not on...your...shoes!"

It's weird, on one calloused hand, I've always trumpeted the virtues of the Andrew types who work hard, study hard, and work out hard.

But on the other, I often revel in the Eduardo types who say fuck-you to convention, believe in the philosophy of not doing anything you don't want to do, embrace *fun* because you're going to die soon enough, who like to dance with Chlamydia, the Greek Goddess of promiscuous sex.

Of course, I may be giving Eduardo too much credit as the notion that this mutt actually has a philosophy of life is a little far-fetched.

But these two represent such extremes that I have zero respect for either.

The tale of Eduardo and Andrew is a lot like Aesop's fable about the grasshopper and the ant. The grasshopper spends the warm summer months singing and screwing while the ant works June through September to store up food for the winter. When winter comes and the grasshopper finds himself dying of hunger, he asks the ant for food but is turned down because of his idleness.

Of course, if Aesop were writing his fable today, the ant would develop blood pressure problems because he neglected to have any fun. That, and the IRS would slap a huge capital gains tax on the ant because of his recently accumulated wealth. His wife would end up leaving him and shack up with Eduardo...er, the grasshopper, at which point the ant would kill himself in a botched murder/suicide.

In our modern day, parallel fable, my pecker is now a poster board for Adidas. In our modern day fable, Eduardo orders his Mojito "shaken, not stirred," and somehow gets hot women — sometimes two at a time — to actually do what we've been trying to get them to do since our sleepy fetal balls plopped into our scrotums.

In our modern day fable, Andrew's superficiality and fake sincerity will allow him to earn trust and obscene amounts of money in a financial world gone mad.

Adolescence, while it's a place I like to visit periodically, shouldn't be a lifestyle. Tragic maturity, while appropriate at times, will kill your soul if practiced perpetually.

The irony is that Andrew and Eduardo need what each other has. If you disassociated their molecules and reconstituted them as one person, you might have a legitimate human being there. Then maybe I wouldn't have to bear the penile scars invoked by a man-child and shake the hand of a prematurely old polo boy.

Becoming a self-actualized man is a helluva thing. Knowing when to do the right thing under difficult circumstances, or knowing when to do the *wrong thing* when it harms no one but reminds us of what it is to be fucking happy, is hard but essential. Unfortunately, neither Andrew nor Eduardo are capable of making either decision.

If you spend your days in the mind-set of a twelve year old or in the mind-set of a seventy-year-old, you miss out. You might as well grab your nuts and fall over now because the soccer ball of life is sooner or later going to hit you square in the nuts and unlike me, you won't get up.

-- 2008

Hygiene for Real Men

The stark truth is that my willie is easily the cleanest part of my body. You never know when you're going to get some action, so I tend to it with all the attentiveness of one of Marie Antoinette's handmaidens.

The latest stakeout by the "hand washing police" revealed some seemingly disturbing facts. One-third of men don't bother to wash up after using a public restroom, compared with only 12 percent of women who don't.

The report, compiled by researchers who spy on people in public restrooms but *don't* happen to be members of the Minneapolis airport police department, was presented this past week to a meeting of infectious disease scientists.

Washing up would do away with the *yuck* factor, but according to microbiologists, it's also the single best thing people can do to avoid getting sick from colds or the flu.

Uh, I'm not sure how to tell you this, but I don't always wash my hands after I pee-pee.

Before you make a mental note (punctuated by a lot of exclamation points) never to shake my hand again, let me explain.

First of all, my hands don't usually touch my unit when I pee. You see, I'm a busy guy so I'm forced to do something efficiency experts call *multi-tasking,* which means doing two or more things simultaneously.

In this case, it means practicing what my Yogi calls "mountain pose," where you stand with your palms pressed against each other in front of your chest, while I'm peeing. This allows me to void while simultaneously gaining inner peace. I tell you it saves a heckuva' lot of time.

But beyond all that, even if I did touch my unit while peeing, it wouldn't matter if I washed afterwards.

The stark truth is that my willie is easily the cleanest part of my body. You never know when you're going to get some action, so I tend to it with all the attentiveness of one of Marie Antoinette's handmaidens. Why the nightly exfoliation alone takes the better part of an hour! (I recommend Clinique's *Cock Scrub* and a small pumice stone.)

I mean, excuse the expression, but you could literally eat off my schlong. In fact, just last week, a couple of girls were enjoying a selection of

Mediterranean *tapas* off my unit. Sure, they took their food outside when some patio seating opened up, but still.

The real problem comes not so much from touching one's own schlong, but touching the toilet door, toilet paper dispenser, or flush handle. That's where the bad-boy germs in the bathroom hang out.

Even so, most of those germs are no worse than those that linger on your cell phone or your computer keyboard, which are, according to some researchers, more of a safe harbor for bacteria than the average toilet seat in a public restroom.

But those are just the usual suspects — the OJ's of the bacterial world. Any hack can peg them as guilty, but it's the microbiologists — the bacterial detectives -- that see the horrific microscopic world that escapes the masses.

Let's examine your daily routine, your average morning for instance, with an imaginary all-seeing microscope.

As you get up and make your way to the bathroom, there are hundreds of thousands, maybe millions, of the bacteria known as pseudomonads hanging from your face by tiny mucus-like strands, struggling to cling to their moist, warm, oily, nutrient-dense home.

They're so tiny that a pile of a few hundred thousand wouldn't be visible to the naked eye. They're little sausage-shaped creatures that zip around by means of a tube-shaped tail with propeller action. They swim along at a speed of about 0.0001 miles per hour, or roughly seven body lengths a second.

For the sake of comparison, if we could talk world-class sprinter Justin Gatlin into allowing us to shrink him down, *Fantastic Voyage* style, to the size of a pseudomonad, the pseudomonad would run him down easily and suck him into one of its food vacuoles. Sure we'd have a lot of explaining to do to his family, but think of the pay-per-view receipts.

You retrieve your morning newspaper and throw it on the kitchen counter, oblivious to the fact you've created havoc for a multitude of pseudomonads and their ilk. Tens of thousands are killed by the sheer impact of this gargantuan tabloid asteroid, while others die horrifically, slowly smothered by microscopic paper fibers or drowned and poisoned by tiny droplets of loose ink dislodged by the impact.

As you prepare your breakfast, you periodically pick up the dishtowel to clean up afterwards, never realizing what a perfect little ecosystem you're holding in your hands. By itself, this weave of cotton threads contains tunnels laced with minerals, proteins, and soluble fats, held together by a sugar-based grid work. That's tasty and hospitable enough by itself to bacteria, but once you wipe off the counter tops, you're adding additional fats, proteins, sugars, and most importantly, moisture!

It's bacterial heaven!

The pseudomonads living in the towel, along with members of the rough and tumble salmonella gang, can get along fine because there's plenty of food for everybody, political and ideological differences be damned.

But unfortunately, you *touched* the eco-system! Some of the salmonella gang decided to branch out into new territories by latching onto your finger.

But they wouldn't have it any other way; they're not at risk at all on your fingertips. In fact, they love it there!

To them, it's a warm, swampy world filled with deep crevices and protective overhangs and refreshing pools of slime and grease. And all that sweat? Manna from heaven! It's filled with stuff to make them grow like potassium, zinc, glucose, Vitamin C, riboflavin, and over a dozen amino acids.

Only there are other bacteria living there already. They don't like the intrusion. A war right out of *300* ensues. The natives start hosing the invaders with streams of antibiotics. Others surround the invading salmonella and eat their food so they'll wither and starve.

The salmonella are slaughtered at first, but they retreat and soon recover. They wage their own counter-attack, spewing their own chemical weapons, the same weapons that make you sick if you ingest enough of these tiny warriors.

The war continues on your fingertips, but as you go about your duties, you touch the refrigerator door! Then the sink. And then your *food* — food filled with tiny, moist, nurturing embryonic-like pockets!

But that isn't all you have to worry about. Wafting in from the open window are tiny, invisible bits of broken-off insect hairs. They land on your food and almost all of them carry between one and fourteen different species of bacteria.

The father of microbiology, Louis Pasteur, was so painfully aware of this phenomenon that he carried a magnifier with him when he was invited to dinner. Whenever a particular dish looked suspicious, Pasteur whipped out his magnifier and examined the food for beasties. Historians believe this is the reason he spent so many holidays alone.

But you're oblivious as you eat your blend of oatmeal, protein powder, flax seed, and Tibetan goji berries. Suddenly though, you feel a disturbing rumbling in your lower intestinal tract. All that fiber, or maybe all those weird Tibetan goji berries, give you a sense of bathroom urgency and you rush, pseudomonad like, to the toilet.

After you flush, you create a bit of an aerated froth that forms on the uppermost layer of the toilet water. It's only a few hundredths of an inch thick, so the froth separates from the swirling water and goes soaring up where it forms a fine mist, breaking up into maybe five to ten billion droplets of water.

Gravity doesn't have too much effect on these tiny droplets, and the slightest draft or air current will send them jetting across the room, into the hallway and the rest of the house.

Most of these droplets evaporate quickly, but many house bacteria or viruses. These droplets will form a tiny ball around the microbe and stay intact in the air. Trouble is, these microbes are mostly pathogenic. Their return address is your bowels and anywhere from 60,000 to 500,000 of them remain in the air after an ordinary flush.

Some land in a few minutes, some stay aloft a few hours, while others remain in the air until the next day. As they float down, some land on the floor, the bathroom countertop, doorknobs, the sink...or even your toothbrush.

Some go into suspended animation and can survive up to 11 days until the water bubble around them dries up.

Go ahead and close the lid before you flush, but you know that quarter-inch gap between the porcelain and plastic? Ha! On a bacterial scale, that's about 5 miles high; plenty of space for that aerated bacterial froth to escape from.

Business done, you do some minor-league primping to ready yourself for the gym. You brush your teeth, blissfully ignorant of the bacterial haze around you and the fecal bacteria that have homesteaded your toothbrush. You primp your hair a bit and apply a little deodorant to hopefully take the place of a shower for a brief while.

Luckily, the deodorant coats and suffocates many of the round, fuzzy, odor-producing bacteria that live in your armpit. The deodorant might also contain some insecticide and bactericide — stuff that's as potent as the stuff in your garden shed — and that takes care of most of the others. Most die in 30 minutes, but some live as long as two hours.

However, other more resourceful bacteria cling to the hairs and escape suffocation and poisoning. Like tiny Tarzans, they cling to mucus vines, eventually falling to your shirt.

Later, as the deodorant wears off, your shirt will rub against the skin and you'll reinfect yourself with the odorous bacteria.

My point of all this is that you can't win. You can win the occasional battle, but you can't win the microbial war. In fact, there's evidence to suggest that maybe we shouldn't even try; or at least not try so hard.

Since the mid-nineteen-hundreds and continuing into current day, infectious diseases that ravaged mankind have been quelled by better sanitation, antibiotics, and vaccinations.

In the Western world especially, young mothers have done everything shy of turning their spawn into bubble boys and girls, each protected from the supposedly harmful ravages of dirt and germs.

Unfortunately, a lot of researchers are convinced this has caused problems. Their theory is called the *hygiene hypothesis,* and essentially it says that pristine environments don't allow our immune systems to develop properly.

There's an arm of the immune system called Th1 lymphocytes that direct attacks on invading cells throughout the body. The hygiene hypothesis postulates that the Th1 system can't get stronger without exercise, this exercise consisting of fighting infections or even through fighting harmless microbes (those found commonly in dirt and even in the household).

Since so many coddled children are kept from coming into contact with these innocuous and semi-innocuous microbes in dirt and water, they never fully develop their immune systems. Immunologically, these children remain 98-pound weaklings.

This, the theory posits, is partly the cause of the epidemic of childhood and adult onset asthmas we're seeing, along with conditions or diseases like allergies, and even such autoimmune diseases like rheumatoid arthritis and Type 1 diabetes.

I'm not suggesting we don't wash our hands after using public restrooms, but don't do it just because your hands touched your schlong; do it because it's a virtual certainty that a few of the hundreds or thousands of people who visited any given public restroom were carrying some really nasty bacteria, bacteria that are now likely on the flush handle, the door handle, or anything else in the restroom you might have touched.

Likewise, wash your hands before preparing foods and after eating them. No use making it even easier for salmonella bacteria to proliferate. If you want to use someone's cell phone or computer, wear freakin' welding gloves.

I'm kidding, sort of.

Lastly, if you have kids, throw them into a nice pile of dirt once in awhile, and in general don't attempt to disinfect your whole damn house unless you want to see your kid sucking on an asthma inhaler all his life.

Now excuse me, I have to go practice mountain pose.

Author's Note: The passages about microbial life in the household were inspired by the book, "The Secret House," by David Bodanis.

--2007

The Influence of Playboy

Playboy mags were never thrown away. They were carefully preserved and archived, like National Geographic which, ironically, was where men of the previous generation had gone to see naked women, even though their 3rd-world, sun scorched, gravity-abused breasts weren't quite as appealing.

T*he vaginas are disappearing! The vaginas are disappearing!*

It's the midnight ride of TC! One if by land, two if by sea!

The vaginas are disappearing! The vaginas are disappearing!

Hey, I've got photographic evidence. I'm not just some troublemaker shouting "fire" in a crowded massage parlor. This is serious stuff.

The amazing thing is that it took a woman to point it out to me. There we were, flipping through a recent *Playboy*, scanning to see if they'd discovered any especially tasty morsels that might transcend their centerfold status and become part of popular culture, when she stuck her finger smack-dab into a cellulose hoo-hah and said, "*What* is *that*?"

Momentarily confused, I didn't know what she meant...until I looked more closely at the vagina. Sure enough, it looked odd.

It was barely a slit. The color was uniformly the same as her flesh without a hint of capillary infusion. Neither was there a hint of the labia minora, which isn't necessarily that odd, but something about the whole package looked strange. It was just too small, too pale, too tidy, and too shy.

Maybe the Playmate was a veteran of the Iraq war, the victim of a roadside bomb that had blown off her vagina. Sure, they'd just fitted her with a pink-colored prosthetic made out of one of those old-style vinyl change purses that insurance agents used to hand out.

The "Playmate Data Sheet" indicated her ambition was to work with animals and to travel the world and that her turn-offs included "rudeness" and "bad hygiene" (imagine that), but nowhere was there mention of military service.

Hmm. I quickly flipped to the "Girls of the Big 10" pictorial. They too, had odd-looking female parts! Same with the "Girls of Wal-Mart" pictorial!

There wasn't a loose lip among them. No hoo, no hah. And in many cases, the top of the vulva seemed to have been lopped off as if some Puritanical airbrush artist had taken it upon himself to turn these flesh and blood mannequins into real mannequins, devoid, of course, of private parts.

What in the previously wide, wide, world of snatch is going on here?

Howzit gonna' avail ya', when ya' got no genitalia?

Playboy has always been famous for airbrushing away any imperfections, but it seems they've now turned their attention to the vagina.

Could it be that Hugh Hefner, in his old age, has developed a little bit of an obsessive-compulsive disorder? Perhaps Hef, in addition to having an aversion to excess lettuce hanging over the edge of his sandwiches, loose locks of hair, and a lack of hospital corners on his bed, insists that his hoo-hahs be as trim and tight as the sails on an America's Cup schooner.

Maybe you're wondering why I should even care what a dinosaur magazine like *Playboy* does or thinks. That's probably a somewhat valid point, but if you're under, say, 30 years old, you probably don't realize the part *Playboy* played in most men's lives while they were growing up. Neither do you realize the role the magazine played in developing our current sexual culture.

Hugh Hefner was 27 in 1953 when he laid out the first issue of Playboy on a card table in his Chicago apartment. He'd borrowed $8,000 and he spent $500 of it to buy the rights to some nude photographs of Marilyn Monroe.

This first issue also contained an editorial penned by Hefner. It described what was to become known as "the Playboy Philosophy":

> *We like our apartment. We enjoy mixing up cocktails and an hors d'oeuvre or two, putting a little mood music on the phonograph, and inviting in a female acquaintance for a quiet discussion on Picasso, Nietzsche, jazz, sex.*

What a load. Still, guys who were 50's and 60's versions of TV's *Earl* suddenly saw themselves as sophisticates, as playboys. Within five years, Hefner was selling a million copies a month. At its peak, in the seventies, *Playboy* sold over 6 million copies a month and it continued to thrive into the 80's.

Playboy also became known for publishing articles by famous mainstream authors, thereby allowing men to buy the magazine under the pretext of wanting to read the articles. Most of the articles were throwaways, though, and *Playboy's* lower-rent competitors were the ones that published the truly innovative work.

Prior to the widespread use of the Internet, men depended on *Playboy* and its knock-offs to get their fill of naked pics of women. There was no place else to go. And for young boys, me among them, *Playboy* was hallowed ground. With trembling hands, we'd hide issues in the closets, under our mattresses, under a loose floorboard, in our pants (*oh!*), anywhere we thought mom wouldn't find them.

But it wasn't necessarily whack-off material. Somehow, it would have seemed wrong to splooge on the angels depicted within. These women were to be worshipped as unobtainable feminine ideals. These women were the ones who'd someday shun us and tell us "drop dead" if we mustered up the courage to talk to them. As such, they deserved our geekish veneration.

Playboy mags were never thrown away. They were carefully preserved and archived, like *National Geographic* which, ironically, was where men of the previous generation had gone to see naked women, even though their 3rd-world, sun scorched, gravity-abused breasts weren't quite as appealing.

I've subscribed to *Playboy* for about 20 years now and I can't really explain why. I suspect it's just habit, or sentimentality. The mags occupy a dusty shelf in my closet and I haven't had any reason to look at back issues until now.

Looking at them, though, seems like looking at a naked time machine — a long naked conga line of beauties arching their backs into the pulchritudinous past.

As I look at the old issues, it's difficult to say whether *Playboy* influenced the feminine ideal or merely *reflected* it. A case can be made for either scenario.

While it's often said that beauty is ever changing, skin-deep, and superficial, that line of thinking is largely bunk. Regardless of cultural preferences, two things remain timeless and irrefutable markers of beauty -- facial symmetry and the mystical .7 waist-to-hip ratio, or WHR. If you haven't heard of the WHR before, Professor Devendra Singh of the University of Texas at Austin originated the concept in a paper he wrote in 1993.

Quite simply, the .7 WHR reflects the ratio of waist size compared to hip size. Non-obese men, obviously, have a WHR closer to 1, while non-obese women, more wasp-waisted, have a WHR smaller than 1, the ideal being close to .7.

Singh came to the conclusion that across the ages, across cultures, regardless of body fat levels or preferences for fuller breasts or butts, the .7 WHR remains a rock solid predictor of female desirability and it's tied directly to endocrinology.

Estrogen, quite simply, inhibits fat deposition in the female waist and stimulates its accumulation on the gluteofemoral region, thus accentuating the .7 ratio and thus signaling the primitive inferior temporal cortex of the male brain that the woman in question is as ripe and as primed for birthin' babies as a libidinous lagomorph, which, not surprisingly, just happens to be the *Playboy* logo.

For its entire history, the *Playboy* centerfold has reflected this magic ratio, regardless of whether you were looking at the American edition of *Playboy* or the Brazilian, German, Croatian, Italian, Polish, Japanese, or Taiwanese version.

Case in point, a female friend recently brought me back a copy of the Brazilian *Playboy*. The centerfold had smaller breasts and a bigger bottom than is typically seen in an America centerfold. Surprisingly, despite the fame of the Brazilian wax job, the model had a full bush, as dark and foreboding as the Amazon jungle itself, complete no doubt with its own pygmies and wonderfully colorful macaws that arise at sunrise each morning to fly en masse to their fruity feeding grounds before returning at sunset to spend the night in their cozy enclave.

Despite these differences, the centerfold had a WHR of approximately .7.

However, I've been noticing a funny thing in the American version of the magazine. In addition to the nipped and tucked hoo-hahs, the typical *Playboy* centerfold is *changing*. She's getting softer. She's getting further and further away from the hard body look of the 90's. Some even have WHR's that look to be approaching .75 or even .8.

Likewise, there's at least a slight, sporadic movement back to natural breasts. Butts are flatter and in some cases, flabbier. Omental fat has, in many instances, taken the place of flat, hard bellies.

Beyond all that, it's amazingly difficult to find a really sexy picture in the Playmate of the Month feature. Yes, yes, they're all naked or nearly naked, but the pictures aren't titillating. They're cute and quaint and almost antiseptic. In fact, the ads in *Playboy* are often sexier than the photos.

Maybe you don't have to look further than the *Playboy* West Coast Editor, Marilyn Grabowski, to figure out what's happening. Ms. Grabowski has been in charge of the centerfold for 40 years now. Working in conjunction with Hef himself, the two pick all the shots that appear in the centerfold pictorial.

I suspect that Ms. Grabowski, surely menopausal now, has long since lost her .7 WHR and is now, at least subconsciously, less in tune with what men like. Likewise, Mr. Hefner is probably hormonally challenged himself, despite the heroic pretense posed by living with seven beautiful blond women who, like the seven dwarves, must toil mightily to get the job done.

We jerk jerk jerk jerk jerk jerk jerk from early morn till night

We jerk jerk jerk jerk jerk jerk jerk everything in sight

Heigh-ho, Heigh-ho

Heigh-ho, Heigh-ho

Heigh-ho

(Whistle)

Of course, I understand that Hef has recently culled the herd down to three women. I guess we all slow down.

The inescapable truth is that Hef's and Ms. Grabowski's glands are too withered to recognize a truly sexy picture, but despite the marginal photos, the annoyingly formulaic features, the lackluster writing, the recycled jokes, the bad advice, pictorials of stars we don't want to see at all, let alone naked, and the overall out-of-date feel to the magazine, I think *Playboy* still influences the look American women strive for.

American women seem to have opted for a softer, less toned, less muscular look, just like the one apparently prized by the *Playboy* magazine of the 21st century. Personally, I prefer the slightly harder look of the 90's Playmate, but Hef never bothered to consult me.

Oh well, I just hope American women don't try to get rid of their vaginas, too.

--2007

Rogue Males

For some reason, we want our leaders and politicians chaste. We want them to screw their wives and only their wives for 50 monotonous years and then die miserable like the rest of us. If they have any sexual desires, we want them to subjugate those desires, or maybe channel them into something else like bowling.

"Si, si, the old man is here," said the Mexican housekeeper into the phone.

"Tell him I love him very much!" exclaimed the 18-year-old Cuban girl on the other end of the line.

The housekeeper turned to Alex and translated the message.

"She says she loves you very much." Then she dutifully followed the Cuban girl's lead and made some less than enthusiastic smoochie noises through her pouted lips.

Every Friday, Maria would call from Cuba to speak to her 50-year-old lover in California. Unfortunately, Maria didn't speak English and Alex didn't speak Spanish; the only language they shared was the language of *love*, or more realistically, the financially but not linguistically related languages of dinero and pussy.

Given the Mexican housekeeper's bilingual abilities, she'd become the unwilling third party in their long-distance ménage a trois.

The housekeeper listened intently to the phone, her face grimacing a bit at the prospect of translating the next few words.

"She says...she says next time you come, you don't even have to *pay*."

While the housekeeper was clearly embarrassed to share this last bit of info, Alex didn't give a damn. He didn't embarrass easy. He'd been doing the "Cuba thing" for years and Maria was just the latest of a string of terribly young hired girlfriends, all presumably looking for a way out of Cuba by latching onto some rich American's withered dick.

It wasn't like Alex couldn't find young girls in America. His American girlfriend, a comely little Filipino with one of those female anchorwoman news-at-six-and-eleven voices, was about 20 years his junior.

Unlike his Cuban girlfriends, Alex didn't even have to pay her, except of course in the traditional American way of fine meals, jewelry, and skiing trips to Aspen.

Alex only asked two things of the Filipino...well, two things other than fucking his myopic eyeballs out several times a week.

One, she always had to wear a little negligee while she was at his place. She came to look at it almost as kind of a uniform. As soon as she walked into his house morning, noon, or night, she'd go change into some little baby doll number. Of course Alex wasn't totally intractable on this point; he occasionally allowed her to scamper around his house wearing the type of panties and bras where the manufacturer's tag was the biggest single piece of fabric on them...*if* her negligees were in the wash.

The second rule involved high heels. She had to keep them on all the time during non-bed hours. That's a given. But even if she got up naked in the middle of the night to pee, she had to put the stilettos back on.

"I just like the way it looks," he'd explain.

Lord knows he wouldn't want to risk waking up in the middle of the night and see her terrestrially bound ass walking away from him. No, better to play it safe and have her enhance that brown bottom by perching it atop some 5-inch heels whenever she got out of bed.

The Filipino girl worked out real well, but if Alex wanted to go young, real young, he had to go to Cuba or Thailand or maybe even some former Soviet Republic where your dollar had more pussy power.

Alex, you see, was what I call a rogue male.

Now the word rogue has several definitions, but I'm thinking of the third most common usage, which refers to a mischievous person or scamp. Of course, the fourth definition, "a horse inclined to shirk or misbehave," isn't too far off the mark, either.

Like a lot of rogue males, Alex had all the rogue accoutrements, like a Ferrari and a 50-foot boat that was essentially a diesel-powered floating bedroom.

And before you label Alex, before you fix him in a formulated phrase, before he's pinned and wriggling on the wall, you should know that he was and is an extremely loyal friend with what's normally a fairly sturdy set of most traditional values. He just likes young women an awful lot, and his justification gland kicks in a little too easy where they're concerned.

"Hey, they're getting something out of it, too," he'd rationalize.

But Alex is no longer a rogue male. He got married and almost overnight, he changed. Gone are the trips to Cuba and given his track record, he's been surprisingly faithful to his wife. Gone too is the Ferrari; it's been replaced by a Prius.

He's still got a boat, but now it's an electric one that looks pretty much like one of those aluminum patio additions you slap on the back of your house. It tops out at a speed of six miles per hour and he and his wife motor silently around the harbor while drinking Pinot Noir.

The new Alex wears Crocs and worries about his lawn. He's a lot less rogue-y and a lot more old-fogie.

I have to tell you, I miss the old Alex.

Some of you are probably glad to hear that Alex changed, that he "got religion" so to speak. Others are probably sad to hear the stallion was finally broken.

Regardless, the new Alex could easily run for political office or be a captain of industry; the old Alex could not. And therein lies the schizo nature of us all.

For some reason, we want our leaders and politicians chaste. We want them to screw their wives and only their wives for 50 monotonous years and then die miserable like the rest of us. If they have any sexual desires, we want them to subjugate those desires, or maybe channel them into something else like bowling.

I maintain that a person can be a rogue male and still maintain high ethical standards in all the things that count. Hell, Gandhi supposedly humped the dots off his mistresses' foreheads. Martin Luther King allegedly was against segregation except when it came to women's thighs, which he was more than happy to keep apart. JFK came a lot in Camelot.

Even Benjamin Franklin and Thomas Jefferson were guilty of multiple sexual transgressions. And speaking of founding fathers, Cokie Roberts writes in her new book about how when one of the very first Congresses broke for recess, 40 illegitimate children were left behind in Philadelphia to wonder exactly which father had founded them.

More lately, various politicians and luminaries are up to their now blue balls in scandal — Larry Craig, Eliot Spitzer, Detroit Mayor Kwame Kilpatrick, husband of Michigan Senator Debbie Stabenow, and possibly the current gold medal winner, Formula One poobah Max Mosely.

Mosely hired five hookers, dressed them up in leather, and lightly whipped them while speaking in German. This was followed up, I assume, with some conventional sex. Unfortunately for him, a video of the party found its way to the *News of the World* website and created a huge blitzkrieg of scandal and ill will.

Jody Sheckter, the 1979 Formula One Champion, urged Mosley to step down from his position as head of Formula One, explaining:

> *"There is absolutely no question in my mind that Mosley should resign. From a purely motor racing point of view you can't have somebody like this running the sport or any other sport come to that."*

Well sure. Having sexual desires that aren't exactly vanilla means you're unfit to participate in the high-minded world of fancy dinosaur-fuel guzzling cars banging off walls and racing around in circles.

Personally, I think Mosely's party sounds like fun. He's getting beaten up further over the Nazi overtones, but hell, if you're going to whip a hooker with a cat-o-nine tail, it makes *sense* to speak German. Just try and whip a hooker while using, say, an Irish accent. You'd break out laughing:

> *Duz yer arse be wantin a feckin baytin? Der, you durtee thang, that'll larn ya for takin the shillin of a daycent chap like me.*

See? Doesn't work a lick.

And forget the humiliation and fall from grandeur that men caught in sex scandals experience, I think the first thing they think of, the first regret, comes not from anticipation of the inevitable shitstorm, but the realization that they're probably never going to be able to have this kind of fun again. Nope, it's back to conventional sex — if any — for the rest of their hellish days.

Unbeknownst to most, Barack Obama is at least partly in the place he is because of a sexual scandal. Now I certainly don't want to diminish Barack's accomplishments, at least partly because I owe him a debt of gratitude. Thanks to him, I can now say, "rhymes with Obama" when people want to know how to pronounce my last name.

I used to say, "rhymes with *Osama*," but that always aroused suspicions that I was a blond Jihadist and people would sneak peeks at my Skechers to see if they were harboring some C-4 and a burning fuse.

Anyhow, most people don't remember that Obama's opposition candidate in the 2004 Illinois Senatorial race was one Jack Ryan, who'd been famously married to actress Jeri Ryan, who's better known as Borgbabe Seven of Nine of *Star Trek:Voyager* fame.

Candidate Ryan was forced to hang up his Senatorial aspirations when it was revealed that he'd taken Seven to private sex clubs in several cities and tried to talk her into assimilating his cock in public.

Barack Obama was left to seek the office pretty much uncontested.

Again, having sex with your wife in public sounds kind of fun, especially if, like Jeri Ryan, she's endowed with Borg nanotechnology in the chestal area. Anyhow, this slightly roguish behavior certainly isn't a reason to shelve your ambitions to public service.

I think we should give (and get) a pass on most sexual conduct. Sexual transgressions should be judged and sentenced by affected spouses and the Almighty, not popular opinion.

Needless to say, I'm not talking about gross sexual misconduct like rape, molestation, or blackmail/coercion; I'm talking about the stuff that most of us have lying just underneath the surface, the slightly kinky stuff, the roguish stuff.

I mean, really, who among us is totally pure? Sure, the best of us will probably quell the sexual beasts, but if the occasional dip into kink is the worst part of your character, is that reason enough to kill your career, your life?

If I can offer myself as an example, think of the stuff I've written in the past. Think of the stuff I've written in this particular column. Any of it would disqualify me for a run at public office. Any of it would likely disqualify me from a normal job in the private sector. I'm clearly deviant by conventional standards, clearly a little too kinky for primetime.

Of course, given the seeming societal pervasiveness of all this kink, kink might actually be the norm. Maybe we'd best accept this, lest we find ourselves with no one pure enough or chaste enough to lead us.

-- 2008

Married at the Spearmint Rhino

Oddly enough, I didn't realize just how much sex affected me until recently. I was like Scrooge, who, despite lugging around the ponderous tits and ass chain he'd forged in life, the one he'd labored at mightily, couldn't see it.

I was a sweat jockey, you know, a personal trainer, a jock. So who do you think they give me? The Dalai Lama himself, Twelfth son of the Lama. The flowing robes, the whole bit.

So we're over at the bench press. I hand him the bar. He sets himself up and nails it — big lifter, the Lama. He pumps out 10 reps with 400 pounds. Do you know what the Lama says? "Gunga galunga...gunga, gunga lagunga," which is natural, given the amount of iron he'd just pushed.

So we finish off the session and he's gonna stiff me. And I say, "Hey Lama, hey, how about a little something, you know, for the effort, you know?"

And he says, "Oh, uh, there won't be any money, but when you die, on your deathbed, you will receive total consciousness."

So I got that goin' for me, which is nice.

But it ain't enough. Maybe Carl Spackler, who got a similar offer from the Lama, is content to live life rudderless, taking comfort in the fact that he'll get total consciousness on his deathbed, but I want it *now*. I'm not willing to wait for it.

I started looking for it early, too. I'm not talking about five-o'clock-in-the-morning early; I'm talking about 10-years-old early.

I wanted to know what the secret to life was, what the secret to happiness was. I started reading about mythology and religion, and later, philosophy. I studied literature; the good stuff they force you to digest in high school that permanently ruins serious reading for most people.

All I picked up were bits and pieces of insight, mere clues, clues that lead to further questions to which no one, it seemed, had any real answers.

When my parents had friends over, I eavesdropped on their conversations, hoping to glean some wisdom. I got none, unless you count the elements of a good martini as wisdom. I took a job at an assisted living center so that I could learn from the really old, who'd presumably, along with their dry skin and wrinkles and scars and rheumatism, also picked up something worth knowing.

It turned out they were no wiser than the average high school kid. It seemed they'd learned nothing about life. They formed the same cliques, had the same insipid rivalries, the same stupid conversations, and the same obsessions over whether their next cafeteria meal consisted of beanie weenies or sloppy Joes.

I took meditation courses, repeating mantras until my pulse was on par with a hibernating turtle, but it gave me no insight to life.

In fact I got nada. Granted, I could spit out little philosophical one-liners all day long, but it didn't amount to anything. Nothing I'd read had given me any real wisdom nor any real clues to what life was all about.

But there was always something holding me back, something serving as an anchor to my personal growth, only this anchor was formed not of iron, but of flesh. Yep, my anchor consisted of my dick and balls and the links that formed the chain that held it was a long conga line of tits and ass and tits and ass and oh yeah, tits and ass, most of it barely covered by really cool underwear with tassels and metal studs and stuff.

Oddly enough, I didn't realize just how much sex affected me until recently. I was like Scrooge, who, despite lugging around the ponderous tits and ass chain he'd forged in life, the one he'd labored at mightily, couldn't see it.

Just how bad was (or is) this roadblock to my personal growth?

At the age of 8, I started a scrapbook that had pictures of babes in it. I started lifting weights in the hopes I could get girls. I quit grad school because I was sleeping around so much I rarely made it to class, which is just as well because as a grad assistant, a bit of quivering but underachieving flesh came to my office and said she'd do anything for a better grade in English comp, and I was *this close* to agreeing to let her orally conjugate the verb *fellate*.

I used Land O' Lakes butter because there was a cute Indian babe on the box. I bought Mrs. Butterworth's because it's not often you see a bottle of maple syrup with tits.

I believed that sex was the most wonderful, spiritual, natural, life-affirming act that money could buy.

I not only had my bachelor party at the Spearmint Rhino, I had the actual wedding ceremony there, too. It was lovely. Instead of walking down the aisle to the *Wedding March*, the bride came sliding down the stripper pole to the strains of *Du Hast* by Rammstein, and not one person complained about how fuckin' ugly the bridesmaid's dresses were.

I even named my first daughter *Cameltoe*, not only to de-stigmatize the term, but because Cameltoes are one of nature's most beautiful sights, and it's really no different than naming your daughter Meadow or Blossom.

I worry about driving because girls in halter tops cause me to torque my head and neck so forcefully that I'm generally forced to book a session with a therapist, only the therapist is naked and uses her nonnies to rub hot oil into my body, but I have to be honest with you, it really doesn't help my neck much at all.

I collect Victoria's Secret catalogs and know most of the models' names.

My will has a provision that insists I be buried in a large crate of unlaundered thongs.

I buy neatsfoot oil not to condition my baseball mitt, but to keep my penis soft, supple, and pliable. Along the same lines, I periodically put a baseball underneath my schlong, wrap them both up with twine, and soak them overnight in a bucket of water, but I suppose all that belongs more in the cock-maintenance category than in the sex category.

I went to the San Diego Comic-Con last week under the illusion that I'm a comic book nerd, but when I got back and looked at the pictures I'd taken, they were all of babes, all except one of Leonard Nimoy. (Hey, we're talking about Spock, after all.)

And speaking of Spock, he only had to endure the *Plak Tow* every seven years, while I'm perpetually in it.

It took my latest "guru," or teacher, to point out just what a distraction sex was in achieving "total consciousness." Paul Hatherley, as a child, had the same questions I'd had, but he didn't give up as easily as I had.

He earned a PhD in psychology and practiced it for 25 years, only to find that it didn't meet his needs, didn't meet his patients' needs, so like the time-honored guru on top of the mountain, he went to live in the woods for ten years, by himself, to ponder the imponderables.

When he emerged, he tossed out his therapist's license and started teaching a "curriculum" for mental and emotional development, one that teaches how to make human life satisfying and meaningful.

I know that it might sound like so much new age mumbo jumbo unless I spent at least 5,000 words describing it, but that's not my goal here. Suffice it to say that it's teaching me to master my emotions, my motivations, my personal and professional relationships, and moreover, understanding living.

It's an absolute ball buster, kind of like being in a Marine boot camp for the mind and I'm continually reminded, in a kinder, gentler way, that I'm pretty much an emotional maggot while being metaphorically reminded that the only things that come from San Diego are steers and queers and then asked which category I fall under.

Anyhow, he's absolutely convinced my preoccupation with sex is holding me back, serving as a huge distraction. I attribute disproportionate importance to it, thereby diminishing the importance of other things that might serve me well in my search for mental and emotional mastery.

He became even more convinced when I told him that I keep my Testosterone levels super high using specific nutritional and physiological regimens.

He gave me some advice that I've been turning over in my mind ever since.

He said, and I'm going by memory here, "Have you considered keeping your Testosterone levels at a point where you maintain normal sexual function and health, but where it isn't such a distraction to your personal growth?"

Holy turgid tamale, Batman.

Now as a student of Mother Testosterone, I know full well that the physiological range of Testosterone is considerably higher than necessary to maintain normal sexual function, so I don't "need" higher T for sex.

Trouble is, I'm not sure I'm willing to be "normal," not only for reasons of sexual performance, but for a host of other reasons. For one thing, I'm a lifter, and maintaining mid-range Testosterone levels is like asking a basketball player to wear Crocs on the court. Sure he could perform, but at what level?

Likewise, I'm convinced that higher levels of T are good for you in a whole bunch of ways and current research backs it up.

There's an inverse relationship with free Testosterone levels and coronary heart disease; it's associated with improved insulin resistance, better glycemic control, higher bone density, and reduced visceral adiposity.

Moreover, higher T almost invariably leads to better mood, an increase in feelings of well-being, and that overall *joie de vivre*. Oh, and it also gives you the dick of death, meaning you can sustain a rebar-like erection for longer periods of time, along with having shorter refractory times, you know, in-between.

But there I am, back to sex.

You've probably guessed by now that I'm not going to go back to "normal" Testosterone levels.

I'll agree that high Testosterone is, at times, a detriment to my emotional and mental development, but I'm just going to have to regard it as a speed bump instead of a roadblock. It may take a little longer and I may suffer the occasional torqued neck, but I'll get there.

-- 2009

Like Hell You Could

Maybe the next time I'm given the "I could look like you" line, I'll just print this rant out and staple-gun it to the offender's forehead.

I lift weights, but I'm not a freak, not by a long shot. In competitive bodybuilding standards, I don't cut it by a long shot.

It probably has just as much to do with personal choice as it does my height or my unreasonable reluctance to Roger Clemens my ass with a lot of illegal chemicals. Since I'm well over six feet, I'd have to weigh about 30 pounds more to even come close to the modern, hulking, competitive bodybuilding esthetic.

In other words I'm no fireplug, but that's perfectly okay with me. I like looking good in a suit, even though it still has to be custom made. I like being relatively light on my feet. When I'm naked, I prefer it that women gape at my grossly enlarged and veiny pecker instead of my grossly enlarged and veiny pecs.

Neither can I haul, hoist, lift, or press enough weight to win any serious powerlifting contest unless I deceitfully hacked, wheezed, and phlegmed my way into a contest for powerlifters afflicted with tuberculosis or emphysema.

If I had to describe my body type or physique, I'd have to say I look more like a football player, maybe a tight end, the rare in-shape quarterback, or even a linebacker. I am, however, by regular-folk-on-the-street standards, a big guy, a "built" guy, a "buff" guy, an in-shape guy.

Non-lifting friends want me to go to the IKEA store with them so I can help them lift unpronounceable Swedish furniture into the backs of their SUVs. Non-lifting friends often point at me in any number of situations and say, "See that guy? He'll kick your ass."

I'm somewhat of a physical novelty to these people, probably a lot like a girl with really big tits is to her friends. Just as her flat-chested buddies tease her by hoisting up their tiny tits and pushing them together to make one good one, my non-lifting friends will often greet me by "making a muscle" with their arm or, worse yet, hitting a sad most-muscular pose.

Of course, with the big-breasted girl and her friends, they probably all strip down to their panties and have a pillow fight afterwards, so it isn't all bad.

But with the guys who "make a muscle"? They just snort and snicker at their wit.

Oh yeah, it's a riot. Humor at its best.

I feel like striking them.

Likewise, I'm big enough that strangers look at me and think *meathead.* The brave ones try to make conversation with me by talking about sports or the latest steroid scandal.

Mongo know very little about ways of world, so Mongo thank you for trying to relate to him on simple level. Mongo hungry now. Mongo want to know if you carry any lunchmeat in your pocket.

I'm sure a lot of you fall into the same sturdy Dreadnought of a boat.

The thing that bugs me the most, though, is the line the non-lifters, the Zach Braff clones, lay on me at least once a week. It's their attempt to provide a plausible but woefully untrue excuse for the condition of their ectomorphic or gelatinous body. Here is that rationalization, the one I hear all the time, the one I'm sure you hear all the time:

I'd look like you too if I had the time to work out all day.

Like hell you could.

But I don't say that. I usually respond with a tight-lipped smile and go on my way, but in their minds, "my way" is off to a long day at the gym or to the wheatgrass stand to quaff a liver, barley, and whey protein shake.

It's okay, though. It doesn't matter.

Still, if I were a vindictive or snarky kind of guy, I might not let that rationalization pass so easy. I might, *if* I were a vindictive or snarky kind of guy, say something like the following:

"Hey Ryan Seacrest, listen up. First of all, the notion that I spend my entire day in the gym, eschewing all worldly pursuits like women, assorted passions, friends, hobbies, business dealings, areas of study, etc., is offensive to me.

"But maybe your view of me is more charitable than that, maybe you think that I can spend the entire day in the gym and still enjoy worldly pursuits because I'm some sort of multi-tasking savant on the order of the Clive Owen character in *Shoot 'Em Up* who could fuck Monica Belluci while simultaneously engaged in a rollicking gunfight with a number of hired assassins without breaking pelvic stride.

"Fair enough, Soy Boy, but the truth is I only spend maybe five hours a week in the gym. I can do that because I know what I'm doing.

"Sure, sure, maybe you have your own little exercise program. Maybe it's some leotard wearing, mat-sniffing yoga class you joined so you could see women make bizarre but strangely arousing pretzel-like contortions where they aim their herbal-tea infused hoo-hahs at the celestial heavens; maybe it's your *Tap Kwan Do* class where you learn the ancient but hugely gay Martial art of emotionally disarming assailants through the enchanting beauty of tap dancing; maybe it's the 10 half-assed naked push-ups — the ones where your shriveled pecker barely grazes the Berber carpet — that you never fail to do upon rising...except on holidays or weekends when you really need to rush down to the cafe before they run out those yummy raspberry white-chocolate scones, but none of that's really a workout, is it?

"To know what I know, to do what I do, you'd have to actually read, study, think, and practice. I'm as in tune with my body and the precise motor-movements it takes to do even the simplest biceps curl as Tiger Woods is when he nails a chip shot out of the rough or when Dirk Nowitzki drains a 3-point shot from 25-feet.

"When you try to do a squat or deadlift or curl, you might as well be trying to perform a handstand on a balance beam. Oh, you may be able to approximate the motion, but your muscles are retarded by inactivity, a sluggish nervous system, and tiny little vestigial testicles that fossilized a long time ago, whereas people like me are as in tune with their muscle fibers as one of those strange Tibetan monks who can slow their heartbeat to a standstill.

"We can get more out of one set of barbell triceps extensions than you can from an hour of Nautilus pushdowns or pressdowns or whatever machines you have in your *24 Hour Fitness* center.

"You have virtually no knowledge of your body, either conscious or subconscious, technical or intuitive. You're like a drunken chimp that was given a car and somehow learned to crash it forward into the outhouse by pushing on the gas pedal with a long banana. It may not look pretty, but yeah, you're driving...sort of.

"So don't tell me you could look like me if you spent all day in the gym.

"Besides the factors you've mentioned, I doubt you have the *drive*; I doubt you have the character; I doubt you have the concentration to fully apply yourself to working out *the right way* for five hours a week.

"I think you have to be a bit of a killer to work out correctly. I don't exactly mean that literally, but I mean you have to have the makings of a killer who, by the Grace of God, was able to redirect his warped passions into something other than slitting throats.

"You want to know how most of us feel? Okay, here's a random snippet from the hard drive of our brain, apparently from a historical file:

'The greatest pleasure is to vanquish your enemies, to chase them before you, to rob them of their wealth, to see their near and dear bathed in tears, to ride their horses and sleep on the bellies of their wives and daughters.'

"It wasn't Hillary Clinton who said that, Slacker Boy, but one Genghis Khan. By the sounds of it he could have been a pretty good lifter. We don't of course hold with the conqueror's sentiments 100 percent, but it kinda *feels* right, you know? And maybe we're not really warriors in the standard sense, but do yourself a favor and don't test us. We tend to get a little irritable with people like you.

"People like us have a dynamism you can't comprehend. Go ahead, call us elitists; we relish the term. With apologies to the Constitution, we were not all created equal. Some of us are just plain better. What are you gonna do about it?

"Maybe we're not really better, but what business do we have doing *anything* if we don't go into it thinking we're the best, or at least have the capability of being the best?

"That's the mindset it takes to do what I do, Princess.

"So the next time you feel like telling us you could look like us if you spent all day in the gym, either shut your pie hole or prove it.

"Have a nice goddam day."

Maybe the next time I'm given the "I could look like you" line, I'll just print this rant out and staple-gun it to the offender's forehead.

You know, just to save time so as not to detract from all those long hours I need to spend at the gym.

-- 2008

Rude Bastards

So turn your car stereo down, dumb ass. You aren't cool. You're Nigel from Spinal Tap, looking for a knob that goes to eleven instead of ten.

China is freaking out. The Olympics are coming, and that means the *world* is coming.

Oh, they're well on their way to finishing the venues and they've stocked up on Mu Shu pork, but the government is worried because China's citizens, by and large, are rude bastards.

Don't get me wrong, most are extremely cordial, particularly in social one-on-one settings, but things get a little rockier once you stray from the gilded palaces and go into the hinterlands.

The vast majority of Chinese think nothing of taking cuts in line. The world is their spittoon. Most disturbing to Westerners is that "holding it" is largely an unknown concept to Chinese men of all ages. If you've ever traveled to China as a tourist, you were probably hard-pressed *not* to take a photo that didn't include some old guy in the background who happened to be taking a leisurely dump next to The Great Wall while puffing on a cigarette.

It makes me want to write the Photo Shop people and suggest a feature where by clicking on an icon of a Chinese guy crapping, you can instantly replace the offending image with a flowering pistachio tree.

Oh, and Chinese babies? They don't wear diapers. Instead, they wear these little crotchless pants — *kai dang ku* — and when they go, the mother or father just holds the little pissant out at arm's length like it was a leaky milk carton while it waters or poops the sidewalk.

Your travel agent didn't tell you about all that, did she?

Bitch.

So the Chinese Government, in addition to spritzing up the place, is also trying to bring a little Emily Post to its citizens so that visitors will have a better impression of China.

I really don't know what they're worried about. By the sounds of it, American visitors should feel right at home...well, except for the minefields of poop, that is.

You don't need me to tell you what a nation of boors and bastards we've become. Guys like me — probably guys like you — have to be careful when we go out lest we run into some of these rude bastards and lose our temper.

Personally, I haven't been to a nighttime showing of a movie for almost 2 years. I go during the daytime, say on a Tuesday, when there's no one in the audience except a couple of depressed old guys and maybe the occasional hooker who's too coked up to get any shuteye.

That way, I can be sure no one puts their stink-bomb Skechers on the back of my chair, mere inches from my nose. That way, I can be sure to avoid some John Facenda, NFL Voice of God wanna-be doing a scene-by-scene narration for his apparently brain damaged friend:

"Pedro is telling Napoleon that he shaved his head because it was hot. He took a bath, you see, but that didn't help so he shaved all the hair off."

Thanks. I hadn't caught the *nuance* of the scene.

By going to a daytime showing, I can avoid blowing an aneurysm; I can avoid being arrested for assault.

I don't even go to ballgames much anymore because most of the people there are too stupid to realize that every time they stand up — almost always in the middle of a pitch — to get yet another order of cheese nachos, they obstruct my view and the view of about a hundred people behind me. By the time the seventh inning stretch rolls around, I've usually missed 6 home runs, three triple plays, and a suicide squeeze and I'm so red-hot apoplectic that my Arizona Diamondbacks face paint is running down my face in purple and teal globs.

I flew to San Francisco a couple of weekends ago and I bit the bullet and bought a First Class ticket so I could avoid some of the usual *coach* rudeness: the seatback jammed into my knees, the jockeying for the arm rest, and the spastic kid who's so happy to be temporarily free from his tether and padded helmet that he's chosen to channel all his joy into repeatedly kicking the back of my seat.

But *noooo*, the louts are in First Class, too. Some guy in parachute pants brings his wife and kid on the plane and junior spends the bulk of the trip running up and down the aisle playing Whack-a-Mole with the elbows and knees of everyone sitting on the aisle while his oblivious father reads *People Magazine*

Luckily, I've got a window seat or there would have been Air Marshals restraining me from ripping off his dad's pants, tying them to the kid and screaming, "LET'S SEE IF *PARACHUTE PANTS* ARE NAMED PARACHUTE PANTS BECAUSE THEY DOUBLE AS A PARACHUTE! FLY LITTLE PARCHUTE-PANTS BOY, FLY!!!!" while prying open the airplane door.

It's all around me. There's the moron taking a cell phone call right in the middle of a funeral — the dead guy's family no doubt appreciative that the ring-tone version of *Love in an Elevator* makes a fine musical accompaniment to the eulogy.

And there's the mutt in the crowded restaurant who recognizes the people sitting at the table next to me. He wrestles his way through the crowd and squeezes between my table and his friends' table and *stands there* so his overflowing ass is in my face, not just through my spinach and pear salad, but all the way through my free-range-chicken-in-raspberry-sauce.

Hey buddy, if your ass doesn't isn't a female underwear model's, I don't want it in my face, okay?

And as long as we're on the subject of asses, what's with guys who don't flush toilets in public restrooms? I can't remember the last time I walked into a stall and wasn't greeted by one of Mr. Hanky's relatives. Is this some sort of territorial thing? Some pathetic stab at immortality, your way of saying "I was here"?

The only humans who've reached some sort of true immortality are Richard Nixon and the Apollo 11 astronauts, whose signatures are on a plaque that was left on the moon. Leaving a pile of doodie floating in a toilet bowl is hardly the same thing.

The Internet is almost worse than real life. While telling someone to "fuck off" takes effort in real life — you have to put your pants on and leave the house and raise your middle finger — telling someone to *fuck off* on the Internet is oh-so easy. According to moderators on most sites, *fuck off* is apparently the most popular message, right up there with "I'd hit it!" but hardly as congenial.

For some reason, most of the rude bastards also have gym memberships. Of course, the gym is just a microcosm of the real world and it's natural that rudeness would feel just as homey there.

The list of rude acts is long: the weights that weren't put away; bumping into you while you're in the middle of some movement where balance and concentration are crucial; breaking wind right next to you and then doing a quick vamoose so that the cute girl doing dumbbell curls thinks you did it; personal trainers shouting out the rep count for his or her numerically challenged fat-ass client while you're quietly trying to count your own reps; insensitive bastards drilling eyeball holes at the ass of every cute girls who's bold enough to do leg curls...wait a minute, that last one's me. Ah, what the hell, nobody's perfect.

And I'm not just sensitive to rudeness directed at me. I get mad when I see people being rude to other people, like waitresses or clerks. Hey, you think that you're somehow higher on the evolutionary scale than that store clerk? Einstein was a clerk. Madonna worked at an ice cream parlor.

Madonna! She of the beauty's where you find it, not just where you bump and grind it! You wanna' be rude to the next Madonna, for crissake? Do ya'? Huh? Do ya'?

Well, maybe you do, but you get the idea.

I'm a cordial bastard. I open doors for people. I say *thank you* and I say *hello,* but when I don't get a response in kind, I get pissed. I feel like grabbing the offender by the lapels and screaming, "Don't you know I'm the guy who would help you if you were being mugged in a dark alley? But now, since you didn't say hello, I'll hear your pathetic screams, rush into the alley, notice it's you and say, 'Oh, excuse me, carry on,' to the mugger."

But I don't grab his lapels. Instead I eat my anger and grow a big honkin' tumor.

Maybe people got boorish and rude from watching shows like *Beavis and Butthead* and *South Park* and *Hurl*. Maybe they don't get that breaching behavioral norms in this way is funny on TV, but it's not all that funny in real life.

Maybe we're all suffering from an entitlement disorder. If we didn't get served right away, if the raspberry scones were gone and all that were left were cranberry, if traffic didn't clear out of our way, if the very heavens didn't break open and shower gold coins on our head, then by God it's a clear case of our civil rights being trampled on and so we are going... to...get...very...*angry*! Angry and rude.

Go ahead, be rude, but I'm not going to save your sorry ass from being mugged, and no woman who doesn't have a self-esteem problem is going to bed you.

David Kupfer, a Falls Church, Virginia clinical psychologist says this about the rude bastards:

> *"There's a failure to understand their own importance on the planet."*

Amen.

Society often equates being a high Testosterone guy with being a lout who cares about no one other than himself. Maybe that's true a lot of the time, but I wish it were different. I know it's a pipe dream, but I'd love to see everyone, not just high T guys, adopt some of the notions of *chivalry*.

Keep in mind that I'm not talking about etiquette; you know, that stuff about what fork to eat your salad with or how to gracefully dispose of gristle at the dinner table. I'm talking about the medieval institution of *knighthood* where the knight was taught to be merciful, humble, and courteous...except when someone didn't deserve it, at which point he'd swing a mace at the ingrate's skull pan.

Yeah, Testosterone Knights. I like it.

So turn your car stereo down, dumb ass. You aren't cool. You're Nigel from *Spinal Tap*, looking for a knob that goes to eleven instead of ten.

Fuck your leaf blower that you pull out at 7AM. Toss it in the trash. Besides, it's a little known fact that there hasn't been any new trash produced in this country since 1963; we just keep blowing the same shit back and forth from coast to coast.

Don't cut me off in traffic unless you're rushing to the hospital because a loved one just got his arm lopped off in a tractor accident. You know what would happen to you if we were walking on the sidewalk and you suddenly leaped in front of me, forcing me to slow down? That's right, a foot up your ass. Just because you've got a shell of metal around you is no excuse; it just means you're cowardly.

Turn your cell phone off. We don't care if your stockbroker is trying to get a hold of you because Amalgamated Panty Shields just went up half a point. We're going to dinner to enjoy ourselves, not to listen to your drivel.

Just think about someone else for once. I could go on for pages. So could you.

I'm telling you, being polite is *bad ass*. Being polite keeps your food from being spit into. Being polite gets you favors. Being polite would allow me to go to a ballgame again. Being polite gets you *laid*, despite what you hear about bad boys getting all the chicks. Bad boys might get laid *once*, but polite boys — chivalrous boys — get invited back again, especially if they say, "Thank you for that fine piece of ass, miss."

(And if she's equally courteous, she'll respond, "You are welcome, fine sir. Prithee come into my chamber and partake of my fine ass again.")

See? All good stuff.

Thank you for reading this.

-- 2008

My Speech to the Graduates, 2010

That's why you don't want to admit that someone's right and you're wrong. It's damaging to your self-esteem. It actually hurts. It hurts so much that you tend to select friends who support you and agree with you. It hurts so much that you select books, blogs, websites, magazines, political figures, radio stations, and television stations that support your firmly entrenched ideas, feelings, and beliefs.

Honored guests, lusty ladies, distinguished bad-ass members of the faculty, and graduating students of the Testosterone Academy of Big Swingin' Balls, I'm honored to have been chosen to speak to you this afternoon.

I'm going to do something a little different today. This speech may be wildly misunderstood or just plain wildly disliked. Most of my previous graduation speeches have been lighter fare, like a nice chicken broth with corn niblets floating on top. This one, however, may be perceived as a heavier meal, something like a hearty stew made thick with monkey brain puree.

Likewise, I'm fully aware that some of my offerings take the listener somewhere profound, but most often they take the unfortunate person behind the railroad tracks, de-pants him, jam a clump of freshly unearthed Jimson weed between his butt cheeks, take any money he might have, and then leave the ersatz potted-plant of a listener lying there feeling cheap and humiliated.

I sincerely hope this speech is an example of the former instead of the latter.

Not long ago, I read an interview with two accomplished powerlifters.

They told about how they were both flying to a symposium and one of them said that the coolest thing about flying was the virtual certainty that they'd be "the strongest motherfuckers on the plane."

That story was fresh in my mind when I went to a choral recital at the local Episcopal Church. A troupe of gifted vocalists was performing a selection of Bach *motets*, which are choral compositions of sacred texts.

Between the choralists, the musicians, and the audience, you had a low-Testosterone mélange of geezers, geeks, pencil-necked music students, high-pitched castrati, and pale, thin, bespectacled girls in plaid skirts and black turtlenecks.

I looked around, puffed out my chest, and thought, "I'm the strongest motherfucker at this Bach recital."

Okay, so being the strongest motherfucker at a Bach recital ain't no great shakes. It's like being the best tambourine player in a group of deaf double-amputees.

More importantly, though, is why I'd even *care* about being the strongest motherfucker in the church, or for that matter, anywhere outside a powerlifting competition or in an anxious crowd of nerds at Best Buy jostling to grab the last copy of the Blu-Ray release of *Avatar*.

By the way, if you've ever wanted to use the line, "I have already chosen, but this female must choose me," to get laid, even in a crowd of *Avatar* nerds at Best Buy, don't bother. It doesn't work.

Anyway, it's my observation that wanting to be the strongest guy in a crowd, or the smartest guy, stems from some sort of neurotic, but perfectly "normal" need to feel superior. It's your ego's effort to raise its grimacing head above the crowd and implore the otherwise uncaring universe that you're somehow *spay-shul*.

(And this isn't a dig against the two powerlifters; I think they'd agree with me; I hope to God they agree with me.)

It's just another form of competition, the stark reality being that most of your other avenues of competition are gone because mom sold the Yahtzee game at the last garage sale and your Ping Pong table is now being used to support your dad's model train set and your Wii is on the fritz because, during a raucous session of Rockstar, your hand got sweaty and the wand flew out the window, fell 8 stories, and hit some hooker on the head, after which she hollowed it out and used it as a meth pipe.

Sure, sure, competition is normal. It's hormonal, neurological, sociological, and historical. But it sure has fudged things up in the arena of human discourse.

Next time you're at a restaurant or coffee shop, listen to the people next to you; watch a political talk show on television; log onto any forum on practically any Internet site in the world and you'll immediately see what I'm talking about.

I know I've pointed this out before, but people don't converse; they have dueling monologues, monologues about whether your opponent's political party is made up of Fascists or Pinkos; whether the Yankees are better than the Sox; whether your god is mightier than his god, or whether she's the selfish one for only granting you sex once or twice a week or whether you're the selfish one for wanting sex twice a day.

I say what I think but you're not listening because your views are right, by God, and you're just being semi-polite and waiting for a brief interlude, a little gap in my discourse so you can verbally crowbar your way back in and take the lead.

And then I watch your lips move, formulate my next response—without really listening to what you're saying—and wait to jam in my verbal crowbar once again.

Beyond that, you're most likely—if you're like 99% of the rest of the population—talking out of your ass. You're simply regurgitating ideas, beliefs, or, puke, feelings.

Most often, these ideas, beliefs, or feelings were formed in the cauldrons of childhood, cast by your parents, your older siblings, your schoolteachers, your clergy or religious figures, the books that were lying around, the TV stations that were left on, or your peers.

Usually, it was done so efficiently that you pretty much decided you'd never have to think again.

Unfortunately, if anyone has a belief based on ideas or feelings instead of facts, then having a discussion with that person is moot. Say that person thinks that Kim Kardashian is the human avatar of a Supreme Being and that once we die, our souls are stored in her infinite ass. Say that person thinks one political party is good and the other is daft.

There's about as much chance of changing that person's mind as there is of the old man on the *Pawn Stars* TV show paying big bucks for a retainer once allegedly worn by teen heartthrob, Justin Bieber.

Ideas and beliefs are formed in the imagination. Feelings are a reaction to something. Each is complete upon creation. In other words, they sprang out of Zeus' head fully formed. No matter what you say, what evidence you produce to the contrary, you can't sway a person from an idea, a belief, or a feeling.

Those notions are set in concrete, sheathed in copper, and formed into a giant decorative lawn jockey that's holding a "gone-out-of-business" sign.

But there's another formidable roadblock to understanding and it has to do with what's known as *loss-aversion*.

A few years back, a couple of wild and wooly psychologists by the name of Kahneman and Tversky conducted an experiment with two groups of physicians. Doctors in both groups were asked to choose between two ways to treat an epidemic. For both groups, option A remained the same, but each group had an option B that was described differently for each group.

Option B, for one group, was described as saving 200 out of 600 lives. For the other group, the same option was described as allowing 400 out of the 600 to die.

The "saving 200 lives" option was chosen by 72% of the doctors, whereas when the same option was framed negatively as letting 400 out of the 600 die, only 22% chose it.

It's obviously the same scenario, but framed two different ways, one "positive" and one "negative."

Why did saving 200 lives sound so much better than losing 400? According to Kahneman, "In human decision making, loss looms larger than gain."

Jonah Lehrer, author of "How We Decide," took the observation further, suggesting that loss aversion looms not only in hypothetical situations, gambling, or investing, but also partnerships, whether they're personal, romantic, or business.

In fact, Lehrer says that for such a relationship to be sustainable, positive outcomes have to outweigh negative ones by five to one. Why five to one? Because negative encounters strike the individual as five times more significant than positive ones.

This loss-aversion reaction is thought to extend to all sorts of scenarios. Every discouragement, every little inadvertent slight dealt by a friend, business partner, or lover, registers as a loss.

That's why you don't want to admit that someone's right and you're wrong. It's damaging to your self-esteem. It actually *hurts*.

It hurts so much that you tend to select friends who support you and agree with you. It hurts so much that you select books, blogs, websites, magazines, political figures, radio stations, and television stations that support your firmly entrenched ideas, feelings, and beliefs.

Similarly, loss aversion probably makes people seek to justify their prejudice (against anything) by exaggerating real or imagined differences between the person or group with which they disagree with, or wish to exploit.

And people use this same perverted process to judge religions, political groups, businesses or business practices, and even friends, lovers, or family.

And if you stumble on someone who disagrees with your ideas, feelings, and beliefs? Why you get sanctimonious, of course. You don't just attack the view, you attack the person who holds the view. He's a cocksucker! She's a stupid moron!

To do otherwise, to listen, perhaps to reshape your ideas, beliefs, and feelings would involve too much pain, too much damage to your self-esteem, and not satisfy your need to compete at all.

And so people continue to have their dueling monologues and nothing gets resolved, nothing changes, nothing is learned and confusion and dissatisfaction reign forever and ever.

And this is what we see today, maybe more so than ever. It seems that everybody disagrees vehemently with some real or imagined enemy. Screaming and insulting each other is the national sport, and currently in the standings the Cocksuckers lead the Shitheads by 2,000,000,001 to 2,000,000,000, but it's a seesaw battle.

It's fucked. Beyond that, if negativity or criticism were suddenly outlawed, the population would probably experience mass pseudo-aphasia, which is not to be confused with Fantasia, a condition characterized by seeing imaginary American Idol contestants.

So why am I telling you graduates this? Well, I'm hoping your brains might still be saved, that maybe they're malleable enough so that they can be shaped into a duckie or a horsie, or better yet a serviceable, well-functioning, even-tempered brain that works on logic and that might be a boon to society.

Maybe I can pull a Morpheus on you.

> *Morpheus: The Matrix is everywhere, it is all around us. Even now, in this very room. You can see it when you look out your window, or when you turn on your television. You can feel it when you go to work, or when you go to church or when you pay your taxes. It is the world that has been pulled over your eyes to blind you from the truth.*
>
> *Neo: What truth?*
>
> *Morpheus: That you are a slave, Neo. Like everyone else, you were born into bondage, born inside a prison that you cannot smell, taste, or touch. A prison for your mind. (Long pause, sighs.)*
>
> *Unfortunately, no one can be told what the Matrix is. You have to see it for yourself. This is your last chance. After this, there is no turning back. (In his left hand, Morpheus shows a blue pill.)*
>
> *You take the blue pill and the story ends. You wake in your bed and believe whatever you want to believe. (A red pill is shown in his other hand.) You take the red pill and you stay in Wonderland and I show you how deep the rabbit-hole goes. (Long pause; Neo begins to reach for the red pill.) Remember — all I am offering is the truth, nothing more. (Neo takes the red pill and swallows it with a glass of water.)*

Let me try to prove that most of you took the blue pill.

As I wrote above, most of us look at the world through ideas, beliefs, and feelings. Those three things also define our roles as a friend, mate, child, or parent. The trouble with this is that it gives us pre-programmed answers for almost any situation we may face.

You can check it out yourself. Do you have pre-determined beliefs on how kids should be raised, on how your mate should treat you, how you should treat your parents, or the role of government? Maybe you have religious beliefs that shape your opinions about the universe or life after death. Maybe you have political ideas that determine what people should do and what they shouldn't do.

And obviously, if you have these pre-programmed ideas, almost everybody else has their own pre-programmed ideas and they usually don't match yours, which is a perfect recipe for the war of ideas—WWE-like in its demeanor and cast of characters—going on around us 24-7.

The trouble with having these pre-determined ideas is that they shape your response to every new circumstance. As a result, you never absorb or learn from a new circumstance and we make the same mistakes over and over again, yet you trudge through life, taking great pride in your ideas and beliefs.

To me, that's just like being in the imaginary, programmed everyday world portrayed in the Matrix. It's fine for some people, but I'd rather have the truth.

That's why I took the red pill a while ago.

The red pill changed the way I see the world. The red pill made me believe in not believing.

A Yoda-like paradox you think that is, huh? Not really. What I try to do is apply the *scientific method* to the world, as opposed to processing it through the usual ideas, beliefs, and feelings.

For those of you who flunked Biology 101, the scientific method involves pursuing knowledge by using observation—sight, sound, taste, touch, smell, and asking questions—to gather information. The scientific method then requires that you use reason to draw conclusions, after which you create experiments to prove or disprove your hypothesis.

The scientific method can be used to accurately observe politics, business practices, interpersonal relationships, and ethics…even religion, if you dare. Practiced honestly, the facts are observable to anyone.

And the facts will stop any argument cold. What's more, they may lead to a satisfying discussion that changes and elevates both parties. Take for example the widely held belief that killing is wrong. There's no debating that, is there?

But what about in war? Is it okay to kill someone then? What if someone were threatening your family? How about then? What if someone told you he was on his way to blow up a school? You okay with killing then?

See what I mean? It gets tricky. Obviously, that wasn't exactly a complete example of how to use the scientific method, but it should show the shortcomings of pre-programmed thinking.

As another example, when I was a child I learned that Bugs Bunny could usually get out of trouble by dressing up like a female. I was pre-programmed by what I'd seen, and copying his tactic worked pretty well when I was a slim-hipped, golden-locked teenager.

Now? Not so much.

Anyhow, even if the situation defies being tested by the scientific method, can you see that having pre-programmed ideas is detrimental to intellectual progress?

Even so, if your purpose is to be competitive or argumentative, or if your loss aversion is so great that you can't risk anything contradicting your beliefs, nothing will dent your thick skull, even using the scientific method.

That's why I'm throwing it at you graduates. It might not be too late to adopt a mindset that is free of the bullshit that's been poured into it by all the well-meaning but usually misguided teachers you've had, whether they were parents, friends, television, or the rest of the usual culprits.

Now go out into the world, flex your logic muscles, and kick some ass.

With special thanks to Dr. Paul Hatherley, who offered me the red pill.

-- 2010

What Women Find Attractive

They also wanted bosoms bursting with milk, while women wanted a man who could break bone and tear flesh with his bare hands while having the skill to catch an array of tasty animals instead of just saber-toothed weasel, which can get damn tiresome if you eat it every day.

The next time you're seated at a dinner party and bored stiff because the conversation has turned towards mutual funds or how the local PTA really has to get its act together, discretely take the water glass from the table, place it between your legs, unzip your pants, and ejaculate into it.

Put the glass back on the table and wait a while, being careful to avoid any toasts.

Before long, the milky, floating, mucoid mass will actually start to look like a human baby. It may also look like a horsy or a ducky, but for the sake of argument, let's agree that it looks like a baby.

Okay, so maybe you don't want to do that in public. Regardless, this water-glass experiment was nearly all the evidence that 18th century biologists needed to conclude that this jism baby was the male's *gift* to the female. They believed that in order for the baby to be born, all a woman had to do was incubate the darn thing for nine months. She contributed *nothing* except to give the fetus a place to hang out and eat.

That's right, women were nothing but the fleshy equivalent of a muffin oven; a potful of dirt; a silky garden patch for man's seed.

No wonder men considered women to be nonessential. No wonder women considered *themselves* to be nonessential.

Of course, this only reinforced traditional notions of masculinity and femininity that had been around since day one.

Men were historically quite comfortable fulfilling the two basic levels of need described by psychologist Abraham Maslow: *safety* needs and *physiological* needs. Man provided his mate and offspring with protection, food, and shelter so they'd stay in good health and be ready for the next round of jism babies.

It's easy to see how these basic needs colored what man and woman find attractive in the opposite sex. Men wanted roomy, child-rearin' hips, preferably in the coveted .7 waist-to-hip ratio.

They also wanted bosoms bursting with milk, while women wanted a man who could break bone and tear flesh with his bare hands while having the skill to catch an array of tasty animals instead of just saber-toothed weasel, which can get damn tiresome if you eat it every day.

> "You know, like nunchuck skills, bow hunting skills, computer hacking skills.... Girls only want boyfriends who have great skills."
>
> — Napoleon Dynamite

These traditional views of womanhood and manhood continued well into the last century and the American cinema provides a celluloid testament to these views. The early matinee idols like The Duke, Humphrey Bogart, Bob Mitchum — all the epitome of traditional manhood — were replaced in the next generation by Steve McQueen, Marlon Brando, and Clint Eastwood.

But then something started to happen. Things started to get fuzzy.

Those tough-guy actors were replaced with Keanu Reeves, Tobey Mcguire, Ben Affleck, Topher Grace, and that blond-haired elf from *Lord of the Rings*.

Nightmare Scenario: Aliens have landed. They're harvesting Earth's women because they're good eatin'. You and a few other men are the only survivors. It's up to you and them to save the women. The names of your allies? The names of Earth's warriors? Keanu, Tobey, Topher, and Orlando.

Christ!

If you've got any brains, you'd develop a taste for roast buttock of flight attendant and join up with the aliens.

Do women even want masculine men anymore? And what the hell does *masculine* mean, anyhow?

The reason for this apparent demise of masculine men, in American popular culture and real life, may lie in an upheaval of Maslow's needs. Oh, the need for safety and physiological needs still exist, but how they play out has been changed. In America, women can do just fine without men, thank you. They have virtually equal opportunities for employment and the police and legal system provide a reasonably adequate source of protection.

So who needs broad shoulders? Who needs skills and strength and high-Testosterone stoicism? Yep, Darwinian theory has been sent packing, its possessions having been tossed out the apartment window into the street below while it tries to dodge the occasional thrown flower pot.

What modern American women need is someone to satisfy the occasional itch and, should they choose to get married and procreate, someone who doesn't mind changing poopie diapers who's willing to step in by God and start *lactating* should momma run dry.

Of course, why even get married? *Why buy the cow if they can get the milk for free?*

So what's the effect of this upheaval of social structure? It appears women are increasingly drawn towards men who look like little boys, or better yet, look like girls. Today's women are increasingly drawn toward *boy toys*.

In 2002, research psychologists at the University of St. Andrews in Scotland gathered together 34 female "raters" to determine the ideal male face. Their creation had big, doe-like eyes that were "expressive." He had a smooth skinned symmetrical face with a straight nose and rounded hair and jaw line. He looked kind of like Charlize Theron, albeit with an adorable little pecker, or maybe like one of those male figure skaters, albeit with a pecker.

Anthropologist Desmond Morris thinks this growing interest in the pool boys of America reflects women's increasing dominance.

> *"Smooth skinned and feminized looks are characteristics of youth. It's possible these looks stimulate not only sexual but also maternal feelings. If women want to be more dominant, they will look for a little boy face."*

In order to test this theory, I printed off two pictures, one of George Clooney who, by most standards, is considered to be very masculine looking, and the other of smooth-skinned Brad Pitt, and polled a number of local women.

I asked 6 American women between the ages of 20 and 40 — all career women — which face they thought most appealing, and 5 of 6 chose pretty boy Brad Pitt. Of the over-40 women I polled, most of whom were housewives, 4 of 5 chose George Clooney.

While my "study" was decidedly unscientific, the results fell in line with some of what the Scottish study inadvertently predicted. The over-40 women who were brought up with traditional views of masculinity preferred the chiseled looks of George Clooney, while the younger women, raised in an age of equal opportunity and female super heroes, chose baby-faced Brad Pitt.

However, when I asked 5 hot-blooded *Brazilian* girls — all under 30 and all recent immigrants — which they preferred, 4 of 5 chose Clooney.

Brazil still has very traditional views of masculinity. Machismo is as part of the norm as is soccer or Samba. The Brazilian girls still harbor those traditional notions of what constitutes a worthy mate: the ability to protect and provide.

But I also showed all the women a picture of a rugged looking bodybuilder who was muscular but not overly large.

The physique represented what most young men would consider ideal: moderately big, ripped, and powerful looking. It was a look that most men think would appeal to women.

Of course! Why, anything else is inconceivable!

Uh, not so fast, Bubba. My results didn't exactly agree with our assumptions. Before I give you my results, it's best if we first look at another, more professional study that was designed to determine what type of *body* women prefer.

A group of college-aged men were shown a male image on a computer screen and asked to manipulate it so the image would represent what women considered the ideal male body.

Most of the men added 20 to 30 pounds of muscle to the figure.

When women were asked to manipulate the same image, they didn't add any muscle. Their ideal image looked like a silhouette of Topher, Tobey, Orlando, or Keanu, the Four Cabana Boys of the Apocalypse.

When they gave the same test to Taiwanese men and nomads from the plains of Kenya, they had no trouble in figuring out what type of body women liked! Maybe the ideal Taiwanese man looked like Yao Ming and the ideal Kenyan looked like he could both herd goats *and* whip the tar out of Western marathon runners, but either way the men knew what their women found attractive.

Muscle didn't figure into it a whole lot.

Are American men completely misguided? We work hard to build our body so that we're more appealing to women, but what we're working for isn't appealing to women at all!

What irony! It's like a goddam soap opera where two lovers have conflicting life goals:

> *Lance: "Well, I've done it, Susan. I've sold everything I had and bought a McDonald's franchise so we can live here together in Bay City forever."*
>
> *Susan: "No Lance, no! I'm President of the local PETA chapter! I can't be with someone who doesn't respect animal rights!"*

Oh death, where is thy sting?

And my little poll didn't do much to dissuade the findings of that study. The American women over 40 found the physique picture "disgusting," "overblown," "unappealing." Almost all the American women under 40 thought the same things, a couple adding that "anyone who spends that much time on his body isn't going to have any time for me."

The over-40 women, despite having traditional views of masculinity, didn't have any frame of reference regarding the muscular body. Hell, John Wayne didn't look like *that*! And the younger women can't conceive of *mothering* something that looks like it was born of a crocodile and a pitbull!

Likewise, almost all the Brazilian women furrowed their brows and shook their heads at the muscular pic.

All is not lost, though. I left something out of my report. The women who I considered most sexual — more flirtatious, more flamboyant in dress — *liked* the physique in the picture. Even one of the Brazilian girls — one who I consider more overtly sexual — smiled and turned red at the notion of a one-night stand with the muscular body. Despite growing up with lean, lanky soccer players, she was drawn to a hyper masculine physique.

I also polled another group that I didn't mention: *hotties*. Girls who work out and had pretty good bodies themselves. They aren't that numerous, but they've got a powerful lobby. They were all over it. They liked the muscular body.

And while my "study" sure as hell didn't take into account whether the girls were ovulating, studies show that women who *are* often tend to prefer roguish, more masculine males while those that aren't sometimes prefer the *emo*-boys who can lactate when called upon. Good, healthy, masculine genes are still coveted, but once the uterine field's been plowed, women want a good, conscientious farmer to nurture the baby crop.

So hormones still rule. Higher Testosterone women are often drawn to strong physiques. They're also more likely to "get" the mental makeup of a man and enjoy sex as much as males. They might even help you jack off into that glass...you know, for science.

It seems that despite social conventions, despite societal and historical influences, biology trumps sociology, at least in some situations.

So don't worry. Keep working out. Your convictions are safe; your goals are still worthwhile. The women who are most likely to sleep with you in the first place — the hormonally driven women — are the ones most likely to find your body attractive.

And even if they don't, what the hell, there are plenty of other good reasons to build a great body.

(Special thanks to the book, "The Future of Men," by Marian Salzman, Ira Matathia, and Ann O'Reilly for many of the facts in this article.)

-- 2006

Fruit of the Loins

I have memories, or at least memories of things I read, of a time when children were merely ancillary fixtures in the household, like sofas or lampshades. Nobody made a big deal about them or ascribed to them any notoriety. After all, there were so many of them running around.

You gotta' come see the bay-bee!

I used to laugh at that *Seinfeld* line, but now it's become reality and the line ain't so funny anymore. I mean, it's been *ten weeks* and I still haven't mustered up the will to go see the damn thing.

I mean, really, what man is interested in someone else's baby? First and foremost, that baby is the living embodiment of some other male's success in mating. Mating is our biological imperative and the father of the wretched thing *won;* beat us in this biological imperative. We're the loser. We've let him succeed in perpetuating his genes.

That bawling, drooling thing will grow up to compete for resources, *our* resources. By the rules of the jungle, we should by all rights devour the baby right then and there, put an end to the humiliating reminder of our own reproductive failure and the eventual competition for resources.

Secondly, this baby pretty much represents the death of the friendship, at least friendship with non-baby friends. The dreamy eyed parents don't realize it, but they've walked through some *Twilight Zone* door of perception ruled by weird hormones and even weirder perceptions of reality. They're on a drug every bit as powerful as crack, but their drug is called *prolactin.*

More commonly known as the "nesting hormone," prolactin, much like cortisol, drove down his Testosterone levels. The father's become docile. He's become lovey dovey. He's donned permanent coke-bottle thick rose-colored glasses.

The father doesn't even know the incubus is sucking the Testosterone out of him. The day that thing was born, it somehow, either by its touch or its demonic cooing or even its mere visage, coerced the father's brain into producing more prolactin. In the mother, the prolactin causes her to lactate, but instead of lactating, human *males* start wearing goofy utilitarian clothes, the better to withstand the vomit and excrement they'll be wearing for the next couple of years; the better to make them less attractive to any other female that walks the earth.

He'll probably start wearing Crocs (because you can hose the puke off them) and the closet will be filled with all kinds of X-Vest like accessories designed to make tending to the baby easier, only instead of lead weights they're jammed with Wet Wipes.

Prolactin will compel the parents to sell their modern, multi-level naked-Jacuzzi party-deck paradise home with the great view because they don't want their child to do an Eric Clapton off the balcony, even though the infant's many months away from being able to crawl, let alone toddle. Besides, the yard is "only" a third of an acre, and apparently babies/children are like sheep, cattle, or other ruminants in that they need acres and acres of land so they don't develop sour gut or cholera.

They'll buy some ranch house in the burbs with 3.5 bedrooms and a swing set and they'll invite you over on Sunday afternoons and they'll tell you about the baby's wonderfulness. You'll hear about what a good eater it is. You'll hear about how alert it is. How the way it throws its poo against the wall is indicative of some future prowess in throwing the John Heisman prolate spheroid; how even its post-pabulum belches are as lovely and harmonic as some castrati Pavarotti.

They can't help it. They're like some old couple that took up canasta. They're really into canasta, live and breathe it, and when they're out with friends, all they want to talk about is canasta, so much so that non-canasta-playing friends want to kill themselves. Eventually, the canasta couple only wants to hang around with other couples that play canasta and you're thankful for it.

You might be stupid enough to invite them out to dinner, assuming that like any sane people they'll get a sitter, but you guessed wrong. They'll bring it along. Dad will be wearing it on his chest, the baby strung up on some modern-day contraption that's a blend of Hannibal Lecter's U-Haul dolly and an Arapahoe funeral sled that makes the father look like some demented rapper wearing a novel piece of bling, only this bling screams and shits.

If you're lucky, they'll have the decency to put the thing under the table like a piece of luggage so you won't have to look at it, but all the same you'll still be creeped out because you're familiar with Ray Bradbury's short story, *The Small Assassin.*

You see, Alice thought the baby was trying to kill her; kept crying all the time to keep her awake so she'd be weak;

insisted that somehow, it had learned to crawl months ahead of schedule; thought it had placed things on the stairs to make her trip and fall.

The doctor didn't believe her until he came over to the house and found David in a twisted position, dead at the bottom of the stairs. Upstairs, he found Alice dead in her bed. An electric cord plugged into the wall had sparked, blackening the wall. The doc follows the cord to Alice's bed, where he sees a safety pin has been pushed into the cable.

The doctor heads for the crib, but the baby's not there. He sees, though, that the wind has blown the door shut, preventing the baby from returning to its bed. Now he knows Alice was right; the baby is a killer. The doctor hears something rustling behind the curtain. He pulls out his scalpel and says, "See, baby? Something bright, something pretty... "

Ought to be mandatory reading for any couple, but they wouldn't believe it anyhow; the prolactin wouldn't let them.

And it won't get better when the kid gets a little older; it'll get *worse*; worse because now you can't talk about anything they couldn't print in the *Reader's Digest*. The prolactin will have approached more normal levels, but regardless, hanging out with these humanoid loaves of Wonder Bread is like being sucked into a G-rated movie filled with whimsical stories of dogs eating the family turkey and dad confusing the pimple cream with the toothpaste.

Puke.

There's no denying it, the friendship's on life support. Who needs to be exposed to that drudgery, that ho-hummedness?

Now I obviously used to be a kid myself. In fact, you might have seen me in *Jerry Maguire*. I played Ray, the cute little moppet who told Jerry Maguire the human brain weighs 8 pounds, which is a line right out of *TC's Big Damn Book of Knowledge*.

Sure I look too old to have played Ray, but I did an awful lot of blow with Mary Kate and Ashley so I aged a little quicker, but what the hell, the light that burns twice as bright burns half as long. And I burned so very very brightly.

So, since I was a kid myself, you might ask, why all the agitation over children?

My answer is that it's not the children so much, but the fact that the parents have made their child the center of the universe. These kids will grow up believing their needs are more important than anyone else's and there's a rock-solid chance they'll grow up to be the self-centered pea-brains that seem to be the dominant species nowadays.

I still blame it on the prolactin. Who knows, maybe there are hormonal mimics or hormone disrupters in our environment that end up increasing or exacerbating the release/effects of this hormone that make it more powerful or prevalent than in the past?

I have memories, or at least memories of things I read, of a time when children were merely ancillary fixtures in the household, like sofas or lampshades. Nobody made a big deal about them or ascribed to them any notoriety. After all, there were so many of them running around.

But let's consider marriage in general. After all, it often leads to birthin' babies. In fact, according to author Susan Squire (*I Don't: A Contrarian History of Marriage*), marriage is an institution created to regulate birthin' babies:

> "*Once people figured out that the endgame of sex wasn't ejaculation but conception, something had to be done. The overriding concern was to avert confusion over paternity, no easy matter given the universal assumption — sustained until around 1800 — that women were nymphomaniacal by nature. The solution was marriage, instituted in concert with the double standard: A woman could only have one sexual partner at a time, her husband, while a man could marry and/or fuck any woman who didn't already belong to another man.*"

While Squires agrees that modern technology has separated sex from reproduction, and even though the double standard has become, theoretically, a single one, she maintains that marriage is still the foundation of the family and that it still regulates sex.

But beyond the fact that marriage regulates sex is the fact that *hormones regulate marriage*, or at least successful marriages that lead to reproduction in the first place.

Just this week the *Proceedings of the National Academies of Science* published a Swedish study of 552 pairs of twins that showed that successful pair bonding — the type that usually leads to having babies — was related to a "bonding gene."

This bonding gene modulates the hormone *vasopressin* and levels of it are strongly tied to how well men fare in marriage.

Lead researcher Hasse Walum first became interested in the role of vasopressin while studying vole rats. Males with higher levels of vasopressin were more inclined to hang around and mingle with the female after copulation. Rather than eat crickets and shit on the heather, they snuggled and asked the female about her day.

Obviously, voles and most humans are usually quite different, so Walum wasn't sure the association would hold.

But it did.

Men with a certain variant of the vasopressin 1a gene tended to score low on a psychological test called the Partner Bonding Scale. They were also less likely to be married than men carrying another form of the gene, and carrying two copies of the gene doubled the odds that the men had undergone some sort of marital crisis over the last year.

In other words, low vasopressin made men, like voles, less likely to canoodle after copulation.

Interestingly, there's also a relationship between vasopressin and prolactin, the nesting hormone. The higher the vasopressin level, the higher the prolactin level. The same hormonal combo responsible for successful pair bonding is apparently also responsible for couples making baby the center of the universe!

Now there's more to marriage and reproduction than just the sum or minus of our hormones but it's a telling relationship, one I'll try to keep in mind when, eventually, I gotta go see the bay-bee!

Disclaimer: I'm not suggesting people shouldn't get married; I'm not suggesting people shouldn't have children; I'm not suggesting your child isn't the center of the universe; and I'm not suggesting people mate with vole rats, so before you get your blood all angried up, either read the article again or get your prolactin levels checked.

-- 2008

The Hadron Collider
in My Pants

You know the somewhat mysterious female G-spot that has all sorts of orgasmic power attributed to it? It developed from the proto-prostate. The same cells that develop into a prostate in men develop into the G-spot in women.

The biological Hadron Collider in our pants, better known as our testicles, are constantly banging out the dark matter we call Testosterone and that, frankly, is why women will never, ever, understand us.

Women — at least most women — don't understand the intensity of our biological imperative, or should I say, our false biological imperative. Nature or the Almighty put the imperative there in the first place, the imperative to bear offspring, but we done thwarted it by using rubbers and birth control pills and coming on her stomach.

As such, the sex drive remains, but it's mostly directed at non-reproductive sex.

Women? They have a biological imperative too; they feel some sort of *yearning* for a baby and they too have libidos and they surely indulge in their share of non-reproductive sex, but their libidos are still driven largely by fertility; ebbing and flowing based on when their eggs are most ready to be peeled by head-banging sperm.

But what's their yearning and their comparatively weak hormonal drive compared to what we go through every day, the endless, constant, all-consuming, destroy everything, risk everything, cut down forests, fight heaven and hell drive to get all the pussy we can shish-kabob on our members?

Maybe you've gone to a baseball game where they pick two schlubs from the audience to come down to the field and race towards a pile of one-dollar bills. Each gets to keep as many bills as he can shove in his pants, stuff in his mouth, and carry in his greedy hands.

That metaphor describes our sexually harried lives, only instead of competing for dollar bills, we're racing against each other to grab up all the pussy we can carry. If there were naked women lying in a pile instead of dollar bills, we'd try to cart off the whole lot of them, even attempting to spread their legs and affix them to our skin, hoping the suction would keep them from falling off and we wouldn't give a damn if the buzzer sounded when time ran out.

They'd have to shoot us before we'd give up. I don't know if it's heroic or pathetic.

Do women even realize the extent of these appetites? I think most of them think our insatiable sex drives are mere posturing, but you and I know better.

I wonder, if it weren't for societal constraints, just how far would men go in their quest for pussy? Would we ever pull the ripcord on our libido?

Look at the one-time emperor of Morocco, Moulay Ismail the Bloodthirsty. He fathered 888 children through his seemingly endless stream of wives and concubines. Lord only knows how many couplings failed or resulted in miscarriages.

If you ask me, it sounds like Moulay was thirstier for *bootay* than blood.

Or consider Chou, king of China in the 12th century, who built a lake of wine and forced naked men and women to chase one another around it. The forest surrounding the wine lake was strung with human flesh. Why did he do it? To please and impress his concubine, but I kinda' think he got off on it more than she did.

If you want a modern example, look at the current king of Swaziland, Mswati III, who hosts a yearly "Reed Dance" in which thousands of bare-breasted virgins vie to become the king's next wife. And before you think old Mswati is just following some ancient time-honored tradition started by his tribal forefathers, the randy bastard instituted the ceremony himself in 1999.

Hugh Hefner, 82-year-old Hugh Hefner, too old, too tired to sleep with seven women anymore, has downsized to just three sizzling hot women, any one of which most of us would probably trade our souls just to drape their panties around our heads while we traipsed through the Alps singing, "The hills are alive, with the sound of mu-sic..."

Who knows? Maybe those examples are tame and tepid compared to what a man might do if there were no moral or legal restrictions or if he didn't care about being ostracized and maybe even shunned by society.

If none of that convinces women that our sexual appetites are more than just posturing, consider what risks males in the animal kingdom are willing to take for sex.

The most famous example of this kind of "kamikaze sex" is the praying mantis, females of which usually eat the heads and sometimes the bodies of their mates. In fact, male heads are the staple food of the female Chinese mantis, comprising 63 percent of their diet.

Regardless of the risk, males don't waver in their quest for mantis pussy.

Or consider the plight of the giant squid. Females typically grow to lengths of 40 feet, while males typically top out at 30 feet. That size disparity in itself isn't a problem, but given that there's no way for the male to have sex with her without making her mad, it often proves dangerous to the male.

The problem is that the female doesn't have a vagina. To get around, or rather, *through* this problem, the male sports a cartilaginous lance on the end of his penis and he uses it as a type of hypodermic to pierce one of the female's arms. He then "injects" a four-inch-long tadpole-shaped spermatophore, which contains thousands of sperm.

While it's unclear how the sperm actually fertilize the eggs, what is clear is that it's no fun for the female. Fishermen often dredge up dead males, or just as often, their bitten-off five-foot-long penises.

Another proportionally well-endowed, but ultimately cursed, member of the animal kingdom are certain mosquito fish. Females of the species are irresistibly drawn to males who are hung, but unfortunately, their giant members create drag in the water, making them easy prey for larger, quicker fish.

Que sera, sera.

While human males typically don't risk life or penile limb for sex, they very often risk careers or marriages or bank accounts or social standing just to get some new nookie.

And it's all determined by Testosterone, a hormone that determines physiology and psychology almost from the moment of *conception*.

While popular belief has it that all fetuses start out as females, biologist Patricia Labosky of Vanderbilt University explains that, "You actually have the plumbing for both genders in early embryos." At eight weeks, both males and females have a proto-penis and a proto-prostate, as well as a proto-uterus and a proto-vagina.

You know the somewhat mysterious female G-spot that has all sorts of orgasmic power attributed to it? It developed from the proto-prostate. The same cells that develop into a prostate in men develop into the G-spot in women.

Some women have more of a developed "prostate" than others, and stimulating the spot in the right way induces them to ejaculate or "squirt" much the same way men do. What's more, the fluid expelled actually shares many common ingredients with semen!

Similarly, male fetuses keep some of their female parts. At about 8 weeks, the testes of the fetus start to produce Testosterone, which promotes the development of the Wolffian ducts (which go on to form the export tubes for sperm). Simultaneously, the male fetus begins to produce something called anti-Mullerian hormone, which "kills" the Mullerian ducts that would ordinarily go on to form the fallopian tubes, uterus, and upper part of the vagina if the fetus lacked a Y-chromosome.

However, the lower part of the vagina hangs around in males to become something called the prostatic uricle, which, as a duct to nowhere, has no discernible function.

Likewise, since there's no anti-nipple hormone, we develop with them intact, even though they're non-functional.

So wrap your mind around this: women have prostates and men have vaginas and tits.

Things get ever more mixed up when some sort of genetic anomaly swizzle sticks the DNA, though. The world is full of women who look, talk, and act like women, but when you examine their chromosomes, turn out to be men. They have Y-chromosomes but a defect on another chromosome makes it impossible for their bodies to react to Testosterone.

When his/her Y chromosome kicked in while he/she was in the womb, it prompted his/her then-neutral gonads to become testicles and start producing Testosterone, but he/she lacked a critical protein that carries Testosterone to the cell nucleus. Since her body wasn't "hearing" the Testosterone, she started to react to her mother's female hormones.

She developed a vagina and was in some ways more female than other females since she had practically no body hair and never developed acne, which most women develop from their small cache of Testosterone.

And then there are what the Dominicans call *guevedoche*, which translates to "penis at twelve" or "balls at twelve." These are individuals who, at birth, look like girls. Their parents raise them as girls and then, at the onset of puberty, it's "Momma-come-quick-Lupe's-got-balls!"

Here's the problem: for "maleness" to occur, you need Testosterone to convert to dihydrotestosterone, and this conversion needs the enzyme 5-alpha-reductase. The *guevedoche*, however, have a deficiency of this enzyme.

As such, they never looked like boys when they were born. Their testicles never descended and their genitalia look perfectly normal... for a little girl.

However, when puberty hits and there's a tsunami of Testosterone, what passed for their clitoris morphs into a penis. Often, the undescended testicles drop into place like rocks dropped off a highway overpass.

While the *guevedoche* are almost always raised as girls, they choose to live their lives as boys and men after the transformation takes place.

If this info has caused some of you fathers to cast a worried eye towards your tomboyish adolescent daughters because you're fretting that you put too much chlorine in your gene pool by attending all those smoke-filled Rasta concerts in the 90's, there probably isn't too much to worry about as *guevedoche* occurs most often in the Dominican Republic, New Guinea, and Turkey.

In the case of the male whose body wouldn't react to Testosterone, she is mentally a female and will remain so. In the case of the *guevedoche*, they have no trouble transitioning into males. The difference is that in the first case, Testosterone didn't influence brain development while he/she was in the womb, whereas in the *guevedoche*, Testosterone organized the undifferentiated fetal brain in a sex-specific manner.

Clearly, the key to our sexual identity is driven largely by Testosterone, and Testosterone is directly responsible for men being hounds, hounds of a magnitude most women will never fully grasp.

But there are those women who do have an inkling of what most men go through on a daily basis. They're the women who, for some reason, have Testosterone levels that approach those of men. Maybe they got an extra dose of maternal Testosterone in the womb, or maybe, like the alpha-female Hyena, their ovaries pump out a little extra androstenedione, which converts to Testosterone.

I've often written about this, but one indication of high-female T might be the length of the fingers or, more specifically, the relative length of the ring finger compared to the index finger. In men, the index finger, on average, is 96 percent as long as the ring finger, while the average woman's index and ring fingers are almost exactly the same length.

However, there are some women who have finger ratios much closer to that of males. The women with this more "masculine" ratio typically have fewer children. There are also a higher percentage of lesbians in this population. Conversely, men with a more "feminine" finger ratio have lower sperm counts, but there's no evidence yet to suggest that a higher percentage of them are gay.

It seems clear that Testosterone, while shaping our brains and genitalia in the womb, might also have affected certain skeletal elements, like finger length, but what about sex drive? Which is where we began this story.

Do these women with masculine finger ratios have a higher sex drive?

Watching two women make love is almost a universal turn-on for men, but does watching two men have sex turn women on? The answer is almost never, *except* for many of those women who have the "masculine" finger traits described above.

Catherine Salmon, a psychologist at Redlands University in California, recruited 40 female fans of guy-on-guy sex (they do exist) and 30 non-fans and measured their fingers. The non-fans had a very "feminine" index-to-ring finger ratio of 1.04, while the fans measured, on average, a more masculine 0.97 ratio.

I only wish we could determine which sex enjoys sex more. Then we'd have a more complete idea of the sexual nature of men and women.

Unfortunately, our only real reference point on this matter is Greek Mythology. It seems that Zeus and Hera were arguing this very point about which sex gets the more pleasure out of sex. Zeus thought women enjoyed it more, while Hera thought men did.

In order to settle the bet they consulted Tiresias, a man who'd been turned into a woman for 7 years before being turned back.

Given his unique experience on the matter, Tiresias said that women enjoy sex more, thus winning the bet for Zeus. Hera got pissed and out of spite, turned Tiresias blind, thus proving perhaps the only thing we know for sure about sex is that we should always lie about it.

REFERENCES:

Flam, Flaye, *The Score: How the Quest for Sex has Shaped the Modern Man*, Penguin Publishing, 2008.

Jacobs, A.J., *The Know-It-All*, Simon and Schuster, 2008.

Luoma, T.C., *Luoma's Big Damn Book of Knowledge*, 6th Edition, Penguin Classics.

Nieschlag, E., *Testosterone: Action, Deficiency, Substitution*, 2nd Edition, Springer Publishing, 1998.

-- 2008

The Little Death

It's eating Jack up inside! And then, then comes
the ultimate, Mike Tyson, break the tiny little
bone at the base of your nose and drive it into your
brain, *punch* — he realizes that while Gustavo
will be getting his rocks off *times two*, he'll be out
searching for an all-night drugstore so he can buy
the colicky, caterwauling baby a *pacifier*.

Jack's brain is reeling. He can't believe this little slip of an Asian girl just said what she said. There are things another human being can say to you that can completely short circuit your brain, things like, "I'm pregnant," or, "You've got six months to live," but *this*...this caught him completely off guard.

Her little off-the-cuff announcement feels like an ice pick to the brain, one delivered by a comely little assassin who clearly enjoys her work.

Forty-ish Jack is on a much-needed night on the town and nothing in the last year has prepared him for this moment, quite the contrary.

He and his wife had been doing great. The business was finally taking off and their adolescent daughter was growing up to be just the kind of bright, cheerful, and upstanding young girl that the human engineering specs call for. But then, out of the blue, out of what might have been some sort of liberal yuppie guilt, his wife decided to adopt a baby of mixed racial parentage.

And so, just when he was starting to feel a little freedom, a little success, Jack's been thrust back into the sometimes-stark parental existence. He's bleary eyed most of the time because of the nighttime feedings and his sex life is down to a trickle and he doesn't get to the gym much any more and his circle of friends is once again restricted to a bunch of similarly shell-shocked guys who've recently become parents and whose off-hours conversation is restricted to painfully mundane discussions of the superiority of one brand of stroller over another.

But on this night, his wife has given him a precious few hours of freedom with one proviso -- he has to buy a *pacifier* for the teething baby before he comes home. Fair enough. Anything to escape for a few hours.

So Jack and his single friend, a Brazilian player named Gustavo, are at popular nightspot. The women are everywhere and they're all supremely gifted in enhancing their physical strengths and camouflaging their weaknesses so that the bar resembles the post-production party of a high-budget erotic video. Every man in the place is walking around with dilated pupils, a damp brow, a heightened respiratory rate, and a southerly trending flow of blood.

Gustavo is hitting mightily on two women, one of them the aforementioned Asian. Unlike the stereotypically demure Asian, this one is a sexy Lucy Liu, but with a pair of the enormous attributes so highly prized by the Western male. She's wearing a tight button-down blouse but only the middle button is in use, thereby prompting many of the nearby men to collectively muster up whatever telekinetic power they might have to make that one solitary button pop off and spin across the room like one of those Chinese fighting stars, thereby exposing the twin emperors.

The other girl is a flaming redhead. She's wearing a grey denim skirt so short that if Gustavo practices just a little patience — waits for her to shimmy onto a barstool or maybe just *hiccup* — he won't have to ask if the carpet matches the drapes.

Jack is feeling left out. While he doesn't have any intention of messing around on his wife, he sure as hell wouldn't mind at least *talking* to a woman who didn't have baby vomit in her hair and didn't consider him to be just a tag-team nanny instead of a man. So he shakes off several months of rust and talcum powder and offers up the only lame introductory statement he can think of, which is, "So what are you two girls doing tonight?"

And that's when the Asian sticks the verbal ice pick in Jack's brain:

"We're going to double-fuck Gustavo!"

It started out as a flush behind Jack's ears, and then it manifested itself as a bubbling sensory soup of confusion that swelled upwards from his brainpan. It was utter jealousy and desire and regret and depression and immense frustration all rolled into one big old psychic matzo ball. And then this panoramic slide show of his recent life fires across his glassy stuffed-antelope eyes, the wife, the baby, the crying, the nagging, the exhaustion, and the lackluster infrequent sex, and then it morphs into a vision of Gustavo fucking with wild abandon! Only Gustavo is now Alex in *Clockwork Orange* and the girls he's banging while the William Tell Overture keeps him in rhythm are the Asian and the redhead!

It's eating Jack up inside! And then, then comes the ultimate, Mike Tyson, break the tiny little bone at the base of your nose and drive it into your brain, *punch* — he realizes that while Gustavo will be getting his rocks off *times two*, he'll be out searching for an all-night drugstore so he can buy the colicky, caterwauling baby a *pacifier*.

It's too cruel. It's too pathetic. He finishes off his double-scotch in one bitter gulp and leaves to angrily scour the town for a, *cough*, plastic nipple. Afterwards, pacifier in hand, he went home, waited for the light, went without the meat and cursed the bread, but fortunately did not put a bullet through his head.

I ran into Gustavo a couple of days later and asked him about his night. I gave him the requisite nudge, nudge, wink, wink, slap on the back, but he pretty much shrugged off the whole experience.

While he enjoyed the, "you know" (he makes a short punching motion with his fist), he confessed that he felt a little depressed afterwards.

I was surprised initially, but I knew exactly what Gustavo was talking about, only I haven't thought about it for a while. The French call it "la petite mort," or "the little death." It's a once-popular reference to orgasm. Most regard the term to mean the post-orgasmic fainting spells that lovers sometimes experience, but I think that's a definition favored by females, poets, and romantics in general.

The same goes for "post coital bliss" and warm after-sex fuzzies. These are feelings more common to women than men. In truth, most men feel the *opposite* way after sex, and it's something few women realize. After orgasm, men often feel depressed. They feel a little dead. And that, I believe, is the derivation of *la petite mort*.

But I'm hardly the first to point this out. In the mid-seventeenth century, the philosopher Spinoza wrote that "...after the enjoyment of sensual pleasure is past, the greatest sadness follows." But he was probably paraphrasing the 2nd century Roman physician, Galen, who wrote, *Triste est omne animal post coitum*, which translates roughly to, "After sexual intercourse every animal is sad."

I can't speak for squirrels and such, but as a man I know this to be true. And I don't know if this type of sadness is specific to sex, or if you can simply reduce it to the realization that *having* is often not so good as *wanting*.

While in sexual pursuit, our senses are heightened and there's a general single-minded purpose. The hunt is good. The hunt is fine. But, afterwards, when lying in the dark, drained of all that life affirming lust and drive, our purpose is less clear. Maybe it's the subconscious realization that there will never be enough sex or enough women to make us truly happy.

Something else became clear as I pumped Gustavo for details. He said he was tired of this smorgasbord of ass! He wanted one...steady...female!

Amazing. Jack wants unfamiliar sex and Gustavo wants familiar sex. Neither is content, nor is it likely they'll *ever* be content.

I hardly think they're unusual, though. We're all in the same boat, but when we're in that boat, we long to be on land and when we're on land, we can't wait to be at sea again.

We're pathetic creatures. Maybe fat boy Buddha figured it out while sitting under his Bodhi tree. Part of his epiphany was that the pursuit of pleasure is an unquenchable thirst; that it can never be satisfied. Give up the endless desire or you'll have to deal with endless suffering. I'm sure endless desire for ass was part of his enlightenment.

Trouble is, shy of cutting off your manhood, it probably ain't gonna happen. The damn thing knows what it wants, philosophy or religion or psychology be damned.

So we're left with a few choices of how to combat the little death. There's castration, of course, but I think that's a little extreme. We might opt for having a wife and mistress or two or three, but that can be problematical in that there just aren't a whole lot of wives comfortable with that scenario. Certainly, we could go Buddhist and try to put an end to desire, but like I said, the penis isn't going to go down that route willingly.

Lastly, we could just maintain the status quo and realize that the little death is only going to stop when the big death says so.

-- 2006

Happy Dress Like a Whore Day!

As any male who's ever stuck his snout out the door on Halloween knows, the holiday miraculously transforms the entire world into a Copenhagen brothel. The Starbucks girl, the flight attendant, the receptionist, the cashier, all miraculously transformed into wanton sluts!

Poor, miserable Ashley.

It's 4 AM and the alarm is sounding, just like it has five mornings a week for the last year and a half. If things go right, if she doesn't have to wait too long for the shower to heat up; if she doesn't spill any coffee on her blouse; if some idiot doesn't ram a semi on the freeway and cause a 5-mile long traffic jam of rubbernecks, she just might get to work by 6 AM.

Ashley works as a customer service rep for an Internet shoe retailer. When someone can't get the website to accept their gift code, or if some fat cow with poor reading comprehension in Bethesda wants to know if the extra-wide Mephisto sandals come in *taupe* instead of *bone* when the page clearly states that bone is the only shitty color available, they call Ashley.

It's not exactly the kind of work she pictured herself doing. In fact, if in junior high, some gypsy palm reader had told her what her future had in store, she might have gotten serious about her studies. That, or maybe killed herself by *inhaling* next to Mr. Hickman, the smelly custodian.

But the future caught her unprepared. She grew up to be a female Biff Loman.

So from 6 AM to 3 PM, Pacific Standard Time, 'Biffina' answers the phone in the basement of the Internet shoe store. She's a pretty girl, but you wouldn't know it to see her at work. Her mousey brown hair is a little lank because most mornings she doesn't have time to wash it and set it and poof it up with her Vidal Sassoon pro-vitamin infused mousse. Her dry eyes won't accept her contact lenses that early in the morning, so she begrudgingly wears her thick, brown, tortoise shell glasses that she's been meaning to update for the last five years or so.

She works in the basement and doesn't interact face-to-face with the public, so she often wears sweats, or at best, some J.C. Penney, high-waisted old lady slacks.

Ashley sits in one of a half-dozen cubicles, each populated with another girl who pretty much feels the same way she does. Management doesn't even know if any of them are alive. Neither does anyone else at the office who works on the floors above them.

But that was before the office Halloween party. She doesn't know if it was the alignment of the stars, something she ate, or the subconscious influence of her favorite slutty *Desperate Housewives* characters, but Ashley decided to vamp it up a little with her costume.

She scrounged around her closet and found an old ballet tutu, a winged fairy getup she'd worn in a grade school production of Peter Pan, and some outrageous high-heeled "bedroom shoes" an ex-boyfriend had once sheepishly presented her.

She tore, cut, shortened, hemmed, and painstakingly tailored each abbreviated piece of fabric so that any one who might have assumed her ass had flattened out from all those hours of sitting would be proven terribly wrong; so that anyone who assumed her breasts were anything but amazingly perky would get an eyeful of gravity-defying reality.

She poofed her hair up to its genetic potential, slathered on enough lipstick and eye shadow to shame a Shanghai whore, and climbed atop her towering shoes. Hence was the "Customer Service Fairy" born.

Other than having to hear, "I didn't know we sold shoes like that!" from just about every guffawing drunken fool in management, she had an incredible, Cinderella-like night. She even thought about leaving one of her "slippers" behind as a symbolic joke, but she worried that someone would trip over the towering thing and break their neck, or maybe drive their Hummer over it and break an axle.

Management might not have known her before that Halloween, but they knew her now. Within 3 weeks of that night, she was made the manager of the Customer Service Department. Within 3 months of that night, she was a Vice President in charge of new accounts, all because she dressed like a whore on Halloween and got noticed.

She hadn't slept her way to the top, but she sure as hell sexed her way up a few rungs.

But Ashley's costume was actually pretty tame by modern Halloween standards. As any male who's ever stuck his snout out the door on Halloween knows, the holiday miraculously transforms the entire world into a Copenhagen brothel. The Starbucks girl, the flight attendant, the receptionist, the cashier, all miraculously transformed into wanton sluts!

It's glorious.

While women don't generally sex themselves up on Halloween for occupational advancement, their real motives are fuzzy at best. Maybe you have to go back to the origin of Halloween to understand its evolution to chief boner holiday of the year.

It goes back to the Druids, a Celtic culture from Ireland and Britain and the holiday's roots lay in the Feast of *Samhain*, which occurred on October 31st, the last day of the Celtic calendar. Of course, if you ever saw the *Halloween* movie — one of the sad few where Jamie Lee Curtis didn't bare her breasts — you'd already know about the Feast of Samhain where the terrible killer in a hockey mask kills all the couples that fornicate out of wedlock.

Okay, Michael Myers wasn't part of the original ritual, but Samhain did signify summer's end and on that night the dead did roam the streets. Gifts and treats were left out to pacify the evil spirits, which would presumably lead to plentiful crops the next year. However, the dead soon got bored with candy corn, Mars bars, and those dreadful circus peanuts.

The dead, much like the living, want nookie. So women, in a valiant effort to erect the ectoplasmic and to ensure healthy crops, showed plenty of bare midriff and more cleavage than the Grand Tetons and perched themselves atop 7-inch heels, making their asses as easy to admire as a bowling trophy atop the credenza. Hence the holiday we know today.

That pistachio crop in California that went bad this past year? All because there weren't enough stripper-wannabes on the streets last October. You women out there simply have to quit being so...damn...*modest*. Don't do it for me, do it for the crops.

Okay, I made some of that up. I'm really not sure why women sex it up so much on Halloween. All I know is that you don't see women dressing up as nurses, nuns, witches, or flight attendants any more, at least not nurses, nuns, witches, or flight attendants that aren't openly displaying neon-colored thongs and Wonderbras with heels so wonderfully high, a lot of men would have to back up 30 yards and get a running start just to jump up and graze the underside of one of their breasts with their outstretched hand.

This evolution of women's costumes has been so abrupt and so wonderfully pervasive that it prompted comedian Carlos Mencia to rename Halloween, "Dress-Like-a-Whore-Day."

Even adolescent girls are wearing bare-midriff costumes with crude, built-in pre-fab breasts that probably make eerie spirit noises when adolescent boys squeeze them.

So what is it really that causes "good girls" to be so bad on Halloween? Why do women dress sexy while men dress like buttheads? Okay, so a straight man dressing "sexy" automatically elicits cries of "Hey, homo!" from his friends, but that still doesn't explain why women embrace their inner whore.

*New York Times*writher Stephanie Rosenbloom tried to figure it out last week, interviewing a number of professors, authors, and wanna-be hussies.

"It's a night when even a nice girl can dress like a dominatrix and still hold her head up the next morning," explained Linda Scott, author of *Fresh Lipstick: Redressing Fashion and Feminism.*

Pat Gill, a professor of gender and woman's studies at the University of Illinois thinks that showing off their bodies is a mark of independence and security and confidence," prompting the author of the Times' piece to wonder why gyms don't have "get in shape for Halloween" specials.

A friend of mine, a clinical psychologist who specializes in sexuality, believes that Halloween provides the "perfect landscape" for women to "pool the power of seduction without the obvious downside of being a real whore." (The downside being that they'd have to blow fat guys with scabby penises.)

Women who dress ultra-sexy are playing out "untenable urges that have been played out by women for the entire history of mankind," he adds.

And the young girls dressing up? He says they don't understand sexuality quite yet, but they do understand *power*, and adult men and women are inadvertently mentoring them into premature sexualization by telling them how good they look.

I buy into the power thing, but I think that's only part of it. Little boys and girls dress like their heroes or role models for Halloween. For boys, this often means a superhero costume and for little girls, it's often a princess, a nurse, or even the Tomb Raider.

While this urge to emulate your role models or fantasy figure doesn't dissipate with maturity, conventional belief systems about what's nerdy or gay don't make it easy for most men to dress like a superhero any more. Besides, few of them have the build to pull it off. So instead they wear togas or beer-themed costumes.

Women, on the other hand, aren't held back by anything, so they dress like hookers or strippers or sexually supercharged female convicts, police officers, or nurses. There's no reason to tap-dance, or should I say pole-dance, around their true rationale. I think they dress like what they are or want to be, and most of the time, it's a whore goddess.

I'm not saying these vixens necessarily want to have sex with undesirable men for money, but I think they do want sex and lots of it. They want to suckle the earth, swallow the galactic penis, and vaginally engulf Terra Ultra Firma.

As I've long maintained, most women are worse than males when it comes to sheer animal appetite, but society puts restraints on them.

In a lot of ways, Dress Like a Whore Day puts me in mind of the typical plight of many Japanese women, who are hugely repressed. They're all Ashleys, or what Ashley used to be. But when the opportunity to cut loose arises, they do it with vengeance.

It's said that almost any *gaijin*, even a Dick Cheney, could easily get the wasabi fucked out of him on any given evening in Japan. The Japanese woman sees the gaijin as *safe* in that he'll be gone in the morning, leaving her reputation unsullied. She can go back to being the dutiful little worker, the dutiful little daughter, and no one will know she spent the night screaming like Yoko Ono wearing a cold, brass, nipple clamp.

Halloween is a condensed version of the repressed Japanese woman's after-hours adventures; a chance to throw off the shackles of repression and don some real shackles, maybe some nice, sexy, fur-lined ones.

I'll readily admit that I might be overplaying the goddess whore angle. Maybe a lot of women are just like Ashley in that they're using Halloween to lash out against boredom and normalcy; to stand out and be noticed, even if it's only for one night.

Either way, we hugely appreciate it. And so do the crops.

-- 2006

Men, Love, and Sex

Would anyone with a functioning pair fall for that claptrap? It's patronizing. That's the kind stuff you say to little children. And really, if the closest your man gets to being an action hero is carrying in the groceries, well you've landed yourself a catch, haven't you? Do us a favor and don't procreate.

D espite being a part of the "fitness industry," I'm only peripherally aware of *Men's Health* magazine.

A lot of writers make fun of *Men's Health*, but it's in the same way mainstream writers all make fun of *Reader's Digest* – despite sneering at it, most would give up drinking rye whiskey to get an article published in "The Digest."

Similarly, most "fitness" writers wouldn't mind getting an article published in *Men's Health*. They also wouldn't mind paychecks fueled by the Jaguar and Porsche ads in the magazine.

Amazingly, *Men's Health* outsells other male mags like *GQ*, *Esquire*, and *Details*. In fact, *Men's Health* sells about 24 million copies every year. But like I said, the mag's been mostly off my radar for the most part, until last Sunday, that is. There on the front page of the "Styles" section of the *NY Times* was a half-page photo of beaver-toothed editor of *Men's Health*, David Zinczenko.

Apparently, Zinczenko is my spokesman. He's your spokesman, too. In fact, he's the spokesman for *Everyman*, declared the *Times*. My God, why else would he have been invited onto the *Today* show on 19 occasions? (Personally, I think he should be a spokesman for the *Scrabble* board game: ZINCZENKO. Holy Mackerel, that's 33 points, even without a double or triple word score!)

His reputation is as a "guy's guy." Even his former girlfriend Rose McGowan attests to the regular guy label, citing the fact that when she first met him, "he was using Irish Springs to wash his face."Listen Rosie, I once washed my 'nads with Lava Soap. That doesn't make me the spokesman of my generation. Regardless, Zinczenko apparently likes to cultivate his image as the anti-metrosexual.

"Metrosexuality is dead," declared Zinczenko during one recent *Today Show* appearance. "And good riddance. But let's be clear here: the trend is a tough calzone to swallow."

Let's forget for the moment that as Editor-in-Chief of *Men's Health*, David is the *mayor* of Metrosexual City, population: 24 million hamsters.

David ol' buddy, if you're trying to declare metrosexuality dead, don't use metaphors like "tough calzone to swallow" because it's something a metrosexual might say. You sound like Nathan Lane in *The Birdcage* when Robin Williams is coaching him on how to emulate a straight guy:

> *Armand (Robin Williams): Al, you old son of a bitch! How ya doin'? How do you feel about that call today? I mean the Dolphins! Fourth-and-three play on their 30-yard line with only 34 seconds to go!*
>
> *Albert (Nathan Lane): How do you think I feel? Betrayed, bewildered.... Wrong response?*

Regardless, the Everyman spokesman has made a bold play to be the Every*woman* spokesman, too, because he's just co-authored a book that tells women how men think: *Men, Love & Sex, The Complete User's Guide for Women.*

"Thousands of men confess their well-guarded secrets about how they think, feel, and behave!" declares the subtitle.

"You see," explains David in the opening chapter, "the truth is men do share their feelings — their fears, their desires, even their deepest secrets. They've shared those feelings with me. And now I'm here to share their feelings with you."

Oh joy! The battle of the sexes is over! Misunderstandings, gone! Conflict, gone! Men and women everywhere, simpatico!

Thanks to der Zinkster, we need to do no more than glance into each other's eyes for a moment to gain complete understanding, to grok each other's essence at which point clothes will magically melt away and women will exact the *exact* amount of foreplay necessary before a naked segue into transcendental sex that is as perfectly conducted as Leonard Bernstein's orchestra, alternating between precise amounts of slow, rhythmic plucking of her string section and just the right amount of tooting on the horn section, culminating in a cymbal-clashing mutual orgasm as explosive, wet, and fizzy as dropping a dump truck of Mentos into a water tower of Diet Coke, followed by the gosh-darn best part, the cuddling and noodling and spooning.

Oh puke.

Zinczenko wrote the guide after passing the results of 5,000 responses to an independent Harris poll through his lavender hued *Men's Health* filter. What the results say about American men, or *Men's Health* readers, I don't know.

All I know is that the majority of the people who answered the survey are quivering pats of butter and it's a wonder any of them have the courage to zip up their fly in the morning, let alone ever talk to a real woman.

Furthermore, for someone who claims to know how men think, Zinczenko hits the mark about as often as Stephen Hawking hurling darts with his amyotrophic laterally sclerotic fingers.

One female survey taker wants to know why, after being married for six years, the amount of sex between her and hubby has dropped off from 3 to 4 times a week to maybe once every two weeks.

Der Zinkster pontificates about how we feel pressure from our job, the kids, and even body issues, and we too wonder if we're giving her the sex she needs. "The rapid-fire sex machine we were when we first met may become more like popguns," explains Everyman.

Please, Zinky. This guy's been working the same terrain for at least 6 years now, probably longer, and it's hard to get the plow out when it's the same crop, every day, year-in and year-out. He knows her pussy better than he know his momma's face, so it's not the job, it's not the kids, and Good Lord, it's not "issues" we have with our bodies.

You want more sex, mam? Put on a wig. Walk in wearing a Catholic school uniform. Put on some dark makeup, a burka, and tell him you came from the Middle East to see if the legend of the Mother of all Penises was indeed true. In other words, give him something other than the run-of-the-mill; give him something *exciting.*

In another one of the books' 25 pithy chapters, Zinczenko lets women know why we're sometimes not as communicative as they'd like us to be. He explains that it's because we're "afraid to say the wrong thing."

I'm sorry, it's not because we're afraid, it's because there probably isn't anything going through our heads. It's like Capone's vault when Geraldo punched through the brick wall. We might be bored, detached from reality, or even confused by your yammering, but afraid? The truth of it is, if we're aware of you at all, we're fantasizing about one of those ball-gags from *Pulp Fiction*.

Then there's all the usual tired ol' fluff about men, why we change channels a lot, or why we don't ask for directions, why we sometimes miss the toilet (surprisingly, Zinczenko doesn't recommend men sit down to pee) and a nauseating amount of type given to what it means if a man calls you right after the first date or doesn't call you right away and what it means if he calls you the next day or three days later.

Sheesh. With all this agonizing, it's a wonder these people ever hook up at all. If I liked a woman, I wouldn't have any qualms about calling her right away. "Oh no, she might know that I like her!" If I get a new game for my Xbox and I have a great time playing it, why would I put it away for a week? What am I, some sort of wanna-be ascetic monk?

Hell no, I want to play it right away, and often, *until my fingers bleed*.

Besides the head-scratching advice, the book is peppered with saccharin-sweet, Testosterone-draining quotations.

Michael, age 30, believes "Men are a lot like eggs. Under the right pressure, we can withstand any stress you put on us, but inside, we are soft and vulnerable."

"I cry every time Lois Lane finds out Clark Kent is really Superman," writes Kevin, age 32.

Jeff, age 30, says, "A woman climaxing is the most wonderful feeling to a man."

Eggs indeed. Would that you had a pair, Michael! You cry during *Superman*, Kevin? You're a hamster! Making a woman climax is indeed a wonderful feeling, Jeff, but no more so than sinking a 3-pointer from your driveway, from behind the trashcans and over the defending arm of the old oak tree.

Adam, age 35, confesses, "Men are starved for affection for the most part — that includes cuddling, foreplay, caressing, soft touches. It's very important for a man's self esteem and ego to have his partner tell him as well as show him through notes, cards, and initiating love-making."

The only note I want from my partner is, "I'm bringing a friend home tonight. Get lots of rest. Oh, and wash that thing."

Then there are lots of highlighted quick-advice sections like SAY THIS, NOT THAT:

> SAY THIS (*to the hamster carrying in some grocery bags*): My God, look at those triceps!
>
> NOT: That goes in the kitchen, next to the window.
>
> BECAUSE: Home improvement is the closest a guy gets to being an action hero.

Would anyone with a functioning pair fall for that claptrap? It's patronizing. That's the kind stuff you say to little children. And really, if the closest your man gets to being an action hero is carrying in the groceries, well you've landed yourself a catch, haven't you? Do us a favor and don't procreate.

Then there are the noggin-scratching surveys. When asked how often men look at other women when they're with wives or girlfriends:

> 53% said, "If there's an opening, I'll take it."
>
> 28% said, "Only in extreme cases, or if wearing sunglasses."
>
> 19% said, "Never, I like to keep my parts properly attached."

What a fantastically trained bunch of poodles you all are! Tell me, do you know any other tricks?

Another survey suggested that the favorite fantasy of 68% of male respondents was "he's a patient, she's a nurse."

Apparently, nobody wants a threesome, anymore. Personally, I think the nurse/patient thing is only a rung or two above the fantasy evolutionary ladder of pretending you're a baby and you need her to change you because you just made a boom-boom.

I'm hoping that most women ignore this book because it could set back male-female relations hundreds of years. You think global warming is a problem and we've got to cut back on our carbon footprints? Well, Zinczenko has an *emoboy* footprint and it's about the size of Greenland.

And the men in the survey? I should set up a Testosterone concession stand outside the palace where these eunuchs live.

I'd clean up.

-- 2008

Back to the Butt

Eventually, women developed permanently swollen, hairless breasts, along with full, reddish lips. Holy mackerel! I don't mean to embarrass you miss, but you've got a tookus on your chest and a hoo-hah for a mouth!

What you gon' do with all that junk? All that junk inside that trunk? I'ma get, get, get, get, you drunk, Get you love drunk off my hump. What you gon' do with all that ass? All that ass insigh' jer jeans? I'm a make, make, make, make you scream Make you scream, make you scream. Cos' of my hump, my hump, my hump, my hump. My hump, my hump, my hump, my lovely lady lumps.

— *"My Humps" by the Black Eyed Peas*

Last year, 2,361 American women had their rear ends augmented. No longer content to have their jeans drape limply over their butt like an old bedspread hanging off a clothesline, they decided to pack some junk inside that trunk.

For the most part, they had their choice of one of two methods. The surgeon could either slide in a contact lens shaped silicone implant just above the sciatic nerve, or he or she could remove fat from one part of the patient's body and painstakingly inject it, globule by globule, into her Dickensian butt.

Please sir, may I have some more?

The first method has its drawbacks. The incisions sometimes break open. Infections are a possibility. And patients just don't like feeling like they had two giant George Costanza-sized wallets between them and the sofa cushion.

The second method isn't perfect, either. For one thing, the procedure takes from 6 to 8 hours, and since it's just as much sculpture as surgery, the results are heavily dependent on the surgeon's artistic ability. Hell, accidentally get hooked up with a cubist and you've got an ass that looks more like a Picasso painting than a *Playboy* centerfold.

Furthermore, the body eventually reabsorbs much of the injected fat — up to 40 percent.

In either case, patients have to refrain from sitting or lying on their back for several weeks. That means weeks of lying on their stomach, after which their breasts probably look like the Hostess cupcakes in your sack lunch after the fat kid sat on them.

Despite, the drawbacks, more and more women are choosing to pimp that ride. The cost? About twenty thousand dollars.

While surgical butt augmentation is relatively new, using artificial means to increase the size of the derriere can be traced back to Ancient Greece where women would actually perform a dance where they literally kicked themselves in the rear to make it bigger and firmer.

In fact, the word *callipygian*, meaning shapely butt, comes from the Greek word *kalliphygos*.

While this questionable method didn't survive the ancient Greeks, women in more recent cultures accentuated the size of their rear by wearing bustles, hoop skirts, and dresses designed to grossly exaggerate the hips.

It wasn't until the 1950's that doctors got involved. That's when surgeons from Brazil and Mexico started taking fat *cut* from the abdomen and transferring it to the gluteal area, but much of it was reabsorbed.

After the silicone breast implant was invented in the 70's, a few doctors started cutting the implants in *half* and implanting them in the buttocks, but the result was too close to some weird, four-breasted, hemispherically symmetrical creature from that nuclear fallout movie.

The 1980's saw the advent of the contact-lens shaped silicone implants specifically designed for the derriere, but there just weren't that many women interested in having the procedure, at least in America, where breasts have been king of the hill, or hills, for a long, long time. Most of the women that initially wanted butt implants were either Brazilian or Mexican, where the ass has always had more allure than the breasts.

Enter the 1990's. Enter J-Lo.

My friend, retired plastic surgeon Bruce Nadler, one of the ass-implant pioneers, says, "J-Lo did for the butt implant what Pamela Anderson did for the breast implant."

They, like Will Ferrell, were deeply and totally in love with her jungle rump.

Suddenly, asses were *in* and remain so. They're so *in* that plastic surgeons and amateur aficionados alike spend a lot of time discussing the qualities unique to primo ass.

Two Mexican doctors, Dr. Ramon Cuenca-Guerra and Dr. Jorge Quenzada, by request of *The New York Times*, studied 132 patients and more than 1100 photos and determined that a beautiful ass has the following characteristics:

- Slight hollows on each side

- A curved fold where the butt meets the thighs

- A V-shaped crease that looks like cleavage

- Two dimples in the lower back

- The ability to deflect small-caliber gunfire

Okay, I made that last one up, but it's not hard to believe the butt described above could pass that test.

Another expert, plastic surgeon Constantino Mendieta, was similarly tasked but he came up with a different conclusion. Dr. Mendieta believes that overall butt shape is more important. He concluded that they come in 4 different shapes: square, round, V-shape, and A-shape.

"The prettiest buttocks," he explains, "look like A's, like upside down hearts with a wider bottom than top."

Clearly, Dr. Mendieta never worked at a grocery store. Otherwise, he'd place more value on the square butt, if only because of its stackability. Anyhow, Dr. Nadler tends to side with Cuenca-Guerra and Quenzada, saying that he likes dimples and the lower differentiation between thigh and butt, a characteristic he calls "the smile."

But this butt mania can't be all because of one moderately talented Latino with a piñata-sized butt, can it? I sure as hell don't think so, but my theory might seem even more implausible to you.

I think, and bear with me here, that this butt renaissance has to do with some complex anthropological, evolutionary, and sociological underpinnings that have been partly overridden by alienation and depersonalization.

Boy, ain't that a mouthful? I sound like one of those schmucks on talk radio, but let me make my case that this butt mania is more than just *fashion* before you blow me off.

All mammals, with the exception of humans, mate from the rear, and it wasn't all that long ago, evolutionarily speaking, that humans did, too.

Our primitive relatives (along with most current-day mammals) exhibited periods of *estrus* where the females would be sexually receptive to males. This estrus was advertised by various sexual signals — the rump, breasts, and labial lips would angry-up and increase in size.

These brief periods of estrus would result in multiple couplings in a brief period of time — sort of a biologically determined frat party.

This all appears to have changed, though, about 500,000 years ago when *homo erectus* established permanent home bases with shelter and fire. It was no longer biologically necessary to determine matings based on factors like safety and availability of food.

Consequently, human females lost their estrus cycles and became sexually receptive all the time. To advertise this delightful fact, their breasts and butt became permanently enlarged. Suddenly, the male homo erectus' biologic surname finally made sense to him because us erectus sure were erectus often!

Mating, however, still took place largely from behind, and usually when the unsuspecting female bent over to pick up a shiny pebble.

But something else was happening, evolutionary-wise. Homo erectus' brain was getting bigger, at least compared to Australopithecus, his low-rent cousin. Bigger brains needed bigger heads, so the female pelvis started getting bigger. The pelvic opening grew longer and more round and this adaptation probably forced the female erectus' legs farther apart while forcing her knees closer together.

This adaptation caused her to grow a bigger butt and new muscles to accommodate these changes, along with causing her to sway and wiggle when she walked, as perhaps best illustrated by Marilyn Monroe wearing that wool skirt in *Niagara*.

Now here's what I consider the truly interesting part. When a female monkey mates, she can get up and do monkey things without losing any of the sperm she just collected. She's on all fours, so her vaginal tract stays *horizontal*. She can hang from a tree and that egg will still get fertilized!

The human female, however, with her newfound bipedal, upright locomotion, along with her newly modified pelvis, has a vaginal tract that's practically vertical to the ground.

As such, anything that could keep her horizontal during and right after mating to keep future generations from dribbling down her leg would be a pretty good idea. If you wanted her to bear offspring, you needed to do everything possible to keep her out of a tree, which still pretty much bears true today.

Doggie style sex, because of modifications to the female frame, was on the way out. Sex had to get frontal for successful mating.

Additionally, all the eye-to-eye contact during frontal sex was important for strong pair bonding. Sex had to be not only functional, but *personal* too. After all, it was important for the male to stick around to protect the mother and infant.

The trouble was, all that engineering had gone into making that ass so damn attractive! If the female was going to make the male interested in frontal sex, she had to do something, evolutionarily speaking, to make the front of her body more attractive!

According to anthropologist Desmond Morris in his landmark book, *The Naked Ape*, the "protuberant, hemispherical breasts of the female" are *copies* "of the fleshy buttocks, and the sharply defined red lips around the mouth must be copies of the red labia."

> *"If the male of our species was already primed to respond sexually to these signals when they emanated posteriorly from the genital region, then he would have built-in susceptibility to them if they could be reproduced in that form on the front*

of the female's body. And this, it would seem, is precisely what has happened, with the females carrying a duplicate set of buttocks and labia on their chests and mouth respectively."

Desmond, you just blew...my...*mind*!

Eventually, women developed permanently swollen, hairless breasts, along with full, reddish lips. Holy mackerel! I don't mean to embarrass you miss, but you've got a *tookus* on your chest and a *hoo-hah* for a mouth!

Enter several thousand years of face-to-face frontal sex. Enter millions of children who begat millions more, who in turn begat millions more.

But all that begattin' has sort of run into a sociological diaphragm. Sex is no longer procreational. Rather, it's more recreational than it's ever been. People don't date, *they hook up*. Getting intimate is asking your partner's name...afterwards.

Eye contact is no longer needed. In fact, many would prefer not to look into each other's eyes. That's too...personal. *Besides, it's just sex, no need to get all gushy over it.*

As such, there seems to be a return to the butt. There seems to be a return to doggie style sex, and even a distinct movement towards anal sex, if the reports from the schools and Howard Stern are to be taken seriously.

The butt has hoisted the sexual mantle from the breasts and lips and placed it on its curvy brow.

Consequently, today's female, either consciously or subconsciously, has adopted fashions that call attention to the posterior proclivities like never before. Low slung jeans, tramp stamps, colorful candy colored thongs, and molecule-thick spandex exercise shorts that lift and separate the butt cheeks are the uniforms of the day. Add to that the higher and higher heels that puff the modern female butt clear out — just like her ancestors in estrus — making it increasingly difficult to squeeze by her in the grocery store aisle without getting at least a little bit friendly.

Most women, too, seem to base their entire workout on shaping and toning the upper thighs and butt to the exclusion of all other body parts, save perhaps the stomach.

And then there are all those butt-jobs at the plastic surgeon's office. And the hip-hop songs that glorify ass. And the ubiquitous ad campaigns based on photos of rear ends.

We're clearly in an ass culture, but we'd better watch it, lest the evolutionary pendulum swing the other way and women start evolving into creatures with giant asses and no breasts that look kind of like NFL linemen.

Do your part to preserve the evolutionary status quo -- look into her eyes. Tell her she's beautiful. Tell her you love the way her breasts mimic her fleshy buttocks.

And afterwards, keep her out of the trees.

REFERENCES:

How to Stuff a Wild Bikini Bottom, Natasha Singer, NYT, March 2nd, 2006, page E3

Sexuality — Female Evolution and Erotica — 2nd Edition, Rhawn Joseph, Ph.D. Neurodynamics, Brain Research Laboratory.

The Naked Ape, Desmond Morris, Dell Publishing, 1967

-- 2006

Four, Up! Like Elephant!

If ever a man loved the anatomy of the penis, it's Dr. Hsu. Aside from publishing papers on the subject, he maintains a large collection of specimens he uses for research. He even has a standing order for "leftovers" with local hospitals. Years ago, a careless lab tech threw away a box containing 73 of his penises and the memory still pains him to this day.

"I *better get home or the ducks will have something to eat."*

Oh yeah, the ducks. Those web-footed demons.

In Thailand the mere mention of the ducks — especially when you've been out with your buddies tossing back some Mekhong whiskey — is enough to cause your manhood to grab its testicle suitcases and waddle over to Cambodia.

The thing is, in Thailand, a lot of peasants live in homes that are elevated on pilings. Underneath the pilings live the assorted pigs, chickens, and ducks that the family depends on for a large part of their food.

That of course isn't scary. The scary part starts when a foolish man comes home late and drunk, so late and so drunk that his wife is compelled to believe he's been out steaming someone else's dumplings.

The occasional wife gets so pissed off that she literally slices off the offending penis with a kitchen knife! She waits until the louse passes out and then goes Benihana on his cocky!

Hai! Hai! Hai!

Hey, son of bitch, you want peanut sauce with cocky!?!

Then, *then-oh-my-god-then,* she takes the bloody and bewildered thing and chucks it out the window! Out the window to the ground below where it's often eaten by the goddam ducks...unless the horrified man can gather his wits and what's left of his penis and fire pole down the ladder to win the most important race of his life!

(Why it's the ducks that have a taste for penis and not the chickens or the pigs might have something with the ducks seeking revenge for that foie gras thing, but nobody knows for sure.)

Other less-rural wives flush the penises down the toilet, forcing their husbands to frantically play the "Is it a turd or is it a dismembered cock?" game as they hunt through the septic tank. (Milton Bradley is in the process of manufacturing a home version of this wildly popular game.)

So that's why, "I better get home or the ducks will have something to eat," is now a common saying in Thailand.

Because of this propensity of Thai wives to exact this particular kind of revenge, Thailand is now home to the best penis microsurgeons in the world. Necessity, as they say, is the mother of invention.

As good as these surgeons are, these reattached penises aren't as good as factory originals. They're obviously shorter, but they're also kind of numb and they only stand up partway. They become little hunchbacked Quasimodo penises that, despite having hearts of gold, are so repugnant they rarely emerge from the Notre Dame cathedral of their owner's pants.

It's easy to understand impotence caused by a kitchen knife and subsequent immersion in a septic tank, but there are many kinds of impotence. Despite the introduction of Viagra and other impotence drugs, many men are non-responders.

Often, they have no recourse but to have some kind of surgery.

One of the world's most experienced of these urological surgeons is one Geng-Long Hsu of Taiwan. Dr. Hsu has been fixing penises of all kinds for 21 years.

If ever a man loved the anatomy of the penis, it's Dr. Hsu. Aside from publishing papers on the subject, he maintains a large collection of specimens he uses for research. He even has a standing order for "leftovers" with local hospitals. Years ago, a careless lab tech threw away a box containing 73 of his penises and the memory still pains him to this day.

Because of his studious pursuits, Hsu is extremely well versed in all aspects of the penis. He even knows about penis *direction*. Hsu says, "Most men are communists! Lean to left. Second most common: bow down, like Japanese gentleman! Number three, to the right! Four, up! Like elephant!"

He uses this vast knowledge to restore malfunctioning or injured penises. One day last year, he repaired a penis that had ruptured from practicing a little known martial art known as jui yang shen gong. It's the fifth of the Nine Mysterious Kung Fus and while translations of jui yang shen gong appear to vary, it seems to mean "genitals hanging kung fu."

Practitioners literally lift heavy weights or drag enormously heavy objects with their penis.

The particular penis Dr. Hsu repaired had attempted to lift 220 pounds. Maybe the name is eponymous in that jiu yang shen GONG is the sound a penis makes when it ruptures from lifting 220 pounds.

Anyhow, aside from repairing bizarrely injured penises, Hsu is renowned for a particular type of surgical treatment for impotence, or as it's now more commonly known, erectile dysfunction (ED). Even though the procedure has fallen out of favor with the majority of urosurgeons, Hsu continues to use the procedure.

What Hsu does seems sort of counterintuitive in that he actually ties off and removes certain veins of the penis. This is counterintuitive because, as most of us know, erections are all about blood and not, as they believed in the Middle Ages, pressurized air.

The blood lies in cylindrical chambers known as the *corpora cavernosa* and these tissues are filled with smooth muscle tissue made sponge-like with thousands of tiny hollow spaces. When this smooth muscle relaxes — as it does when signaled by an enzyme-produced nitric oxide gas — it expands with blood.

When the pressure inside gets to a certain point, it literally squeezes shut the veins caught in between the aforementioned coporus cavernosa and the *tunica*, thus preventing blood from flowing out and hopefully maintaining the Thor's-hammer-like erection.

The common cock ring mimics this effect. The trouble is, cock rings sometimes get stuck. In fact, cock-ring emergencies are so common in San Francisco that they now use the designation "C-Ring" on their fire department teletype and everybody knows what they're talking about. They even have their own modified circular saw specifically modified for this purpose.

Anyhow, if a man is impotent, it's often because the erectile tissue isn't expanding vigorously enough to constrict those aforementioned veins and the blood seeps out until it is, according to Hsu, "Like a tire! Flat!"

Part of the problem is that aging causes the loss of elasticity and some of the muscle cells in the erectile chambers are gradually replaced by connective tissue fibers that are too rigid to allow for ample turgidity.

If the tissue is too rigid, it won't expand fully and force those blood vessels to close. Maybe the answer is to get romantic with one of those foam rollers. Regardless, Dr. Hsu prefers removing some of these larger veins so that the rate at which blood flows out of the penis slows, thus allowing the patient to maintain an erection despite lack of elasticity.

While most urologists have abandoned the procedure because of gradually diminishing returns among patients who've had the procedure, Hsu claims to have a patient satisfaction rate of about 90%. Unfortunately, unless other docs can replicate his results, Dr. Hsu will pretty much remain the sole practitioner of this method.

Despite men like Dr. Hsu who use surgical intervention to cure impotence, the reason for the problem has, at least for the last 80 years or so, thought to have been psychological. Limp penises were caused by neuroses, unresolved conflict with parents, or weird obsessions.

If you needed to un-shrink, you went to the shrink. Of course, impotence became medicalized in 1998 when Pfizer introduced Viagra. Granted, there were those who still had problems because they really did have deep-rooted psychological problems or, as mentioned earlier, the penis had merely aged and developed fibrotic tissue.

Regardless, impotence has come a long way since the Middle Ages when impotence was thought to be caused by a demon or a witch. In the late 1700's, blame shifted to men themselves. 1760 saw the publication of a book called *Onaism; or, A Treatise upon the Disorders Produced by Masturbation*. Read throughout Europe and America, the book spread the belief that sperm was a vital source of life energy and bad things happened when you squandered it.

Masturbation and casual sex — especially with ugly women — led to all kinds of medical problems like blindness, heart trouble, insanity, stupidity, acne, clammy hands, acrid belches, "a flow of fetid matter from the fundament," stooped shoulders, flabby muscles, and of course, impotence.

The cure of course was simply to stop beating off.

Entrepreneurs saw an opportunity to cash in on the problem so the U.S. Patent Office was besieged by anti-masturbation devices, some even consisting of adjustable rings lined with spikes. Any nocturnal erections would be punished by extreme pain.

Other devices gave the user an electric shock or, more mercifully, merely tugged on the pubic hairs when an erection reared its sheepish head.

This type of thinking carried over well into the 20th century, perhaps culminating in the 1916 publication of *Practical Treatise on the Causes, Symptoms, and Treatment of Sexual Impotence and Other Sexual Disorders in Men and Women.*

The author, American physician William Robinson, was big on preventing premature awakening of sexual desires in the young, strongly urging parents "to keep their boys away from sensuous musical comedies and obscene vaudeville acts."

(While this may at first seem ludicrous, who among us didn't want to fuck some of those kitties, especially the yummy Bombalurina and Rumplteazer from the Broadway musical, Cats?)

Another party poop, a Dr. Crommelinck, even urged men to avoid touching their genitals at all times -- even while urinating -- lest they got excited. He advised, "Urinate quickly, do not shake your penis, even if it means having several drops of urine drip into your pants." This no doubt gave birth to the old lavatory chestnut, "Shake it more than twice and you're playin' with it."

Luckily, the medical world is now a little more accepting of masturbation and the true reasons for impotence have been pinned down to mostly treatable conditions.

Still it makes you wonder if all this hand wringing is more trouble than it's worth. In many ways, having a penis is like owning an exotic sports car you can barely afford, a sports car that consumes 95% of your thoughts and your energy.

We wonder if we'd be happier, if life would be simpler, if we just got rid of the damn thing.

Yeah, maybe, but we know full well we'd soon be at Dr. Hsu's clinic, begging for him to slap that baby back on and, while we're thinking about it, to give us a few spares from that collection just in case we run into a jealous Thai woman with a kitchen knife.

ACKNOWLEDGEMENT:

The majority of the info in this article came from a great new book by Mary Roach titled, *Bonk, The Curious Coupling of Science and Sex* (W.W. Norton, 2008).

-- 2008

Coma Boy and the Centegenarian

So it seems that life is a cosmic crapshoot. We're the Canadian geese in a flock, looking forward to our next meal of clover and alfalfa when the universe gives us its version of a deadly wedgie by throwing a jet engine into our path. Maybe you escaped Captain Sullenberger's plane this time, but Honker and Mrs. Featherbottom didn't.

On December 10th, my friend Tom went all John Ritter on us and blew a hole in his aorta.

There wasn't any discernible cause; it just blew like an old inner tube that had too many miles on it. The blood started hosing *onto* his innards instead of *through* them.

He didn't lose consciousness right away, though. His first thought was that he had food poisoning, only he couldn't imagine that even eating raw sewage out of a Calcutta gutter could cause him to feel as bad as he did. He managed to call 911 and the paramedics got there in 10 minutes.

They wheeled him into the ambulance and that's probably the last thing he was conscious of before he slipped away.

Given that it was late at night, it took the hospital a little longer than usual to put together a surgical team. By the time the spelunkers/surgeons had worked their way into Tom's chest cavity, the hole was a massive 1.8 centimeters long.

They managed to slap a patch on the hole but by then the damage was done. They figured that his de-oxygenated brain was now more on par with some of the lovely feckin' potatoes of his native Ireland. There was also extensive damage to his kidneys.

While Tom was technically alive, the doctors gave him about a 1% chance of pulling out of his coma and they didn't even mention the "r" word. Of course, recovery is a relative term. In Tom's case, recovery would probably mean — if he were lucky — sitting around some convalescent home where he sports a bucket around his neck to collect the drool and where sadistic night-shift orderlies jam brooms up his oblivious poop-chute to amuse themselves.

Tom's sons flew in from Canada when it happened and they stood dutifully by his bedside, making sure not to trip on or tug off any of the considerable amount of tubes and wires emanating from their father's body. They talked to him all day long as if he weren't a potato and they celebrated Christmas and New Year's with him, either as homage to *Weekend at Bernie's*, or to presumably stimulate what, if anything, was left of his oxygen-deprived brain.

To keep their spirits up, the sons watched DVD's and flirted with the endless stream of nurses that busied themselves around their father.

They thought what they were doing was paying off because they'd happily report that their dad would occasionally grimace or fidget, which to them was indicative that he was somewhere inside that brain, struggling to get out, but they were blissfully ignorant of the fact that even completely brain-dead patients sometimes make facial expressions that are indistinguishable from those of Dick Cheney.

Mutual friends of ours kept asking me, "Are you going to send some flowers to Tom?" to which I'd reply, "No, I'm sending him a gift certificate to Sizzler." I mean, hell, the guy's in a *coma*. Sending a gift — any gift — would be ridiculous, but nobody seemed to see it exactly that way.

Anyway, almost a month later to the day, Tom, wonder of wonders, woke up from his coma! He was... *fine*. Oh, he was a little disoriented and he was weak as hell, but his brain was no worse for wear. The kidneys, too, had healed up.

The doctors consider him to be a bonafide miracle man. Even physicians who weren't involved with the case kept sticking their heads in the door and checking his chart to satisfy their empirical minds.

While I was both thrilled and amazed to see Tom recover, I was most interested in what sounded like a legitimate "near death experience." Sure enough, Tom had seen the light. He'd not only seen the light, but also the hills, the craggy rocks, the deep blue sky and the rolling fields of heather. Tom was convinced he'd been to someplace that looked and even smelled a lot like Ireland or maybe Scotland.

Don't you see? Heaven is like Scotland! Sure! Tom had been there before being pulled back through the ether because he had unfinished business on Earth!

I had my proof of hebben, where de angels am!

Hosanna, Hey Sanna Sanna Sanna Hosanna Hey Sanna Hosanna!

Uh, not so fast, afterlife boy.

Turns out Tom's sons had watched the *Braveheart* DVD three times while he was in a coma. His subconscious mind had not only listened to the movie, it'd filled in the missing images with pictures of Scotland.

No wonder he thought he'd been there. That might also explain why he thought he was racked and disemboweled by order of some angel named Longshanks.

Tom also "remembered" being flown to Scotland by a beautiful big-bosomed pilot in a tight, white, leather jump suit. Of course. His sons also watched *Goldfinger* and Tom's frazzled synapses latched onto Pussy Galore as she piloted Auric Goldfinger around Fort Knox.

Crap.

A couple of days after Tom's resurrection, I had another taste of disillusionment. I'd been invited to a birthday party for Ed, but not just any old birthday party — Ed was turning 100 years old.

Unlike the stereotypical centegenerian, Ed is perfectly sound of mind and body. He doesn't live in a nursing home, nor does he need to. He doesn't own a wheelchair, nor does he need one. His mind is as sharp as it ever was and nobody talks to Ed in that old person dialect where they raise their voice and use the first-person plural a lot.

Hell, if any nurse said, "How are we feeling today, young man?" to Ed, he'd probably give her a titty twister.

Nope, Ed's a wonder.

Seated at Ed's table were all the men he'd trained to become rich. Each had started out as messengers for Ed's mortgage company back in the 50's, 60', or 70's and worked their way up. None were currently worth less than 100 million. Seated to Ed's left was Angelo Mozilo, former CEO of Countrywide, who credits Ed with creating Countrywide's business model (the successful one, not the one that led to the massive stock dump that caused the SEC to investigate Angelo).

The others, less famous but equally wealthy, were all grateful to Ed and they still considered him to be the smartest man in the room.

Midway through the party, the hosts brought out a mermaid piñata. Why they thought this was appropriate for a hundredth birthday, I've no idea, but Ed was urged to take his tennis racket (amazingly, he still plays) and break the thing open.

Ed starts thumping on it, but it looks like some wiseacre made the thing out of concrete instead of paper-mache paste. As Ed continues to whack the mermaid, a morbid epitaph formed in my mind:

> *Here's what's left of poor Ed Katz,*
> *They made him whack a piñata.*
> *Now he rests in an old red urn,*
> *Made of fire-baked terra cotta.*

Luckily, the thing finally broke, scattering the candy within, and Ed's ancient heart was no worse for the experience.

I couldn't help but wonder what Ed's diet or exercise regimen was like. Good God, what discipline he must have! I can only imagine the collective pile of crappy food he's pushed away in his life. Was it the fish oil he no doubt guzzled like a wino that was responsible for his longevity? Or, speaking of wine, was it because he drank two glasses each day and soaked up all that life-extending resveratrol?

What do you eat, Ed? Tell us! What's your secret?

"Well, I never eat breakfast or any vegetables, and my favorite food is steak. And butter. And oh yeah, ice cream."

Noooooooooooooooooo!

And he doesn't use fish oil and he drinks wine only occasionally.

Say it ain't so, Ed! Say it ain't so!

Tell me that everything I believe in isn't wrong; tell me you're kidding; tell me you made an unholy pact with the Devil! Tell me... *something.* Throw me a bone! But no, it seems to be true. The guy does virtually everything "wrong" and he's celebrating his 100th birthday, with quite possibly many more to come.

Crap.

By all rights, Ed should be dead from old age and what some would deem dietary self-abuse. Tom's not nearly as old as Ed, but he's definitely in the coot category and by all accounts, coot-age or not, he should be dead, too, of catastrophic biological malfunction.

The only things they appear to have in common is that they both exercise a little bit, Tom as a morning walker and Ed as the occasional tennis player. Oh yeah, they're both horn dogs, too. Tom carries Cialis with him to church on Sunday morning because that's where he meets women. When Ed's first wife died about 8 years ago, he remarried within a month to a woman 30 years his junior and, based on the bottle of lube I saw on his nightstand a while back, they're still getting it on.

I interviewed Ed a few years ago — not for an article, but just to get a sense of what everyday life was like in the early part of the previous century. While looking for the tape, I stumbled on a box of tapes of interviews I'd done with bodybuilders and athletes in the 90's.

Among them were lots of young and comparatively young *dead people*, including Shelley Beattie, Paula Piwarunas, Mike Mentzer, Sonny Schmidt, Momo Benaziza, Andreas Munzer, and Dan Duchaine. Listening to those tapes is a little ghostly, but I can't help wondering why they're dead and the two should-be-dead coots I wrote about in this article are still alive.

Granted, some of the dead ones pushed the pharmaceutical boundaries. At least one took her life, and the deaths of one or two are still somewhat mysterious. Of course, one of the horrible truths of existence is that sometimes, people just die; often for no real reason.

Regardless, the people I listed died young, and it makes me wonder if I'm fooling myself into thinking I'm invincible, me with my oils, powders, pills, and potions.

Granted, longevity is largely genetic. If I moved one nucleic acid here and another there, moved guanine here and thymine here, I might live another 60 years, but if they stay put, as is likely barring any huge genetic breakthroughs, is an unalterable expiration date stamped on my forehead?

So it seems that life is a cosmic crapshoot. We're the Canadian geese in a flock, looking forward to our next meal of clover and alfalfa when the universe gives us its version of a deadly wedgie by throwing a jet engine into our path. Maybe you escaped Captain Sullenberger's plane this time, but Honker and Mrs. Featherbottom didn't.

So regardless of our age, any one of us might die today, tomorrow, or 80 years from now. Who the hell knows? Regardless, I'll continue to use my oil, powders, pills, and potions to maximize my genetic potential. I know they work. Tom and Ed are aberrations, statistical anomalies. That much I know is true.

And without going too much Mitch Albom on you, preferring instead to go a little Andy Dufresne, *Shawshank Redemption* on you, I've reaffirmed my choice to get busy living instead of get busy dying.

-- 2009

About the Author

TC Luoma was born to Finnish immigrants in Windsor, Ontario, but spent the bulk of his youth and adolescence in nearby Detroit, Michigan. He attended Eastern Michigan University where he earned degrees in Microbiology and English Language and Literature. After college, TC had a host of jobs including stints as an assembly line worker, an armored car guard, a phlebotomist, a used car salesman, a male model, a Freshman English teacher, a short order cook, a technical writer (writing books on how to service cruise missiles), and many other jobs too numerous to list.

Currently, TC is the editor-in-chief of Testosterone (T-Nation.com), an Internet magazine devoted to weight training, sports supplementation, and in general, changing your physique. (Their unofficial motto is "Look Good Naked.") In addition to publishing revolutionary ideas about sports training, the magazine discusses sex, women, the male psyche, and what TC calls the "testosterone void" in America. His diverse educational background and work experience has made him uniquely qualified to comment on the state of the American male. (He can also whip your butt in Jeopardy.)

TC currently lives in La Jolla, California with his heroically tolerant wife, Laurie, and his Staffordshire Bull Terriers, Tommey and Riley. His wife, when describing him, likes to quote Tuco from *The Good, the Bad, and the Ugly*: "He's tall, blonde, smokes a cigar, and he's a peeg."

3245338R00196

Printed in Great Britain
by Amazon.co.uk, Ltd.,
Marston Gate.